# Fundamentals of Interviewing and Interrogation



This book provides interviewers, particularly police investigators, everything they need to conduct effective, ethical interviews with criminal suspects. The author pulls from his training and experience to provide instruction on interviewing and interrogation, an essential area of investigations.

This book provides both the theory behind interview techniques as well as the practical application, which appeals to different learning styles. It can be read as a whole, or it can be picked up and skimmed for ideas on how to approach certain interviews. Unique to this book are the case studies. These discuss cases moving from first considerations, to strategy, to the actual interrogation monologues.

The primary audience is police investigators, but anybody conducting interviews as a regular aspect of their job duties can benefit from this book. This might include military, loss prevention, or arson investigators, to name a few.

**Darrel Lambert** is an active police investigator for a major metropolitan police department. He has been with the department for over 18 years, including seven as a detective. He is currently assigned to the homicide unit, but has experience with the investigation of violent crime, including the physical and sexual abuse of children. In his role as a detective, he has conducted hundreds of hours of suspect interviews in cases ranging from simple assault to murder. He stepped into a teaching role on the subject of interviewing and interrogation in 2020 and with partner Valentin De Los Santos serves as lead instructor on interview and interrogation for his department. Lambert and De Los Santos have taught at the Crimes Against Children Conference in Dallas, Texas, every year since 2022. In 2023, they co-founded Modern Interviewing Solutions (moderninterviewingsolutions.com) to teach police investigators from around the country how to conduct interviews and interrogations ethically and effectively. Lambert holds a Bachelor's degree from Wesleyan University. Most importantly, he is a husband to an amazing wife and a father to two wonderful children.

# Fundamentals of Interviewing and Interrogation

Darrel Lambert

Routledge
Taylor & Francis Group
NEW YORK AND LONDON

Designed cover image: Getty Images

First published 2026
by Routledge
605 Third Avenue, New York, NY 10158

and by Routledge
4 Park Square, Milton Park, Abingdon, Oxon, OX14 4RN

*Routledge is an imprint of the Taylor & Francis Group, an informa business*



ISBN: 9781041122661 (hbk)
ISBN: 9781041122654 (pbk)
ISBN: 9781003663904 (ebk)

DOI: 10.4324/9781003663904

Typeset in Sabon LT Pro
by KnowledgeWorks Global Ltd.

Access the Support Material: www.routledge.com/9781041122654

# Contents

# Introduction

## Introduction

> You gotta say some stuff and get them to say some stuff.
>
> Trent Watts

I am writing this book for the working police detective. The one in the trenches investigating rapes, robberies, stabbings, and murder. Interviewing and interrogation is a crucial tool to being successful in those investigations. I wrote this book to demystify the process. Everybody reading this book can be a good interviewer. Most can be great. Some will be exceptional. None will be perfect. It all starts with the fundamentals.

My particular brand of teaching on interview and interrogation was formed by years of attending classes and reading everything I could find on the subject. Most importantly, I was doing the work by volunteering to do every interview I could. As I gained more experience, I began listening to the thoughts other investigators had on the subject. I noticed that well-meaning investigators had theories on obscure body language topics but no ability to build rapport, manage suspect interactions, or ask questions. This was water-cooler wisdom masquerading as hard-earned knowledge.

Everybody wants tricks and shortcuts. How should you interpret the movement of their eyes or their body posture changes? How should you modify your delivery for their personality type? When I've been to courses teaching a combination of fundamentals and tricks, the tricks get all of the attention. Like real-life clickbait, "Criminals don't want you to know this one easy trick!" There are some tricks out there for detecting deception and gaining cooperation, but, hear me out, there's no point learning them until you learn and work the fundamentals.

This is true for at least three reasons. First, on a practical level, the information gathered with tricks is hard to interpret and means nothing in a court of law. I've never tried it before, but I'm confident if I testified that their eyes looking up and to their right was an indication of deception I'd be asked, "Are there any other reasons the eyes might look up and right?" You can always testify to what they said. Interpreting the meanings of their nonverbal actions? Not so much.

The second reason there is no point learning tricks before fundamentals is this: tricks are percentage boosters that mean nothing if there isn't enough to boost. When I was 20 years old and following the Tour de France, I was young and fit with a cheap and terribly heavy all steel bike equipped with rat-trap pedals instead of the clip-ins. I'll never forget passing an obese man with a $5,000 ultralight bike with all the bells and whistles.

DOI: 10.4324/9781003663904-1

I beat him because the fundamental need for a cyclist is fitness; fancy gear is a bunch of tricks or percentage boosters. If you are new to interviewing and you are focused on reading body language instead of asking questions, you are the obese cyclist with Gucci gear.

The third reason to focus on fundamentals before tricks is that, in my experience, newer interviewers have a limited field of "vision" in the room. In order to expand your vision, you need repetitions in the room. No amount of training can remove the need for real-life repetitions. What do I mean by vision? If you imagine a chess player, they have to learn how the pieces move before they can think of any real strategy. If you don't know how to move your pawn, there is no way to think of moves even two steps ahead. Top players think of moves *twelve* steps ahead because they have vision built on a reflexive understanding of basic movements. As they become better, their strategies become more and more complex. The same is true for interviewing. You *must* learn the fundamentals before strategies and trickiness. New interviewers have limited vision until they do the work to master the fundamentals.

What are some of the fundamentals? Perhaps the most fundamental practice is to *prepare* for the interview. You must know your case facts and, as much as practical, think in advance about your questions. If you are working a case that is still an active crime scene, you may not know all of your case facts or be prepared. In that case, realize that the conversation you have with potential suspects does not have to be the ultimate and final suspect interview. Establish as much ground truth as possible, do not accuse them, get timelines, and build rapport that will encourage them to meet with you again another time.

If your case or type of crime matters at all, you must at least attempt to interview suspects unless there is some articulable reason to believe that contacting them will cause them to hurt others or abscond from the country, for example. When was the last time you interviewed a suspect? Why or why not?

You must cover custodial issues with the suspect. In the United States, if the suspect isn't in custody, you do not have to read them their Miranda warnings, but you should advise them that they are free to leave at any time, they can terminate the interview at any time, they aren't under arrest, and that their biological needs will be met (water and bathroom breaks at a minimum). If they are in custody, by police, and being questioned, you must read them their Miranda warnings. If you aren't sure if they are in custody or not, read them Miranda.

Finally, as a fundamental tenet, you must avoid the three poison pills of interviewing: threats, promises of leniency, and actions that shock the conscience. Promises of leniency are only okay with prior approval from the prosecutor. This might happen in drug cases, for example, where police are allowed to promise leniency on the suspect's drug charge in exchange for more or bigger drug dealers. Otherwise, engaging in any of these three poison pill practices will get your interview suppressed.

### *The Three Levels of Interviewing*

I think of interviewing as occurring on three levels. Think of these levels as blocks making a pyramid with the widest block on the bottom. The first and foundational level is Knowing What To Say (and how you are going to say it). The second level is Hearing What They Say (and in what context they said it). The third level is Tricks. For the purposes of this book, I propose levels one and two as being The Fundamentals.

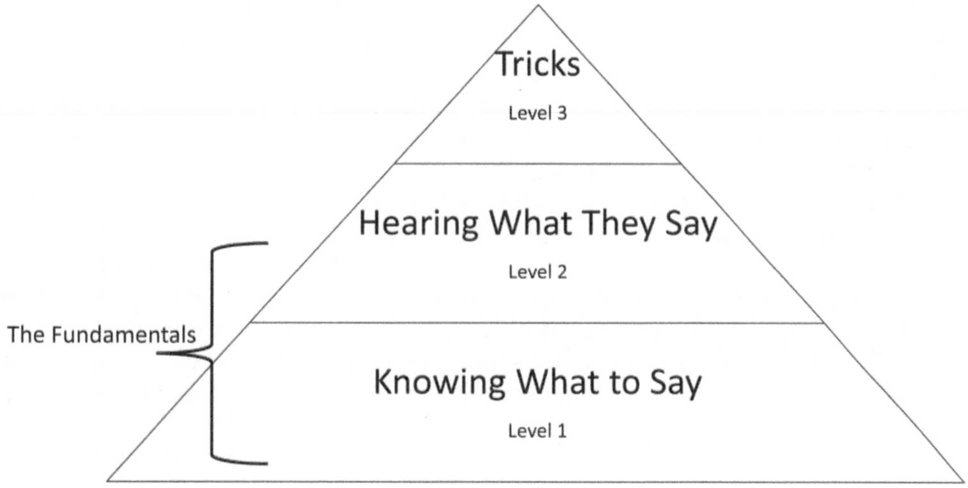


*Image 0.1* The image illustrates the Pyramid of Interviewing and Interrogation. The foundational skills – knowing what to say and actually hearing what they say – should be prioritized over tricks.

The foundational level of interview and interrogation is Knowing What To Say (and how you are going to say it). One of the common fears I hear from interviewers when I teach is the fear of running out of things to say. If you prepare your questions in advance, you will be much less likely to run out of things to say. You should think through topics you want to know about and organize them (within reason) from least concerning to most concerning. For example, if your suspect contacted the victim on Instagram, establish that they use social media including Instagram before asking about the specific account they used to contact the victim. Another tip for not running out of things to say is to ask as many open-ended questions as possible followed by encouragers (go on, because?, and then?). A series of closed questions will be hard to sustain for the entirety of the interview.

Open-ended questions versus closed questions

| | |
|---|---|
| Open-ended: | Tell me about that.<br>What happened?<br>Tell me all about yesterday from beginning to end. |
| Closed: | What color was his hair?<br>What time did you get there?<br>Where were you last night? |

Knowing how you are going to say what you need to say shares the foundational block. This is where skills like avoiding tagged questions (a question followed by another question or statement before waiting for an answer, for example: "Where were you last night? Who were you with?"), controlling your emotions, and using note taking as speed control come into play. It takes a lot of practice to get good at this, but it isn't hard to understand the concepts, and you can practice anywhere.

The first step to being good is to have the humility to start with the fundamentals. I practice the basic techniques described in this book at all times on and off the clock. I note when the checkout person at the grocery store asks two questions at once. I ask my kids open-ended questions about their day, and then I practice listening to what exactly they tell me. I listen for deception from salespeople. I seek out opportunities to learn about others.

If you prepare during low-stress events, you'll be more likely to do it right when it counts. I think one of the reasons newer interviewers focus on the tricks is that the topic feels overwhelming. The way to make a thing less overwhelming is to practice until these basic skills become reflexive. As Kobe Bryant said, "When I prepare, I know what I'm capable of doing."[1] The more reflexive your use of these skills becomes, the more your vision will expand during your interviews.

At level one interviewing, just focus on preparing for the interview and asking your questions. Of course you'll listen to responses, but don't be hard on yourself if you miss deceptive indicators. I've talked to many new investigators tearing their hair out with worry over the possibility that they might miss deception. If you stay focused on what you can control at the skill level you are at, which is level one things at first, you'll catch the obvious lies. First, catch the obvious, then catch the more subtle.

The good news is that sometimes you succeed simply by preparing and asking questions. Don't rush past this level. You can be more successful than most simply by working level one.

When are you ready for level two? You are ready when thinking about what to say no longer clouds your ability to hear what the other person is saying. Michael Reddington, a forensic interviewer and author of *The Disciplined Listening Method*, writes about how the biggest impediment to actually hearing others is our own internal monologue.[2] Many new investigators have their brain space occupied with thoughts of what they are going to say and how they are going to say it when they should be listening. If you keep practicing level one skills, you will naturally arrive at level two.

Level two interviewing, as I conceive of it, is Hearing What They Say (and in what context they said it). This is where the real deception detection takes place. You're at level two when you feel comfortable in knowing what questions to ask and how to ask them. At this level, your "vision" has expanded and you'll be able to hear more of what the suspect says and, therefore, be able to analyze it.

Let me give you an example:

*Interviewer:* Where were you last Wednesday?
*Interviewee:* I usually go to the bar on Wednesday nights.

If you are a level one interviewer, you may hear the person say that they were at the bar last Wednesday, *even though that's not what they said*. They said that they *usually* go to the bar on Wednesdays. Upon further questioning about their trip to the bar that day – which is well within the capacity of a solid level one interviewer – the interviewee may clarify to say that they weren't at the bar last Wednesday. In fact, they were at their girlfriend's house. If you stay diligent, you'll get there in the end.

A level two interviewer hears more because they've cleared their mind to listen. They know what they asked, and they heard what the interviewee said. A level two listener would notice that the interviewee narrowed the response to Wednesday *night* even though the question was broader and about the entirety of Wednesday. It is a possible indicator of deception when the interviewee makes a broad subject narrow or a narrow subject broad.

The level two interviewer would also recognize that the interviewee said that they usually go to the bar on Wednesday nights. This is a *statement*, not an *answer*. They did not say that they actually went to the bar. Maybe they went to the bar and maybe they didn't. The interviewer's attention should be drawn to this response because it is a statement in response to a question.

An insight from one of my favorite authors on the topic of interview and interrogation, Don Rabon: a typical pattern is Question, Answer, Question, Answer. When it goes Question, Statement or Question, Question, you should be alert to the possibility of deception.[3]

This second level is where you'll think more deeply about what the interviewee says (and doesn't say). This is where Investigative Discourse Analysis (IDA) and Statement Analysis (SA) come in handy. These disciplines carefully examine each and every word the subject says or writes. The idea is that a subject will word their statements based on all of their knowledge, which, for a guilty person, includes the knowledge of their guilt. This knowledge will show itself in some way in their statement.[4]

One technique from these disciplines I use daily is to listen for modifying or qualifying terms. These are usually words ending in "-ly". Really. Honestly. Mostly. Basically. These terms serve to either turn the intensity up or down on a statement. The question is, "What is it about that statement causing the speaker to alter the intensity?" If your kid says they "basically" did their homework, you might want to check. If your sexual assault subject says they are "mostly" celibate, you might want to ask about the times they aren't. Practice spotting qualifying terms in conversations, news shows, and podcasts. Think about what purpose they serve.

Another useful technique from Statement Analysis and Investigative Discourse Analysis is to listen for any time the noun changes for a specific person, place, or thing. This is called Changes in Referencing. If I say "my wife" all throughout the narrative and then, at some point, name her as "Jane," there is some reason why that change has happened. It doesn't happen in a vacuum. You should ask questions about the topics under discussion when that change happened.

Level two listening is much more intense than level one listening. Whereas level one listening is gathering the gist of what they say, level two listening involves attention to exact wording and the context in which it is offered. In order to really hear what the person says during an interview, I will often repeat their exact words in my mind. This keeps me focused on them and prevents my mind from wandering.

In all of this level two stage, you need to be acutely aware that most people lie by omission. What is being left out of the story? Where are there time gaps? Does this story make sense? Winning at stage two is being alert to the different modes of deception, many of which will manifest themselves in some way in their speech, if you're ready to really hear it. I write more about deception detection in Chapter 3.

Ok, we are almost to level three. Having read the above, do you really feel like you've mastered the first two levels? I've spent hundreds of hours in the interview room, and I haven't. I'm getting to where I can peek into the third level, but I still have a lot of work to do to master the first two. Unless you feel like you've really mastered these first two levels, I recommend not moving on to the third level. I'm not suggesting that you ignore a deceptive nonverbal that you happen to observe; I'm just asking you not to *prioritize* learning about nonverbals until you are consistently good at the foundational skills.

I'd estimate that 90% of your capacity for success in any given interview is in levels one and two...The Fundamentals. The third level makes up the final 10%. The third level, which I'm calling tricks is, among other things, nonverbals, adjustments for personality, eye movements, and dynamic persuasive techniques. There is simply no reason to chase the 10% until you've done your best to get the 90%.

At level three, your vision has expanded within the room. You're comfortable with your ability to ask questions. You're skilled at hearing and analyzing their response, now you're ready to really take off. I do not pretend to be an expert at level three. I've had glimpses of it, though.

Prioritizing the study of nonverbal communication belongs on level three. This is where you may consider eye movements, grooming gestures, and arm and leg crossing as indicators of deception. Nonverbal communication only matters *in context*. **Your preparation on level one and your careful listening on level two are prerequisites for any serious consideration of what their nonverbal communication means.** There is plenty to uncover here. As much as 65 percent of communication happens at the nonverbal level.[5] If you are interested in the subject, Joe Navarro, a retired FBI special agent has written many books on the subject. There is also a very good YouTube channel called "The Behavior Channel" with analysis of nonverbal communication in interviews.

At this third level, you may consider adjusting your communication style to more closely align with how the interviewee prefers to receive information. Dr. Steven Rhoads has an excellent course called Subconscious Communication for Interview and Interrogation. In it, he talks about how to diagnose a suspect's personality type. Armed with this knowledge, he suggests ways to approach the different personality types. This is valuable for an upper-level interviewer.

Have the humility and discipline to work at the level you are at. The vast majority of information you seek can be obtained with working inside of levels one and two of interviewing: Knowing What To Say (and how you are going to say it) and Hearing What They Say. As you become more comfortable working on those levels, seek out training from people teaching on tricks and extras. Slowly, you'll start seeing them with your expanded vision, but first, The Fundamentals.

**Disclaimer**: All cases discussed in this book with any specificity have been finally adjudicated. None of the cases discussed use actual names or case numbers. When necessary, certain details have been altered to further disguise the case from those that might have knowledge of it. In all discussions of interview technique, I have attempted to use the most universal principles possible. You are responsible for making sure any use of the contents of this book conform to your agency's policy and applicable state and federal laws.

Although I am an active law enforcement officer, I purposefully do not list my department affiliation. My thoughts are my own. Nothing I write here should be construed as reflecting the position or opinions of my department.

## Notes

1 A Coach's Diary. (2023, September 26). *Kobe Bryant | Confidence Comes from Preparation.* YouTube. https://www.youtube.com/watch?v=YkPODCYd100

2 Reddington, Michael, *The Disciplined Listening Method: How a Certified Forensic Interviewer Unlocks Hidden Value in Every Conversation* (Charlotte, NC: Per Capita, 2022), 55.

3 Rabon, Don and Tanya Chapman, *Interviewing and Interrogation: Questioning, Detecting Deception and Gaining Compliance* (Durham, NC: Carolina Academic Press, 2019), 77.

4 "Detecting Lies and Deception Using Statement Analysis®." 2024. Statementanalysis.com. 2024. https://www.statementanalysis.com/.

5 Navarro, Joe, and Marvin Karlins, *What Every BODY Is Saying: An Ex-FBI Agent's Guide to Speed-Reading People* (New York, NY: Harper Collins, 2008), 4.

## References

A Coach's Diary. (2023, September 26). *Kobe Bryant | Confidence Comes from Preparation*. YouTube. https://www.youtube.com/watch?v=YkPODCYd100

"Detecting Lies and Deception Using Statement Analysis®." 2024. Statementanalysis.com. 2024. https://www.statementanalysis.com/

Navarro, Joe, and Marvin Karlins, 2008. *What Every BODY Is Saying: An Ex-FBI Agent's Guide to Speed-Reading People*. New York, NY: Harper Collins

Rabon, Don, and Tanya Chapman. 2019. *Interviewing and Interrogation: Questioning, Detecting Deception and Gaining Compliance*. Durham, NC: Carolina Academic Press.

Reddington, Michael. 2022. *The Disciplined Listening Method: How a Certified Forensic Interviewer Unlocks Hidden Value in Every Conversation*. Charlotte, NC: Per Capita.

Chapter 1

# Preparation for Now and Later Cases

### Key Takeaways

1 *Preparation is crucial:* Thorough preparation for both urgent (Now) and delayed (Later) cases is essential for successful suspect interviews, as it allows the interviewer to focus more on the suspect's responses rather than their own questions.
2 *Cases are either urgent (Now) or delayed (Later):* Now cases require quick preparation due to their urgency, while Later cases allow for a more thorough investigation before the interview, with the advantage of having more evidence and information.
3 *Effective interview techniques vary somewhat:* For Now cases, I advise asking suspects directly about their involvement early on, while Later cases benefit from a more gradual approach.
4 *Challenges in urgent cases:* There is a higher risk of false confessions or detaining innocent suspects due to incomplete information. Interviewers must be cautious and avoid confirmation bias.

The first best thing you can do to be successful in the interview room is to prepare. This is a level one, foundational skill. It is also the step that you have the most control over. No great level of skill is needed. The more you prepare, the less you will have to think about what you are going to say, and the more you can concentrate on what the suspect is saying in response.

To get started, review what you know. **It is axiomatic that the best way to distinguish between a truth and a lie is what we know to be true.** If you don't know anything, then all things you are told are equally likely to be true. In order to know things as a detective, look to your reports, your witnesses, and the evidence.

Investigator's cases are generally split into two types: the Now (urgent) and Later (delayed). Now cases just happened. Patrol has made an arrest, and they have notified the responsible detective unit. The detective has from the time they get the call until the suspect is placed in their interview room to prepare. Later cases are the ones that a detective had time to investigate. They've conducted follow-up interviews, submitted search warrants, and generally investigated the case. *While the preparation will be more thorough for the Later cases, it shouldn't be skipped in the Now cases.*

There are pros and cons to both types of cases. Although you have less time to prepare in the Now cases, guilty suspects are more likely to believe they have been caught red-handed. They will feel that their guilt is obvious, assume you have all of the evidence, and be much more likely to tell the truth quickly. The guilty suspect has from the time of arrest until the time you sit across from them to come up with a story, should they choose to lie.

DOI: 10.4324/9781003663904-2

They'll have a story, but it is unlikely to be consistent. Also, there is only so much they can lie about. Even bad technique will get a good amount of admissions here. With good technique, you will almost always be successful.

Now cases have cons to them too. For example, these arrests are often made quickly. There is a high likelihood that some of the information you start with is wrong or incomplete at the time you start your suspect interview. These arrests are much more likely to nab an innocent suspect than investigations that you conduct over the course of a month or more. The innocent suspect is at a high risk of getting wrapped up deeper than he should as confirmation bias sets in.

### A Tip for Now Cases: Ask the Suspect Sooner if They Did It Than You Would on a Later Case

Something like "Were you involved in what happened tonight?" will do fine. I very much mean ask them and do not accuse them. If their shoulders slump and they nod their heads, stay calm, move in, and collect the story. If they cross their arms and grimace at you, settle in for a much longer talk. Although in most interviews my recommendation is to play a longer game, these custodial cases have an aspect to them of needing to strike while the iron is hot. You may give a guilty suspect on the verge of confessing hope that he isn't done for when you circle around the subject for an hour before starting the questioning.

The Later cases have an obvious upside to them: you have more time to prepare by conducting a thorough investigation. You can submit search warrants, talk to witnesses, and get forensic evidence back. For Later cases, your ideal time to conduct a formal interview of the suspect is at the very end of the investigation when you have all of the evidence that you are likely to get. After this much time with a case, you'll be able to talk fluently about the people, places, and things involved. You'll have evidence that you can present to the suspect. This is a strong position to be in.

> What if you are working a delayed case, and, a few days into the investigation, you get a call from the suspect demanding to come in and talk? It happens. What will you tell them? I listened to a detective one time tell a suspect on the phone that he wasn't ready to talk to him yet, but he would call him when he was. I recommended that he call him back and invite him in. "How does next Tuesday at 9 am work?" I've had more than one guy say, "How about now?" Depending on my other obligations, I agree and make myself available.
>
> The fear from the unprepared detective is that they will miss deception or be unable to interrogate with incomplete information. I say that's ok. Develop rapport. Lock them into a story. Ask for alibis or other exonerating information (and of course, check them out later). If it turns out later that he was lying, you'll probably have another chance at the suspect in a custodial setting. A provable lie is almost as good as a confession. Finally, the suspect that is motivated to come in and make a statement today may hire an attorney tomorrow. If they are willing to talk to you, make the time to talk to them.

The downside to a Later case is that innocent suspects lose their memories of events. They didn't do the crime, so they forgot what was never important to them. It is harder for them to prove their innocence. On the other hand, guilty suspects get to plausibly act like innocent suspects that just don't remember. Guilty suspects have more time to destroy evidence, manipulate witnesses, and otherwise manhandle the case.

## Preparing for the Now Cases

"So, yeah. I punched him. He fell. I stole his wallet. He owed me that! Code of the streets, man. You knock a man out, you go in his pockets!" – Robbery suspect as told to me in 2018 while working Nighttime Violent Crimes.

> When I was working on the night shift as a detective, we'd get all sorts of wild cases.
>
> This is the lieutenant, the bomber just hit again. Send me all of your detectives.
>
> Hey Detective, I got a lady across the street from the main that just took an entire gas station hostage with a knife. What do you want us to do?
>
> There's a home invasion here that looks like a dope rip. A couple guys kicked in their door with AKs to steal 'unknown things' for 'unknown reasons.' You want us to mark off the crime scene?

Being a detective in Nighttime Violent Crimes was the hardest and, at the same time, the most interesting job I ever had. We had custodial interviews on Now cases almost every single night. Patrol would bring the suspects in. One detective would stay and interview the suspect while others went to the scene. I learned a thing or two about interviewing suspects in Now cases during my time in that unit.

I've had officers bring me a guy and tell me he's the suspect because the victim described the suspect as wearing a black shirt, and they found this guy with a black shirt in the area looking suspicious. I've also had officers bring me the suspect in a stabbing with video footage of the stabbing, the bloody knife, and two eyewitnesses pointing to the suspect as the one that did it. Most Now/custodial cases will fall between these two with a little more evidence than the first one and a little less than the second.

It's important to discuss a legal point that many detectives seem unaware of: Just because a person is accused of a serious crime does not mean that you get to move them (or order that they be moved) from one place to another without their consent unless they are under arrest. Detention powers do not expand simply because the crime is grievous.

For example, let's say a patrol officer found a suspect standing over the body of a stabbed person with a bloody knife in their hands. It would be perfectly reasonable for the officer to place the person with the bloody knife into handcuffs in order to detain them. Can you, as the detective, tell the patrol officer to bring the detained suspect to your office for questioning? No. You can either ask the patrol officer if that person would be willing to come in and make a voluntary statement (not ideal in this situation) or you can authorize that they be placed under arrest for aggravated assault and then brought to you for questioning.

If the suspect is brought in and able to explain themselves such that it seems that they may be innocent, you could drop charges and release them. Otherwise, they will be booked into jail after the interview. Don't play games with this and arrest people while assuming that you'll un-arrest them later. Stick with what's probable and do what's right.

*I'm not a lawyer, and this book isn't intended to be legal advice. Consult with District Attorneys or your legal team to be sure where they fall on this.

I have observed that detectives investigating Now cases tend to feel over-confident about their prospects in the room. This leads them to skip the preparation stage. You'll see them chatting with co-workers or doing any number of things that aren't actually connected to the issue at hand. They figure that the person has been caught red-handed and a few accusations should do the trick at getting the confession. Who wouldn't confess to a crime that has witnesses, surveillance video, and the gun used in the crime found in the suspect's waistband? Sometimes they are right and the suspect confesses immediately. When they are wrong, though, they have no plan, nowhere to go, and no hope of succeeding in the room. Don't be this person.

Back to preparation for Now cases. In most of these cases, there isn't a report to review. You'll be relying on the officers that were involved. Start your interview with them. Why did they get called to the scene? What did they see? What did they do? How did they identify the suspect? Did he make any statements? What evidence do they have? Spend time on this step.

Interrogate the case facts that the arresting officer presents. I do not mean to interrogate the officer. Interrogate the case facts themselves. You said this was reported by a bystander. Who? A witness described the suspect to you. Who? What's their connection to the crime? A doctor told you he would have to have surgery. Who? Did they provide a prognosis? Is it possible that anybody else was involved in the crime? You said the victim identified the suspect. How? Did anybody else match the description? What evidence did you gather? Can I see it?

More often than not, patrol has made the right arrest. If you gather all of the information from them that you can, you can feel confident in their arrest too. If you don't prepare enough, you'll find yourself in the middle of an interview not sure what's true or false. There will be a decision to be made: should you interrupt the interview and leave to ask about the information, or should you let it slide and hope it isn't that important? Many people opt for the latter with predictably bad results.

I had a case one time where patrol responded to a sex crimes service call. A mother walked into the kitchen to find her 4-year-old daughter with her pants around her knees looking scared. The mother's brother-in-law was avoiding her gaze and looking nervous. Mother took Daughter to a side room and asked her what happened.

Daughter told Mother that the suspect put his private part inside of her private part. Mother called patrol. I authorized the arrest, and I responded in to speak with the suspect.

During the interview, the suspect told me that the little girl came into the kitchen and said that she had to use the bathroom. He told her that she couldn't because his son was in there. She said that she had to pee and she would do it right then. She pulled her pants down and that's when Mother walked in. I took a break from the interview room to walk around and think about it. I remember thinking to myself, "If there's any non-criminal explanation, I suppose that would be it. Is it possible?" Then I remembered what patrol told me, which is that the little girl told Mother that the suspect put his private part in her private part. I wasn't just investigating a suspicious circumstance of a little girl with her pants down. I was investigating an outcry from a child of aggravated sexual assault.

I went back in and got the confession from the suspect. He is currently serving a 25-year sentence in prison. The point is that when you spend hours talking to a person, sometimes what you think you know can get muddled. If you are ill-prepared, the deceptive suspect will absolutely take advantage of your lack of preparation to get their lies past you. Prepare as much as you can.

If the suspect is placed under arrest and brought to your office before you are ready to speak with them, have them put into the room and taken out of handcuffs. Ask that the officer take the suspect to the restroom. This will assist in making them comfortable and make it so that it won't interrupt your conversation later.

You can have the suspect wait for you in the room while you finish preparing for the interview. However, I recommend a maximum of about 45 minutes. This gives the suspect time to settle down and think about what they've been charged with without giving them so long that they get bored, angry, or sleepy. I've seen detectives leave a suspect in the room for much longer than 45 minutes, but I think it is often counterproductive. If you must make a suspect wait for longer than 45 minutes, I recommend entering the room, introducing yourself, providing them with coffee or water, building some rapport, and explaining the wait.

After talking with officers, research the suspect in your report system. Read over past reports. Look into the suspect's criminal history. Then organize what you know. Think about the evidence in your case and how to use it. Write down some questions. Set some goals for yourself.

A baseline goal is to get the suspect to talk to you and offer some version of events that can be verified. This is true for both the innocent and the guilty.

Moderate goals include having the guilty suspect put himself on scene and in contact with the victim during the crime. These goals might also include verifying social media accounts, access to guns, routine contact with the victim, and similar significant facts.

The highest goal is always to get the truth. That will mean gathering evidence to exonerate an innocent suspect or to get incriminating evidence from a guilty suspect.

For innocent suspects, once you get them past the baseline goal of talking, there isn't much to advance your position. The truth is the truth. For guilty suspects, on the other hand, you always want to be advancing. If he starts at baseline (talking to you and giving a version of events), move your expectations to the moderate goals (on scene and in contact with the victim). If he starts at your moderate goals (or your questioning moves him from baseline to moderate), look to achieve the highest goal (the truth). If you arrive at your highest goal, ask why he did it. Ask what other victims there are. Ask for an apology note. You always want to be advancing.

Scenario: You walk into the custodial interrogation. A man has been arrested for murder. He quickly admits to being with the victim at the scene, but he denies doing anything to cause her death. You have evidence that he was involved in her death. Here, you are starting in the middle. Your goal is to continue questioning him until he is either able to explain the evidence against him or admits to being involved in the crime.

If the suspect is in custody, by police, and being questioned, you must read him his Miranda warnings (more on custodial issues in Chapter 7). However, just because a suspect is in custody does not mean that you should launch into an accusatory interrogation immediately after reading Miranda. Slow down, establish rapport the best you can and ask for his version of events in a non-accusatory manner. Your baseline goal here is to get the suspect to talk and offer some version of events.

Your basic flow for a custodial interview will be like this:

1 Greeting
2 A brief monologue
3 Miranda (assuming custodial)
4 Rapport building
5 Ask "Were you involved in what happened tonight?" Or similar
6 Fact finding
7 Evidence presentation
8 Interrogate if their guilt is still reasonably certain

## Delayed Suspect Interviews

Suspect interviews in delayed or "Later" cases are often non-custodial. Your preparation for a Later suspect interview should take place before you ever contact the suspect. The ideal time to conduct this interview is after you have all of the case facts you are reasonably likely to obtain. You've submitted your search warrants. Hopefully, you've received your warrant returns. You've interviewed the witnesses and victim(s). Once that has happened, sit down and prepare a list of questions. Think about your evidence and how you intend to present it. Print out evidence that you would like to show the suspect. Put all of this into a packet. Then you are ready to arrange the interview.

A properly prepared case will include the following (at a minimum):

Case number
Suspect name
Victim name
Summary of the alleged crime
Questions
Evidence presentation

This might take an hour or two to prepare. It gets faster with repetitions.

Many detectives don't prepare for an interview until the day of the interview. They call the suspect with a sketchy understanding of the case, schedule it, and figure that they can throw some thoughts together later. I have had the experience of calling suspects to schedule them for some appointment in the near future and having them tell me that they'd rather just come in now. If I didn't prepare, this unexpected interview leaves me scrambling to write out my questions.

Another reason to prepare for the suspect interview in advance is to avoid duplicating your work. I don't have enough working hours in the day to do everything twice. I doubt you do either. Reading a report takes time. Even the least prepared detective will read the report before contacting the suspect. Some reports can be 100 pages long. As such, any thorough preparation should include a synopsis of the case in your working document. Who did what? When? Where? How? What evidence do you have? This is always helpful, but it is even more important in cases where the interview is delayed. The case facts become fuzzy, the case falls to the bottom of your working pile, and then, suddenly, the suspect calls you. If you prepared well, you can get away with reading your synopsis.

Prepare for the interview. Contact the suspect. If he doesn't come in right away, file your prepared notes away. They'll be ready when you need them.

In a recent case of mine, I prepared all of my questions for the suspect in a sexual assault of a child case after I completed the core of my investigation. Then I called him. He refused to come in, but he agreed to talk with me on the phone. Because I had prepared, I was ready. I had a plan. I moved him past, "I don't know who that girl is" to "we made out three times in my truck, yes I impregnated her underaged friend, but, no I didn't have sex with her." This was a lot of progress. I issued a warrant for his arrest.

As luck would have it, he was arrested months later on my day off when I could not possibly get away to interview him. I asked my partner to interview him. He agreed to do the interview. Because I had prepared, I was able to point him to my file that had the prepared questions. These questions included specific pre-written questions and an outline for evidence presentation. My partner went in there and got a full confession.

This case had both of the reasons why we prepare before contacting the suspect in Later cases: he may insist on being interviewed immediately (our phone interview), and there may be a significant break in time between when you prepare and when the interview happens. Doing the preparation at the right time prevents either of these from being a problem.

Suspect interviews in Later cases are often 2–4 hours. Make sure that you have enough time to do the interview. When I have a non-custodial interview coming in, I prefer to schedule it for 9 am, and I make sure that I don't have anything scheduled for that afternoon that can't be moved. You may only get one shot at interviewing the suspect. Do not miss out on that opportunity because you ran out of time.

Prepare yourself for the interview. Before you go into the room, make sure that your own biological needs are met. Don't go in hungry. Use the bathroom first. Get whatever caffeine you need.

Ideally, you should have another detective or officer meet the suspect and show them to the room. Have that other detective point them to where the bathroom is and then settle them in the room. This allows your first greeting to be its own thing, free of mundane details like signing in and restroom breaks. If possible, have the lead detective provide the suspect coffee or a bottle of water. The act of providing the drink is an important part of rapport building and reciprocity. I discuss this in greater detail in Chapter 6.

If your interview in this Later case is non-custodial, do not leave them in the room alone for more than a few minutes. They came in on their own. They may be skittish about the interview. An extended wait will only increase anxiety and lead them to think of other more pleasurable things they could do than sit and wait to talk to a police detective.

A typical flow for suspect interviews in Later cases will be like this:

1 Greeting
2 Discuss custodial issues
3 Rapport building
4 Transition
5 Fact finding
6 Ask them if they did it
7 Evidence presentation
8 Interrogate if their guilt is still reasonably certain

I discuss each of these aspects in different sections of the book. The unique element of non-custodial interviews is how custodial issues are discussed. You should always let the suspect know they are not under arrest, they are free to leave at any time, and their biological needs will be met. At a minimum, the meeting of biological needs will include bathroom breaks and water. You should also let them know that they are a suspect, but that you haven't made any final decisions in the case. If you don't explain these things to the suspect, the defense will argue that their client *was* in custody despite your claims otherwise.

My typical explanation of circumstances sounds like this:

> Thanks for coming in today. I want to make sure you understand that you are not under arrest. At any time you want to leave, the door is open. You can open the door, walk out to your left and head into the lobby. We are here because your name came up in a criminal investigation as possibly being involved, but I have not made any final decisions in the case. At any time you want to use the restroom, just say so, and I'll show you where it is. If you want water or coffee, let me know, and I'll bring them to you. If you are done talking at any point, you don't need my permission to leave. Just head on out and do what you need to do. Does all of that make sense to you? Do you have any questions?

You can use that one or riff on it to make your own. Again, the elements that should be in there are about their biological needs being met and that they are not under arrest. Unlike how most jurisdictions have a standard Miranda warning card, I have never heard of a standard warning for non-custodial interviews.

> What if the person comes in and says, "Let's make this quick, I have an appointment in an hour"? This has come up multiple times. In most cases, I suspect it is a ploy on their part to force me to rush the interview. They plan to come in, say their denial, and get out.
>
> I push back on this one. I'll say something like, "If you have an appointment in an hour, we should reschedule our appointment. I want to hear what you have to say in

response to some serious allegations. That usually takes longer than an hour. Would you like to come back tomorrow?"

Each time I've said this they've agreed to postpone their other "appointment" and sit to speak with me. If they do end up leaving, be pleasant and professional. They may have been testing the waters, and this will show that they can trust you not to be a harsh interviewer.

## Summary

This chapter emphasizes the importance of thorough preparation in both urgent (Now) and delayed (Later) cases to ensure successful suspect interviews. Now cases require quick preparation and direct questioning due to their urgency, whereas Later cases allow for more comprehensive investigation and evidence gathering. Detectives must remain organized, avoid confirmation bias, and be cautious with the information they have. Effective interview techniques, such as rapport building and structured questioning, are crucial in both scenarios to advance toward uncovering the truth.

## Immediately Actionable

In urgent (Now) cases, interview the arresting officers thoroughly before interviewing the suspect. Take time to write down at least a few questions.

You can have the suspect wait while you prepare, but don't allow it to go on past 45 minutes. If you do, they are likely to be more resistant.

Prepare before contacting the suspect in delayed cases. They may insist on coming in immediately, or you may have to interview them on the phone.

Never turn down a suspect interview in a case assigned to you. It may be your only chance.

Chapter 2

# Questioning

### Key Points

1 *Cognitive interview (CI) is ideal*: The most science-backed style of interviewing is the CI. With a little practice, and a little patience, you can almost guarantee you'll gather more information.
2 *Start as open as possible*: Cops are report writers. We naturally question for specifics. What time? Where? What color? As investigators, we need to break that habit and prefer open-ended questions. "What happened?" Instead of "What happened last night at 6 pm?"
3 *Listen closely*: Deception detection starts with careful listening. Listening for main ideas only is not enough. We have to hear exactly what they say.
4 *Ask one question at a time*: Otherwise, the interviewee gets to choose which question he responds to.
5 *Assume nothing*: Deceptive people will capitalize on your assumptions.

The foundational block of interviewing is Knowing What To Say (and how you are going to say it). If you are new to interviewing and have no idea where to start, focus on the skills discussed in this section. If you are an experienced interviewer, look these over and ask yourself if these are skills you use. These skills will be relevant no matter how far you go on your interviewing journey.

This is where some of the art of interviewing comes in. It matters how you ask your questions. In general, you want the conversation to flow from big, open-ended questions. The questions you prepare will supplement the flow of that conversation.

My primary audience is police officers and detectives. A common complaint from both is that recommendations for better interviews take too long. Who has time to build rapport? What about the next call I have to go to? I wouldn't interrupt them if they would just hurry up! I have too many cases to spend 4 hours in a suspect interview! For suspect interviews in serious felony investigations, there is no shortcut. Do the work or give your spot up to somebody that will. There is, however, some wiggle room in misdemeanor cases and patrol work.

There's a food service adage: you can have it good or you can have it fast, but you can't have both. If police interactions were food service, the hours-long suspect interviews a detective might do would be that date night restaurant you like so much: slow but high quality. The average patrol interview is more of a McDonald's: it's fast, it fills you up like real food, but it's nothing to be proud of. Just like food service, there is a middle way that compromises a little on both ends to produce a product that is pretty good and pretty fast.

DOI: 10.4324/9781003663904-3

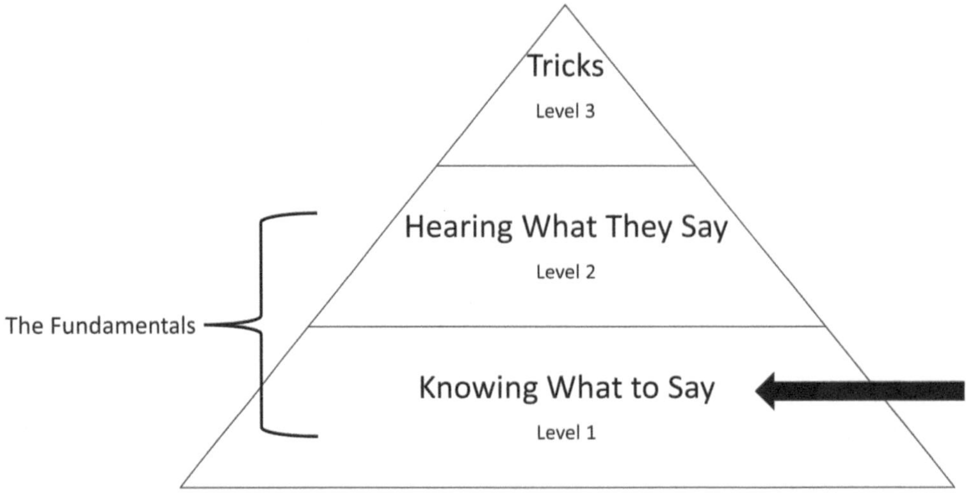


*Image 2.1* Pyramid of Interviewing and Interrogation, emphasizing the foundational skills of Knowing What to Say.

This is the fast casual or Chipotle of interviewing: it takes a little longer than McDonald's, and the food isn't nearly as good as the date night restaurant, but the result is better and healthier than the fastest of food.

If you're the busy patrol cop or an overworked misdemeanor detective, try to elevate your suspect interviews to fast casual dining. Any interview is better than no interview. A little bit of patience and technique can improve your information yield.

In the sections that follow, I will focus first on the CI. What is it? How can you benefit from it?

## The Cognitive Interview

The CI is one of the few scientifically proven ways to gather more information. Research on CI has shown that it yields between "40% and 80% more details than a standard interview."[1] As such, it should be the go-to method for interviewing whenever possible. CI was developed in the 1980s with funding from the US Department of Justice at a time when a survey of law enforcement professionals found that only 2% had received any formal training on interviewing.[2] For a more in-depth survey of the technique, I recommend reading *Science Based Interviewing* by Susan E Brandon and Simon Wells.

One thing Brandon and Wells point out so well in their book is that CI was designed to elicit information from cooperative victims and witnesses, but its principles work well with gathering information from deceptive suspects too. It works with deceptive suspects because it encourages them to provide full narratives with lots of details "and research has shown that credibility assessment is more reliable if it is based on verbal cues."[3] This speaks to why the Federal Law Enforcement Training Center (FLETC) is using Brandon and Wells' work in their advanced law enforcement training.

CI is a rapport-based style of interviewing that recognizes the interviewee as the most interesting person in the room. They are the ones that have the sought-after information.

Its principles teach interviewers how to create an environment conducive to memory recall. Then it espouses listening without interruption. The technique encourages the interviewee to pull from different areas of the brain where memories are stored.

Brandon and Wells list eight steps in the CI process. In the ideal form of CI, they are:

1 Introduction
2 Elicit the narrative
3 Reinstate the context
4 Ask for the story in reverse order
5 Ask for a sketch
6 Ask follow-up (clarification) questions
7 Challenge
8 Review what has been said[4]

The ideal form of CI isn't always practical for working cops. Many of our interviewees are resistant. Time and safety concerns can push us to gather information more quickly. As a practical matter, I use a variation of these steps. Depending on the situation, I may only use three or four of them. The sketch, for example, is not always applicable. I don't always ask for the story in reverse order.

In the introduction, you ease the interviewee's anxiety, and you provide them an example of how you will ask your questions. To ease their anxiety, you might set expectations for the interview, "I ask my questions in a different way. They help you access memory from different areas of the brain. This may take a little bit longer, but you'll be surprised how much you remember." Choose the words that sound right for the way that you talk.

In order to elicit the narrative, you might say something like, "In as much detail as possible, tell me everything that happened. No detail is too small. Think about what you could see, smell, and feel. If you don't know something, please don't guess." This should prompt the interviewee to get started.

While eliciting the narrative, you should listen as attentively as possible. Don't interrupt. When they pause, let them. They may be thinking rather than being done talking. Once they have finished, *ask them to go on*. They will have reached what they consider the end of the story, but this simple technique of asking them to continue on past the "end" almost always elicits more information.

Continuing on with the elicitation, go back to the beginning and break the statement into segments. Go through each one carefully. If a story has, say, six natural segments, you may be dying to talk about Section 5. Do not rush to that segment. Go through them in order. For example:

*Interviewer:* In as much detail as possible, please tell me everything that led up to John's death. No detail is too small.

*Suspect:* Ok. Well, he picked me up after work. He was working. I was at home. From there, we went out to dinner. Everything was fine! He texted with some friends. We talked about our plans for our upcoming trip. On the way home, we argued. It was a silly thing. Anyway, he got mad. Then I got mad. It just kept going on and on. When we got home, he ran ahead of me into the apartment. I remember thinking, "Great. Now we have to argue." He locked himself in his bedroom. I didn't hear from him all night. The next day, his door was still locked. I walked outside, and I looked in his window. It was cold outside. I could see that he was hanging from a rope attached to the fan. I screamed. I didn't know what to do. He was obviously dead. I called 911. I called my friend. Then I just kind of waited until officers and firefighters arrived. That's about it.

*Interviewer:* What else?

*Suspect:* I knew he was dead because he was blue and he wasn't bleeding. I've had some paramedic training. I knew there wasn't anything I could do that would help him then. It's really sad, he has two kids. His wife had just told him that she was filing for sole custody.

During the elicitation phase, the interviewer here hasn't interrupted at all. Now would be a good time to break the narrative down into parts. Most stories have natural divisions. I would break this story down as so:

1 What happened before John came to pick her up
2 The ride until getting to the restaurant
3 The restaurant
4 The ride home and the argument
5 Going back into the apartment
6 What she did from the time John went to his room until she found him
7 Finding John
8 The call to 911 and what happened afterwards

You may be most interested in getting to the part where John hangs himself, but have the discipline to go in order at this point. There is so much more to the story. You might say, "If you could, take me back to before John picked you up. What was going on?" She is sure to add details you hadn't known. These details may be just what you need to complete your investigation. For each segment, prompt the interviewee with where you want to start and where you want to end.

As to reinstating context, the idea here is to try to get the interviewee to mentally put themselves back in the situation. You might say, "I'd like you to mentally put yourself back in the apartment when John went in. What could you hear? What could you see? What could you feel? Really try to put yourself back in the situation and tell me what happened then." This should prompt them to point out visual or tactile sensations they hadn't included before. I have done this before, but I don't do it every time.

Challenging the statement is not the accusatory payoff some of you may be looking forward to. "I've waited so patiently for this very long story to be over. I think they are lying. Now I can accuse them, right?" Not exactly. The CI consistent challenge should be done in a way that maintains rapport, even with suspects or complainants you believe are being deceptive. Using CI, a challenge is going to sound more like, "You said John entered the apartment first, but at another point you said you entered the apartment first. Which is it?" Or, "You said that your brother was in the car, but your brother said that he wasn't even there. Help me understand." Here you use their own words and the case facts to prod at parts of the story that don't make sense.

A challenge can be effective even in situations where you believe the complainant. You might anticipate where others will question the story. "You said that this all happened when you were five years old. That was a long time ago. What helps you remember it so well?" This is a challenge of sorts, but it will also often lead to much stronger statements. To not only have the memory of the thing but also have an explanation of why they remember so well is strong evidence.

Asking for the story in reverse order is a portion of the CI that I sometimes use. In the example above, you might say, "You said that you called 911. What did you do just before? And then before that?" This part is usually a little awkward at first. Your interviewee is likely to seem confused about what it is you are asking them. If so, just explain that this is a technique that helps with memory recall, and it will make sense once they go through it.

I have found that asking for a narrative-based free recall of events is ineffective when interviewing resistant interviewees and those who are less articulate. Not long ago, I was interviewing a suspect when I prompted him, "In as much detail as possible, tell me everything about what happened. No detail is too small." He looked confused. He said maybe ten words and then stopped. I tried again with the CI consistent prompt. He again said a few words and stopped. It was apparent to me that this technique was not going to work in this situation. I had to adapt and switch to a much more direct questioning style. No single technique works all of the time.

A CI on its own is the preferred way to speak to cooperative victims, complainants, witnesses, and suspects. The use of CI in suspect interviews works best when you use it as part of a broader strategy including traditional interview elements. The way that I use CI in a formal suspect interview is to work it into my overall strategy. My typical approach to interviewing a suspect is this:

1 Greeting
2 Custodial Issues
3 Rapport
4 Transition (Identifying the issue at hand)
5 Cognitive Interview
6 Traditional Interview.

CIs are most useful for events that everybody agrees happened and that have a natural beginning, middle, and end. For example, you are investigating an aggravated assault that happened last week. You have a suspect in the room. Even if he doesn't agree that he had anything to do with it, you can still guide his attention back to that day, and ask CI consistent questions about his day, his alibi, and other issues.

How could you use a CI on a child sexual abuse case that happened at some place, some time, 5 years ago? Not only does the suspect *not* stipulate to the fact that such a thing happened, the exact day and time are unknown. Even if they *were* known, it was 5 years ago, and anybody could be expected to have forgotten what happened 5 years ago. In these situations, I don't use CI about the allegations themselves, but I will use elements of the CI when other events come up. If, say, the suspect talks about a time that the child walked in and saw their penis, you could say, "Tell me all about that situation from beginning to end without leaving anything out." Then I would go through the CI process for that event.

Patrol officers reading this may think this technique sounds good for detectives, but not for them. I would argue that it is plenty effective for beat cops too. In 2024, I was working a patrol shift. I responded to a robbery call. The complainant called in to say that he was robbed by two men at an intersection that I know to be an open-air drug market. I had my suspicions going in that the complainant was ripped off while selling drugs, but I set them aside to listen. It was raining outside. The complainant approached seeming to want to stand in the rain and talk through the window. I got out and invited him to step under a nearby awning, where we could both be dry. I told him that I was there to listen to him, and I didn't want him to be uncomfortable. This helps build rapport. It communicates to him that I observe his discomfort and it matters to me.

The complainant was excited. He gestured about as he told me his story before I could prompt him. I listened to what he had to say. When he stopped, I used practical elements of the CI, starting with eliciting the narrative:

| | |
|---|---|
| *Me:* | If you could please tell me all about what happened from the beginning until the end without leaving anything out. **ELICIT THE NARRATIVE** |
| *Complainant:* | I was sitting at Avenue A and Manor on a bench by the MetroPCS store. There are cameras! You can check it out. I'm hanging out. Waiting for my brother. Then I see something. I turn and then boom! He's pointing a gun at me. Then comes the second guy. Boom. He's got a gun too. I throw my hands in the air. They want my money. Boom. I throw it at 'em. $100 in five 20-dollar bills. I give 'em my phone and a lighter. I think I recognized one of 'em. That's it. |
| *Me:* | What else? **PROMPT FOR MORE** |
| *Complainant:* | What do you mean what else? I just got robbed! We got in the car and we left. |
| *Me:* | Ok. I hear you. I ask questions in a way that will help you remember things you may not even know you know, sometimes they sound a little funny. I'm listening to you. This will just take a few minutes. Let's break the story into parts. If you could, go back to the very beginning. Tell me everything that was going on before the robbery up until you see the robbers. **RAPPORT / BREAK THE STORY INTO PARTS** |
| *Complainant:* | What you mean? I was sitting on the bench just…hanging out. |
| *Me:* | Could you describe where you were sitting in detail? **EXAMINING THE SEGMENT** |
| *Complainant:* | It's just a little black thing by the MetroPCS store. Check the cameras! It's all there! |
| *Me:* | Ok. What were you doing there? **FOLLOW-UP QUESTION / EXAMINING THE SEGMENT** |
| *Complainant:* | I got friends there. I got a right to hang out right? |
| *Me:* | Of course. You have any problems with anybody else while you were there? **FOLLOW-UP QUESTION / EXAMINING THE SEGMENT** |
| *Complainant:* | No. |
| *Me:* | Ok. Let's talk about the robbery. You're sitting on the bench. What's the first thing that let you know there's a problem? **EXAMINING THE NEXT SEGMENT** |

The conversation went on. The complainant provided more detail about order of events, description of suspects, and so on. Interestingly, he became increasingly annoyed at my questions, particularly the ones I asked about his brother and what he was doing. The complainant started fidgeting, looking around, and asking how long this would take. I addressed this directly by telling him I was listening and that it wouldn't take much longer. It wasn't long before the interview fell apart. He let me know that he had provided all he wanted to and we should just do our jobs.

If the interview had gone on, I would have continued with the CI elements that made sense for the situation. I would have summarized and asked more direct questions until I understood. I would have asked for sensory details. I would have asked for his story in reverse. Then I would have challenged him with something like, "You said you were hanging out. I hear you. I've worked that area since 2008. I know a few things about it. Does this have anything to do with drug dealing?" This wouldn't be an accusation, but it would hold him to account for the unspoken thing we both know, which is that this probably had to do with drugs.

*Takeaways from Practical Cognitive Interviewing for Patrol*:

- You might not use all 8 steps from Cognitive Interviewing
- Introduce yourself, build some rapport
- Ask open-ended questions to elicit the narrative
- Prompt them to tell you more
- Break the story into parts, and examine them
- Ask follow-up questions
- Challenge the story
- Review what has been said

Overall, this is a good example of how the spirit of the CI can be used on patrol. What really happened? Probably a dope rip. The complainant probably did get robbed, but he didn't want to implicate his brother or admit to dealing drugs. I suspect that the increasing specificity of the questions forced him into a position where he was having to work harder and harder to keep the things out he didn't want to talk about. This frustrated him, and he moved to end the interview.

This entire interview might have taken 5–10 minutes longer than an interview done without CI influence. I approached the complainant in a non-judgmental way *even though it was reasonably likely that he was lying to me about part or all of what happened*. He gets treated with respect. I get more information.

If you find that this area of interviewing interests you, there are many books and articles on the subject. If you'd like to see a practical application of the technique, ask to sit in on a forensic interview at your local childhood advocacy center. The forensic interviewers are experts at using the precepts of Cognitive Interviewing. For the purpose of the working cop, you can improve your interviews by using elements of CI. Use what you can at first. As you get more reps in, your familiarity will increase over time to allow you to use more and more of the technique.

*To summarize*:

- The CI has been used and studied for over 40 years.
- Highly effective at developing more information than a traditional interview.
- Approach the interviewee in a non-judgmental way.
- Ask for the entire story with no detail being too small.

- Listen without interrupting.
- Break the story down into segments and inquire into each of those.
- Ask the interviewee to tell the story in reverse.
- Ask the direct questions that you haven't had answered in the open prompts.
- Challenge the sections of the story that need challenging.

## Start as Open as You Can and Slowly Work Down to Specifics

Cops tend to prefer direct questions. We want the answers right now. If a person tells us that there is a car involved, we want to know what color, what make, and where it went. If they tell us that somebody hit them, we want to know how they hit them, if it hurt, and where the assailant went. The problem with this preference for direct, closed questions is that it limits what the person is able to tell us. It is far better to elicit a narrative response and then go back to clarify details. This takes a little bit more patience, but the information yield is much more substantive.

Start with open-ended questions. These types of questions allow the interviewee to choose where to begin and what to include. *While they are answering, you must have the discipline to let them finish their response without interruption.* When we interrupt, we claim the position of primary importance in the interview, which is the wrong way to go about it. Let them finish. Encourage them to continue. Take notes. Then, once the person has been allowed the time and space to answer, get more specific.

FLETC talks about questioning like a funnel. A funnel starts wide and gets progressively more narrow. You might start with, "Tell me everything that happened." This is broad and doesn't direct the person as to where to start or what to include. Once they answer, narrow the questioning.

If you start with the more specific question about the assault, you are narrowing the possibilities of responses. You may not get the back story that will inform you how it started, who is involved, and what happened afterwards.

Let's look at how this process may play out. First, I will provide you with a typical series of questions that yield incomplete information. Next, I will show you a good interview leading from open-ended questions down to ever more direct questions. You may recognize the way you ask questions as typical of the first style. That's ok! I hope to show why open-ended questions leading to more direct questions are the better way to approach an issue.

*Interviewer:* What's going on?
*Interviewee:* My wife hit me! That's what!
*Interviewer:* Are you hurt?
*Interviewee:* Yes! Can't you see my eye? It's swollen!
*Interviewer:* What did she hit you with?
*Interviewee:* Her fist!
*Interviewer:* Where is she?
*Interviewee:* She went to her sister's house.
*Interviewer:* Do you want to press charges?

In the previous exchange, the interviewer starts with an open-ended question. That's good! From there, though, they elected to ask a series of closed questions. Closed questions elicit short responses, which are consequently less informative than open-ended questions, which elicit longer narrative responses. Let's look at how an interview with the funnel approach to questioning might have gone.

*Interviewer:* What's going on? **OPEN-ENDED QUESTION**
*Interviewee:* My wife hit me! That's what!
*Interviewer:* Ok, could you please tell me everything that happened from beginning to end? **ANOTHER OPEN-ENDED QUESTION**
*Interviewee:* She was mad that I went out last night. Sure, I stayed out late, but I was just blowing off some steam. I came home late, and she was in my ear. "You never do this. You never do that." I just wanted her out of my face. I pushed her to the side so that I could go to bed. She got mad, and she started hitting me! We yelled a bunch, and she went to her sister's place.
*Interviewer:* What else? **ENCOURAGER**
*Interviewee:* Nothing much. She has a temper. I don't think she should be able to do those things. Being out late is no kind of reason to yell and holler like she did.
*Interviewer:* A temper? **REFLECTION**
*Interviewee:* Yeah. Anything can set her off. For example, a few months ago, I didn't have enough money to pay my part of the rent. Instead of trying to figure it out, she started slapping me all over. I didn't make a report or anything, but that's the way she is. Right to violence.
*Interviewer:* Can you tell me more about the argument when you got back from drinking? **A MORE SPECIFIC OPEN-ENDED QUESTION DIRECTING THE INTERVIEWEE TO THE ARGUMENT**
*Interviewee:* Ok. I walk in the door. I'm a little drunk. There she is just waiting to get into it. She got up from the couch and told me I was no good. We argued. I pushed her. She hit me!
*Interviewer:* Tell me more about her hitting you. **ANOTHER MORE SPECIFIC QUESTION ABOUT THE HIT**
*Interviewee:* She got up in my face. She balled up her fists and stood there arguing for a bit. Then she punched me three times in the face. That's why my eye is swollen!
*Interviewer:* Which hand did she hit you with? **A DIRECT, CLOSED QUESTION TO CLARIFY A DETAIL**

This is the way to question a person with the funnel method. It starts with open questions, encourages the person to go on, gets more specific, and finally asks closed questions at the end. Again, a closed question is one that can be answered with just a few words. We only want to ask closed questions once we have provided the opportunity to give long-form responses.

If you compare the first, more common style of interviewing, you'll see that some of the things the first interviewer found out with closed questions, the wife going to her sister's house, for example, are provided in free-form narrative. Many of the questions that occur to you will be answered if you give the interviewee a chance. Have a little bit of patience. Reserve your closed questions for the things the interviewee doesn't provide in response to your open-ended questions.

### Don't Interrupt

How often do you interrupt people after you ask them a question? Probably more often than you think. According to the developers of the CI, Ronald P. Fisher and R. Edward Geiselman:

> Following their initial request for a description of the crime, on the average, police [interviewers] interrupted within 7.5 seconds after [eyewitnesses] began their narration.[5]

Just before making this point, they highlight why interrupting is so devastating to the efficacy of an interview:

> ...interrupting [the eyewitness] in the middle of a response, also discourages [the eyewitness] from taking an active role in the interview. This error is probably the most common and the most severe error [interviewers] make, because it establishes [the interviewer], not [the eyewitness], as the focus of the interview.[6]

Who has the information? If it's the other person, you need to let them talk. Suspects in a police interview room are divided into two main groups: guilty and innocent. You want both of these groups to talk a lot without interruption. Guilty suspects have a hard time keeping their stories straight. They'd love for you to interrupt them and talk more. Don't. Innocent suspects need time and space to access their memory and tell you what they know. Interrupting negatively affects their ability to access memories. Don't.

In 2022, I was sent out to work backfill patrol shifts. I had been a detective for over 4 years, and I taught on the subject of interview and interrogation. I knew the right way to interview people. I was surprised, then, how hard I had to fight not to slip into my old ways of interviewing during calls. That day, my radio earpiece was blocking my left ear so I could only hear out of my right. The body camera was beeping and vibrating. Other officers were looking at me impatiently. Medics were equally impatient. I was standing in the parking lot of a local fast-food restaurant and looking at a man with a torn shirt and scratches all around his face.

In the following exchange, I've put my thoughts into brackets. When the man spoke, though, I didn't interrupt him. I jotted reminders for these thoughts down on my pad, and I followed up with him once he got to the end of his story. You'll find that many times the person will answer the questions that you have if you give them the time and space to do that.

| | |
|---|---|
| *Me:* | What happened? |
| *Man:* | My girlfriend and I got into an argument |
| *My thoughts:* | [Who's your girlfriend? How long have you been dating? Did it get physical? Argument about what?] |
| *Man (continues):* | It wasn't getting any better, so I told her we should go for a drive. We got into the car, and we drove. Once we got on the frontage road, she yelled and hit me in the face. |
| *My thoughts:* | [Where were you when this happened? Were there any witnesses? Were you injured? Do you want to press charges?] |
| *Man (continues):* | I pulled over into a parking lot. |

| | |
|---|---|
| *My thoughts:* | [Which parking lot?] |
| *Man (continues):* | I told her that we should just end it if it was going to be like that. She told me that she would kill me if I left her. |
| *My thoughts:* | [Did she present any weapons? Were you in fear for your life?] |
| *Man (continues):* | I started the car back up. I did the turnaround under the highway. |
| *My thoughts:* | [Where? Which turnaround?] |
| *Man (continues):* | Then I decided that it wasn't right what she had done. I pulled over here, and I called the police. We've been together for 5 years, but I can't handle her anymore. |
| *My thoughts:* | [Here, as he closes, I see that he answers at least one of the questions I had wanted to ask earlier] |

As the man spoke, instead of interrupting him, I listened to what he was saying. As he mentioned things I wanted to know more about, I wrote notes to the side of my notes about the narrative. Relationship? Argument? Hit? When he got to the end of his narrative. I *still* didn't ask him the things I wanted to know. Instead I prompted him to tell me more.

| | |
|---|---|
| *Me:* | What else? |
| *Man:* | She called me a bunch of names. The ambulance got here first. I'm pretty sure that she's telling them that I hit her, but it's a lie. |

Now you can direct the person back to areas of the story you have questions about. Some follow-up questions you could ask.

- You said that she is your girlfriend, tell me more about that.
- You said you argued. What do you mean?
- You said she hit you in the face. Describe that to me.
- You said that she threatened to kill you. Explain that to me.
- Were there any witnesses?

This isn't meant to be an exhaustive list of questions that you could use to follow up with this man about his report. Rather, it's meant to show how to ask follow-up questions after you give the eyewitness or suspect space to talk without interrupting.

A caveat to the principle of non-interrupting: some deceptive people will talk about random topics for extended periods of time. This is often an act of avoidance. Talking about how to install sprinkler systems or your love of anime is so much nicer than answering questions related to the felony crime of which they're accused.

If the person talks about a side topic, let them have a few minutes to discuss it. If it becomes obvious that they aren't leading to a point related to the investigation, say something like, "That's really interesting! Let's come back to that. I had a thought that I don't want to lose. When you were downtown…"

### Listen to What They Say

The single biggest distraction that creates the greatest negative impact on our ability to listen is the voice inside of our own heads - our internal monologues. No one can have anything more important to say to us than we have to say to ourselves. Our internal

> monologue wins every time. The first danger is that it tricks us into believing we have observed our counterparts' messages accurately when we have missed the point altogether. We pick up enough pieces of what they communicate that we believe we understand the totality of their message. In reality, our brains connect the dots and insert the missing pieces based on our perspectives, expectations, and assumptions - not what our counterparts told us.
>
> Michael Reddington[7]

Listening is hard. So hard, in fact, that I regard focused listening as a level two skill. If you're honest with yourself, you do less of it than you think. I never realized how much of my brain space was filled with internal monologue until I read Michael Reddington's book *The Disciplined Listening Method*. After reading his book, I noticed how much I prepared my response to the person speaking while they were speaking. I also noticed how often I thought about entirely unrelated things when others spoke to me. Once I noticed, it was obvious I was missing a lot. If you decide what to say before the person finishes, you didn't actually hear the end of their statement.

We all have the experience of talking to somebody while they are interacting with their cellphones. We intuitively know that they aren't really listening to us. However, I would argue that even without a cellphone in the hand, most people are as distracted as though they did have it in their hands. I'm not sure anybody really listens to anything anymore.

Listening matters when talking to our friends and loved ones because it shows that we really care. The other day, I had this conversation with my son. Brackets show my thoughts.

*Me:* Tell me about your day!

*Son:* I got hurt playing football.

*Me:* Really?

*Son:* Yeah. It was the same boy [which boy? What's he talking about? I wish I could keep his friends' names straight. Maybe I should write them down or something. Did I already do that?] as the other day [there was another day?] he landed on my foot when I reached for the pass [did I send that email to my boss? I probably forgot to fill out the overtime sheet again] now I can't walk without limping.

How much was I really listening to my son? As I've paid attention to my thoughts when talking to others, I'm amazed how distracted I am. It takes a great force of will to really listen. The good news is that intense listening is so rare that it is memorable and even flattering. I still remember the conversations I've had with people when I could tell that they were intently listening to me.

Listening matters with suspects because deceptive people capitalize on your tendency to fill in the gaps with your conclusions and expectations. The person says they are married? You assume their relationship is like yours. They say they went to bed? You assume that they stayed asleep.

In 2023, I was interviewing a suspect in a high-profile case. He told me about how he met up with the victim and brought her to his hotel room. At one point in the story, he said he went home about 8 pm to be with family. Then, the next day, he went back in the mid-afternoon. Although he didn't *say* it, he *implied* that he stayed home all night. Luckily,

I had evidence linking him to further interactions with the victim. So I asked him, "Did you go back to the hotel that night?" He admitted that he did go back around 2 am and hung around there doing drugs until about 4 am.

With careful listening, I may have achieved the same result without having the evidence to guide me. He said that he went home but he *didn't* say that he stayed home. If I avoid making conclusions about his statement, I can ask him:

- Where else did you go that night?
- Did you leave the house between going to bed and leaving the next day in the mid-afternoon?

This is in contrast to how we would talk to friends. If a friend said they went home and went to bed, we would assume that they stayed in bed or at least that there was nothing else they wanted to report. Because we are friends, we don't ask them to talk about things they don't choose to talk about. **Talking to suspects is not talking to friends. We cannot assume they are cooperative. We cannot fill in the gaps for them.**

It may come as a surprise that I regard focused listening as a level 2 skill. Isn't listening to the interviewee essential for talking to them at all? Otherwise aren't we just kind of talking to ourselves? Listening and focused listening are not the same. When you are engaged in passive listening, you are like a fish: you see a shiny object and you snap it up. You're making decisions without understanding the situation. Sometimes you get fed, sometimes you get hooked. Focused listening would be like an evolved fish that saw the shiny object, looked at it, thought about it, and then snapped it up or not as the situation may be. Focused listening involves suppressing our instincts towards distraction and making assumptions and instead really hearing what they say.

## Ask Your Question and Stop

Everything after a question mark complicates the question. There are two main ways we complicate our questions before the interviewee has a chance to answer: asking another question or continuing to talk after asking the question. **When you hear the question mark, stop.** If you don't take anything else from this whole book, remember this rule. This is the one that I believe made the biggest immediate impact on how I question suspects.

Don't ask another question until the first one is answered. If you cared enough to ask the question, listen to the answer. If you thought of a better question after you asked the first one, wait until they answer and then ask the better question next. It's natural to engage in a process of refining your questions. You're going to think of better questions after the first, but have the discipline to stop after asking the first question. The reason this matters is that asking too many questions confuses people trying to tell the truth while giving deceptive people room to lie.

Don't add on statements until the question is answered. The Reid Institute popularized the term "tagging" to describe the second aspect of complicating questions: continuing to talk after asking the question. As they define it, tagging is "a questioning error that involves the investigator asking a direct question and then continuing to talk, perhaps by suggesting possible responses to the question or clarifying the question."[8] In other words, when you hear the question mark, stop.

I once interviewed a robbery suspect that told me he spent the stolen money on crack cocaine. I was impressed with his honesty, but I wanted to know more:

*Me:* Where are you buying crack? And I'm not saying you're going to tell me who your dealer is, but, basically, are you buying it from the street or what?

Here, I asked the question and then added on lots of other words to no purpose. The question is: "Where are you buying crack?" So why not just ask that question? The purpose of all the other words is in order to relieve my own anxiety at having asked a question that I know from experience is unlikely to generate an honest response. Why be anxious? He's the one being questioned about robbing a man and smoking crack. I think I can live with the shame of him not thinking I'm street-wise enough to have known better than to ask. All of those extra words gave my suspect time to think of how to respond.

> The average rate of speech for most Americans is around 125 words per minute. ...This means that, when we listen, we ask our brain to receive words at an extremely slow pace compared with its capabilities...When we listen, therefore, we continue thinking at high speed while the spoken words arrive at low speed...To phrase it another way, we can listen and still have some spare time for thinking.
>
> Harvard Business Review "Listening to People"
> by Ralph G. Nichols and Leonard A Stevens[9]

What do you think deceptive people are doing with all that extra time to think?

I've observed that the smartest people tend to violate this rule the most. My favorite journalist is a center-left New York Times alum named Bari Weiss. I don't agree with everything she says, but she seems honest and willing to listen. Anyway, she's undeniably intelligent. Check out this series of questions she asked her guest on her January 19, 2022 podcast with Alec MacGillis, an investigative journalist:

> Why is all of this happening? Meaning... the spike in...right?...if you look at the statistics from Philly where I think in 2021 there were I think 559 homicides, up from a previous record high from 1990 where there were 500. It's New York. It's Los Angeles. It's San Francisco we could go through ... the statistics all bear this out. Why is this violence on the rise and what does COVID have to do with it?[10]

The first question mark comes when she asks, "Why is all of this happening?" *Everything* after it is tagging the question. Ultimately, she asks three questions and talks a lot. Let's write the questions out here.

1 Why is all of this happening?
2 Why is violence on the rise?
3 What does COVID have to do with it (violence on the rise)?

These are very different questions. If she followed the rule of "When you hear the question mark stop," she would have stopped after question 1. It's not a precise question, but it's enough to let the interviewer respond. *In fact, for the very reason that it is imprecise it is the most likely question of all of them to generate a surprising response*. It's the most open-ended of the questions.

The monologue between question 1 and question 2 is (probably) a way of proving that she is informed. It's not necessary information at this point.

Question 2 is the actual question she is getting at. This is an open-ended question with enough guidance that it is likely to yield information on the particular topic she is interested in.

Question 3 is an add-on. I think the thought occurred to her, she thought it would be nice to know, and she threw it in there. This was more impulsive than carefully thought out.

With a cooperative interviewee, they are going to try their best to answer the spirit of the question-soup, but there is almost zero chance they'll remember all of the questions. They'll probably choose keywords they like the most, and cobble together a response.

What do you think will happen with an uncooperative (deceptive) interviewee? If you guessed that they will selectively choose to answer the least threatening question, you are correct.

For example, let's consider Prince Andrew's BBC interview with Emily Maitlis about the Jeffrey Epstein scandal. I have a section of this interview that I play in trainings I put on. I've heard it dozens of times, and I still can't remember what all of the questions are.

| | |
|---|---|
| *Emily Maitlis:* | So why wouldn't you announce this…this breakup? When you got back. Why wouldn't you publicly explain what you'd done? Did you worry that he had something that could compromise you? |
| *Prince Andrew:* | No.[11] |

Here are the questions:

1 Why wouldn't you announce this breakup?
2 Why wouldn't you publicly explain what you'd done?
3 Did you worry that he had something that could compromise you?

Like with Bari Weiss' question, I'd say that Maitlis came up with her best question second and then threw in a nice to know question. What response did Maitlis get from Prince Andrew? "No." No…what? Because of the way she asked the question, there is no way to know what question he is answering.

The kicker is that her first question was good enough! "Why wouldn't you announce this breakup?" That would be a punchy question. It's not as precise as the second question, but it'll do! He would have little time to think. He would have to talk about why he didn't announce his severing of ties with the disgraced Epstein. He might lie about it, but at least you wouldn't make it easy for him to lie!

We take time to refine our thoughts. We see this in Bari Weiss' and Emily Maitlis' questions. Both of them create their best question on the second go 'round. They had a thought. They worked on it. They produced a better thought.

Liars go through the same process of refinement as they think through how to respond to a question. They come up with a response. They test it. They produce a better response. It's understood that a better response for a liar is one that makes it less likely they get caught. **If you give them more time to think by asking too many questions at once, you are giving them the advantage.**

Practice this one-question-at-a-time technique in your everyday life so that it becomes second nature. Instead of, "How was your day? I hope you picked up the ingredients from the store. I'm thinking about making…" Chastise yourself for tagging the question. Next time just ask, "How was your day?" Listen for tagged questions on podcasts and in TV shows. Think about how the interaction might have been different if you or the speaker had stopped after the first question. Soon, it will become second nature to ask one question at a time, which means you'll nail it in the interview room.

When you hear the question mark, stop.

## Once They Respond, Don't Rush to Ask Another Question

Any time you ask an important question, you should allow the interviewee to answer *and* leave silence after their answer. The silence lets the interviewee know you expect more. Deceptive suspects are likely to feel pressure to add more. Truthful suspects are likely to see this as an invitation to think more deeply about their response. *The best techniques are good for innocent suspects and bad for deceptive suspects.*

I think there is an outdated concept of interview and interrogation where the interviewer seeks to bully the interviewee into telling the truth. The idea is: if you ask questions fast enough, you'll either intimidate them into talking or trip them up as they respond. I don't think either of these concepts is correct.

First, asking questions too quickly means you will run out of questions. My partner and I do a poll at the start of our training sessions. The question is, "What worries you about interviewing?" One common response is, "Running out of things to say." You will 100 percent run out of things to say if you rapid-fire questions like this. In order to *not* run out of questions, **slow down the pace.**

Second, many personality types will resent your attempt to rush them. I know because I'm one of them! I'm a very easy-going type, but I will become downright mulish if you try to push me. Being pushy is an absolute rapport killer. It will make you the enemy. It's easy to lie to the enemy. It's hard to lie to people we like. Don't do anything that makes you the enemy. You're already at a disadvantage due to the nature of the interview.

Third, bullying people into tripping up is just as likely to catch innocent people as it is guilty ones. A single slip-up isn't going to get you a conviction. The only way you can really hold somebody to account for what they said is if you ask the question clearly, give them time to answer it, and then confirm what you heard.

Let's look at an example of rapid-fire questioning. On February 1, 2008, Nicholas Browning snuck out of a sleepover at his friend's house, and he murdered four of his family members. YouTube has video of detectives questioning Nicholas and his friends about their actions that night. I recommend watching the interview for yourself to get the full experience.[12] Here, we will focus in on the detective questioning "Ryan," one of Nicholas' friends.

*Detective:* You guys spent the entire evening together yesterday?
*Ryan:* Yes
*Detective:* At your house? Did you leave the house at all last night?
*Ryan:* Umm…just to walk around the neighborhood.
*Detective:* Okay. How far do you live from where he lives?
*Ryan:* Umm..half a mile.
*Detective:* Half a mile? Did you guys go over there?

*Ryan:* No.
*Detective:* Did he?
*Ryan:* Yes.
*Detective:* What time did he go over there?
*Ryan:* Umm...Like 12:30.
*Detective:* Last night?
*Ryan:* Yes.
*Detective:* What'd he go home for?
*Ryan:* Umm... Truthfully we were going to just take his car out.
*Detective:* I'm sorry. What was his name?
*Ryan:* Nick...Browning. Just take his car out for a little drive.
*Detective:* Okay. Did you guys do that?
*Ryan:* No.

You really have to watch the interview to appreciate how fast the detective is asking him these questions. The whole exchange only takes 33 seconds. Each time Ryan answers, the detective is asking the next question before the last letter in Ryan's word is even fully voiced. It's very fast.

One of the reasons this excerpt illustrates the point so well is that there is at least one occasion when Ryan has a distinct pause before answering. I get the impression that he is attempting to process the question rather than be deceptive.

I'll say again, the best techniques are good for innocent suspects and bad for deceptive suspects. For example, Ask Your Question and Stop is good for innocent suspects because it doesn't confuse the issue you are seeking an answer for, and it is bad for deceptive suspects because it doesn't give them time to think about and refine their lies. Rapid-fire questions are the other way around. They create a situation where an innocent suspect may get tripped up, say the wrong thing, and become a primary suspect. This is bad.

On the other hand, rapid-fire questioning benefits the guilty suspect because it makes you look like a bully, which gives them plausible deniability even if they do slip up and give you something they didn't mean to. I'm sure their attorney will enjoy peppering you with questions to demonstrate to the jury how unpleasant it is. "Your Honor, he didn't know what he was saying much less what the detective was asking."

What if, instead, you asked some of the questions like this:

*Detective:* Did you guys go over there?
*Ryan:* No.
*Detective:* (five second pause)

Or

*Detective:* What time did he go over there?
*Ryan:* Umm... Like 12:30.
*Detective:* 12:30. (Silence)

When you leave silence after the answer, it lets the interviewee know that you aren't fully satisfied with their answer. This will usually lead them to add more information. You're winning when you can get more information for nothing. **Keep your silences to**

**2–5 seconds. That's enough to get more information, but not enough to make it seem like you're messing with them.**

Next time you are in the room with a suspect, leave several seconds of silence after each of their responses to important questions. Maintain eye contact with them while you wait. This is a technique that you can practice (sparingly) around family and friends as well. It's a little bit awkward, but you'll be amazed at how much more people will tell you when you simply wait after hearing their first answer.

## Control Your Emotions

Your goal in the interview room is to gather true information. Displays of negative emotions, particularly anger or disgust, wreak havoc on your ability to accomplish this goal. Nobody wants to talk to another person that is judging them. Feel what you need to feel, but don't let the other person know it. The best approach is pleasant neutrality.

If you've ever seen the interview with Elizabeth Smart's kidnapper, you'll see the investigators engage in techniques that (I hope) are from a bygone era of interviewing. In 2002, Elizabeth Smart was kidnapped by Brian David Mitchell. He kept her for about 9 months before he was caught. He was interrogated by a local cop and an FBI agent. There is yelling, table pounding, and pointing. They express contempt for his actions and his worldview. Unsurprisingly, they don't learn much from the suspect.[13] When you watch the interview, there isn't much to conclude other than that the investigators wanted to either intimidate or shame the suspect into confessing.[14]

Using anger to intimidate a suspect is unlikely to be effective (so we already hate it). In the current environment of law enforcement, even if it did yield information, it would almost certainly be suppressed before ever making it to a courtroom. Ineffective and inadmissible is a devastating blend. You lose if you get your interview thrown out.

It's important to point out that you should watch out for your partners and intervene if they seem incapable of keeping anger out of the interview room. Some cases become personal. There was a child torture case that my partner investigated. The injuries were terrible, and they would leave life-long scars for the victim. I had not been involved in the case at all. I found my partner pacing about his office at an elevated level. He was about to interview the suspect. Even though I didn't know anything about the case, I told him, "You should let me do this one." He was resistant at first, but he ultimately realized that the case had become personal for him, and he let me do it. I'm glad he did. The things the suspect told me were difficult to hear even for me. His anger would have interfered.

Disgust and contempt are the kind of judgmental emotions that need to be kept out of the interview room. Expressing judgment may make us feel righteous, but it doesn't serve our goal of gathering true information. Research has shown rapport-based interviews to be particularly effective in gathering more information from child sex abuse suspects.[15] Contempt or disgust are rapport killers. Are we in the room to make ourselves feel good? Or are we in the room to get the job done? Personally, I want to get the job done.

Your goal is *not* to make the interviewee a better person. There's an interrogation video I reviewed on Jeffrey Sokol's viral *To Catch a Predator* case. In it, Sokol is caught soliciting sex from a 12–13-year-old girl. He is arrested and interrogated. During the interrogation, the detective says, "She's 12!" "A 44 year old guy shouldn't be talking to a 13 year old girl." "She's 12!" "She's still fucking 13 years old dude!" He says a lot of things like that. What purpose do these statements serve? They serve to let Sokol know how the detective sees the world. In the room, we want to know how the suspect sees the world so that what he did seems rational and acceptable to him.[16]

*Tip*: Even if you don't *vocalize* your emotions, other people are remarkably perceptive when it comes to *observing* them in you. Be mindful of what you do with your face as well as with your words.

The best approach in the interview room is pleasant neutrality.

### Use Note Taking as Speed Control

Doing less in the interview room is the best way to get more. Ask your questions then get out of the way and let the interviewee do the work. The thing is, it can be awkward to sit and look at another person after they've answered. They've answered. Now it's your turn. That's where note taking as speed control comes in.

When I go into the room, I have my prepared questions, reports, and evidence, and a notepad. By consistently taking notes throughout the interview, I get the interviewee used to a pattern. I ask questions, and I focus my attention on them during their response and the 2 or 3 seconds after. Then I write notes. While writing, I keep the interviewee in my peripheral so that I can pick up on any major body movements. On especially important questions, I might look up at them in the middle of note-taking and then go back to writing.

Silence is a powerful interview tool. It gives the person more time to add or subtract information, and it gives you more time to examine what they have told you. The thing is, it's weird to sit with another person you don't know and just look at them. They'll start to feel like you're messing with them. Nobody likes to feel like they are being messed with. When you use note-taking to slow your pace down, you get the benefit of silence without the awkwardness. They can see why you aren't talking. You're writing. You're thinking about their answers.

Taking notes like this increases anxiety in the deceptive while having minimal impact on the truthful. Think of answering a question like this: when the interviewee answers, they put a picture between the two of you. A truthful answer may be a slightly blurry picture, but everything is where it is supposed to be. You can look at it and fill in details, but the content stays essentially the same. For example, a *truthful* person's answer comes out like a blurry image you can only really see the outline of. With careful questioning, the picture fills in and becomes sharp.

A deceptive answer is a picture with a detail or details that give it away as being false. The liar would love nothing more than for you to ask another question. The longer their answer sits between the two of you, the more exposed they feel. Their "picture" answer may look like an artificial intelligence images with extra fingers or hallucinations in the background.

At first glance, it all looks fine. Then, as you let the question sit in the open, the strangeness becomes more apparent. You start to notice the extra fingers on the hand or the sign with gibberish in the background. The deceptive person sees the problem faster than you do, and all they want is for you to ask another question before they think you notice it so that the picture can go away. They don't want to focus on this picture. They want to give you a new picture.

Note-taking helps us in all of this. While you are writing your notes, their answer sits between you. You are doing this on purpose, but taking notes makes it seem normal.

A common question I get at training classes: "What do you actually write in your notes?"

The simple answer is that I write what they say. I try to get as much of it as possible. I also note down any major nonverbals I observe. I note vague language, points to follow up on, and certain language features from the Statement Analysis teachings (see Chapter 12). In the room, I use my notes to guide our interview. Later, I use these notes to write my report.

One other point to make about note-taking, after the interviewee answers, if you make any sounds, you will relieve the anxiety in deceptive interviewees. The technique works best when you make no sounds at all. For example:

*Interviewer:* Where were you last night?
*Interviewee:* At home.
*Interviewer:* (Looks at interviewee during response and for several seconds afterwards) (Writes notes for several seconds). Ok…

As opposed to:

*Interviewer:* Where were you last night?
*Interviewee:* At home.
*Interviewer:* (Looks at interviewee during response and for several seconds afterwards) Ok. (Writes notes for several seconds).

The first one holds the pressure on the interviewee all throughout the note-taking. The second one relieves the pressure prior to the note-taking. Try this out in your next interview, and I think you'll notice the difference.

### No Memory Qualifiers

*Memory qualifier defined: a question asked in a way that presupposes they may or may not remember the answer.*

*Q. Huh? You remember how she was dressed at that time?*

A. Uh, I think she had on a nightgown.

*Q. She had a nightgown on?*

A. Think so.

*Q. You don't remember what color it was?*

A. I think it was white.

Excerpt from George Allen interrogation[17]

Memory qualifiers are add-ons to questions that allow a subject to avoid denying a thing by claiming not to remember it. An interview subject might say something like, "I don't remember her being there." How can anyone know what he remembers? This subject is giving himself an out in case it is proven that the person was there. Most people intuitively recognize memory qualifiers from the interviewee as potentially deceptive, but we still use them from the interviewer's side of the table, which makes it easier for the subject to lie.

We see qualifiers all over the place in the George Allen transcript excerpt above. "You remember how she was dressed at that time?" Here the interviewer has used a memory qualifier, which makes it easier for the interviewee to lie should he choose to do so. It's like an invitation to lie. In fact, on the third question, the interviewer combined a negative question with a memory qualifier to create an impressively bad question, "You don't remember what color it was?" If the interviewee were intent on being deceptive, this would be the easiest question to lie to. A simple, "nah," and he's on his way.

Another interview I highly recommend watching is the Stephanie Lazarus interview. She was a LAPD detective nearing retirement after 25 years when she was questioned about the murder of her ex-boyfriend's wife. Her responses are very much worth the watch. In one of my blog posts, I transcribed part of her interview.[18] Let's zoom in on one of these exchanges:

[Detective] **Question asked 1:** You're not sure where he moved to after he got married? You never went over to visit him or his wife...

[Lazarus] **Verbal 1:** No idea! I don't think...I mean, I don't think so. I mean...um...I don't know. I mean I don't think I did. Um. I mean I know he lived on Roscoe for a long, long time. Um (sigh) I mean I may know. He may have told me where he lived. Somewhere in the valley. I mean he may have said he lived over in such and such, but I...I couldn't tell ya specifically where.

[Lazarus] **Nonverbal 1:** Grimace, shoulder shrug, hands out, eyes wide, grimace, hands in a juggling motion, gulp, gulp more hands, leaning forward, shoulder shrug.

[Detective] **Question asked 2:** But you don't remember specifically ever going over to visit him or visit them wherever he moved when he left Roscoe?

[Lazarus] **Verbal 2:** I don't. Honestly, I don't know. I don't think so. But, you know, I don't want to say, "no I don't think so and then he says oh yeah she came over for something, dropped something off" um you know I don't know.

[Lazarus] **Nonverbal 2:** grimace, hands, lean forward again

Here the detective asks a few negative questions (discussed more in the next section) in the first prompt. He then asks a negative memory qualifier in the second prompt: "But you don't remember..." The correct question is, "Did you visit him at the house he moved to when he left Roscoe?" We all ask clumsy questions sometimes. Overall, the Lazarus detectives did a great job with a tough interview.

Detecting deception is hard enough, we don't want to make it any harder by virtue of the way we ask our questions. A memory qualifier can come from either the suspect or the investigator. As Inbau et al pointed out in their book *Essentials of the Reid Technique*, "Deceptive subjects will use memory qualifiers with their answer to a question to reduce personal responsibility within the response....However, if the investigator's question contains a memory qualifier, the deceptive subject feels much more confident in his denial..."[19]

The use of memory qualifiers is one of the most common mistakes I hear when listening to others interview. Once you understand how bad they are for your interviews, it is relatively easy to get rid of them. Tune your ears in to what you and others are saying. You'll start hearing them everywhere. Practice noticing them. Then practice removing them from your speech patterns.

Instead of: "Do you remember where you were last night?"
Ask: "Where were you last night?"

Instead of: "Do you recall how you got there?"
Ask: "How did you get there?"

In the above examples, the second question is clearly the better question. It's like that for all memory qualifiers. You may still hear, "I don't remember how I got there," but you'll have made *them* use the qualifier instead of giving them an easy out.

### Get Rid of Negative Questions

We've talked some about negative questions in the previous section on memory qualifiers. In general, they make it very easy to say "no" to the question because of how they are framed. There *are* instances when negative questions can be used to achieve specific ends, but they are most often used in ways that hurt the interview. It is best to avoid negative questions altogether.

In the Stephanie Lazarus interview mentioned in the last section we saw this question:

[Detective] **Question asked 1**: You're not sure where he moved to after he got married?

The way this question is framed makes it very easy to lie should she so choose. A better question would be, "Where did he move after he got married?"

Here are a few examples from the previous referenced George Allen, Jr. interrogation:

*Q. You didn't cut her?*

A. No.

*Q. You sure?*

A. I'm sure.

*Q. Absolutely positive?*

A. Positive.

Then:

*Q. You didn't touch the knife?*

A. No.

*Q. You sure of that?*

*A.* I'm sure. I didn't touch it.[20]

These negative questions are all over the place. Like memory qualifiers, you'll hear them when you start listening for them. Unless you are using a negative question as a purposeful means to an end, avoid them.

There are two ways negative questions can be used to achieve specific ends. First, is the roadside classic, "You don't mind if I search your car, do you?" This is a question that is purposefully designed to increase the chance of getting the desired "negative" response, "No, I don't mind." This question is effective, which is why it has become such a mainstay in roadside interdiction type interviews.

Second, a negative question can be used to confirm a denial that has already been voiced but that you have evidence is a lie. You can lock them into the denial and then later expose it for the lie that it is. Imagine investigating a case where you have excellent evidence that the suspect shot "Ray":

*Question: Did you shoot Ray?*

*Answer:* No. I didn't. I wouldn't do that.

*Question: So you didn't shoot Ray?*

*Answer:* Uh-uh. That's what I said.

In my opinion, this is an acceptable use of a negative question. In general, though, they should be avoided. With all the things to think about in an interview room, spending the brain power to think about if *this* negative question is a good one seems inefficient.

### Forced Silence

Once you ask a significant question, consider not saying anything until the suspect answers your question. This technique addresses a relatively common counterstrategy of simply remaining silent. In my experience, the questions interviewees use this strategy on tend to be the most sensitive. Most interviewers end up filling the silence and changing the question.

Let your question keep doing its work. They heard your question. Be prepared to wait for however long it takes. A typical forced silence event might take 10-30 seconds. Long ones will stretch for several minutes.

A great example of forced silence is seen in the interrogation of Michael Bailey, a man caught exposing himself in a Walmart. The technique really comes across better in the video.[21]

*Interviewer:* So let's back up. Where does this start? How long has this been going on?

(21 seconds of total silence)

*Interviewee:* I don't know. I guess quite a while.

The concept is easy to understand, but it takes a lot of discipline to get it right. You have to be going slowly enough to recognize the interviewee hasn't answered. You have to wait and allow yourself to feel awkward. Not every suspect will use this counterstrategy. **However, in my experience, of all the questioning techniques discussed in this book, this one is the most likely to lead to a significant admission.** It's well worth practicing.

## Don't Assume Anything. What They Say Is What They Say

A common source of misunderstanding comes from assumptions. The interviewer fills in the gaps of what they are told to create a coherent narrative. This tendency is bad for understanding what it is that compliant interviewees are trying to communicate. It is devastating for understanding what happened when it comes to deceptive interviewees.

Compliant interviewees want to communicate to you what happened. They don't include all of the details because they may not realize how important they are. It may seem obvious to them, for example, that it hurt when the suspect hit them, so they don't say so. They may be embarrassed that they were drunk at the time, so they don't mention it. Ask questions until you understand what the person is telling you.

Deceptive interviewees are trickier. They want to encourage you to make assumptions. If they cause you to make assumptions, they get away with lying by omission without *actually* lying. This provides them an out should you reveal the omission later on. "I didn't *say* that I was at the bar. I told you that I *usually* go to the bar on Wednesdays. You weren't listening to me!" It's important to realize that this is a specific technique employed by deceptive suspects to mislead you.

Don't assume anything! If the interviewee says that they are married, don't assume their marriage is like yours. One interviewee talked about how happily married he was. As the interviewer, I began to fill in the blanks around what that meant by thinking that his happy marriage was like my happy marriage: loving, faithful to one another and the like. Later, however, he told me that he regularly got hotel rooms and had drug-fueled sex with random women. Apparently *his* happy marriage includes sex with random women outside of the home. If I had simply assumed that his marriage was like mine without examining what he meant, I would have missed out on key information surrounding the case.

**A good interviewer assumes nothing. If they say they were robbed, don't assume they were scared. If they say they were hit, don't assume they were hurt. If they say they went to bed, don't assume they stayed asleep.**

### *Encouragers / Reflections*

*My kid:* I don't like my bus driver.
*Me:* Because? **ENCOURAGER**
*Interviewee:* I went downtown with my friends. We visited a few different bars.
*Interviewer:* Bars? **REFLECTION**

Encouragers are single words or short phrases designed to let the interviewee know that you expect more from them. There is no single technique that will get you more information for less effort. Although they are easy to learn, it will feel awkward to use them at first.

Examples of encouragers:

| | |
|---|---|
| Go on... | What then? |
| And? | What else? |
| Because? | Uh huh |
| Oh? | (silence) |
| Really? | How so? |
| I'm listening | Tell me more |

Reflections are one or two-word echoes of what the person just told you said in a questioning tone. These brief extracts of the person's own statement prompt them to keep going with little effort from you.

*Interviewee:* We went downtown last night.
*Interviewer:* Downtown?

*Interviewee:* I only had one drink.
*Interviewer:* One drink?

I imagine a conversation as passing a ball back and forth. Whoever is talking is holding the ball. I want the suspect to hold the ball as much as possible. Using either an encourager or a reflection is like a quick pass back to the sender. They have the ball again, which is where I want to be. They are the most interesting person in the room. I want them to talk and to talk a lot. In this game, the person that holds the ball the least is the winner.

Typical interview

*Interviewer:* Where were you last night?
*Interviewee:* With friends.
*Interviewer:* Which friends were you with?
*Interviewee:* Sam and Joe.
*Interviewer:* Sam? What's his last name?
*Interviewee:* Martin.
*Interviewer:* You said you were with Joe too?

Here we can see that the interviewer says more words than the interviewee. The interviewee held the ball the least so he wins. Point, interviewee (suspect).

Better interview

*Interviewer:* Where were you last night?
*Interviewee:* With friends.
*Interviewer:* Ok... **ENCOURAGER**
*Interviewee:* You see we like to go out to McFadden's on Saturday night. It's like a regular thing.
*Interviewer:* McFadden's? **REFLECTION**

| | |
|---|---|
| *Interviewee:* | I wasn't just there by myself. I had Sam and Joe there. They'll vouch for me. |
| *Interviewer:* | Really? **ENCOURAGER** |

Here the interviewer kept pushing the conversation ball back with continuers and reflections. The interviewer said less, so the interviewer wins. Point, interviewer (detective).

The use of continuers and reflections requires practice. It's un-training our natural response of receiving information and asking a question about it. In order to make sure that you will use them in interviews where it matters, look for opportunities to use continuers and reflections outside of the suspect interview room. This is a technique that you can practice with family, coworkers, and friends.

## Summarize

> The interviewer should close by reviewing the narrative. A review provides the subject with additional cues to memory, so that he might provide new details if he is telling the truth. It also allows the interviewer to check the accuracy of his own notes and his understanding of the narrative; an honest subject is likely to correct inaccuracies.
>
> Science-Based Interviewing[22]

Summarizing the interviewee's statements is one of the most powerful questioning tools you can use. Summarizing allows truthful people to correct inaccuracies, it locks deceptive people into a statement in a way that they can't claim misunderstanding, and it allows you to see things you have missed. When I summarize an interviewee's statement, I *almost always* think of more information I want to know.

First, gather the suspect's statement about a particular issue. Use questioning techniques we have reviewed so far such as encouragers, reflections, and silence. Once you have the statement, simply say to them, "Ok, I heard you say... Did I get that right?"

The following is based on a patrol call I responded to on January 13, 2024.

| | |
|---|---|
| *Me:* | What happened? |
| *Interviewee:* | She woke me up hitting me, yelling about my phone and how I had to get out. That's why my shirt looks like this. I just want my phone and I'm out. |
| *Me:* | Your phone? **REFLECTION** |
| *Interviewee:* | Look, I was on [Facebook] live. I worked that day and I passed out with the phone on. She must have come in, checked the phone, and seen things she shouldn't have. |
| *Me:* | What else? **ENCOURAGER** |
| *Interviewee:* | Then my girl started hitting me. Cussing me. Tell me about this and that. Her sister drove off with my clothes. She told me that she poured bleach all over them! I don't even care about all that. I just want my phone. |
| *Me:* | Your girl? **REFLECTION** |
| *Interviewee:* | I met her. We linked up. She's three months pregnant with my baby. I don't even care about all that. I just want my phone. |

| | |
|---|---|
| *Me:* | Ok. I heard you say that you came home from a day of work. You are living with your girlfriend. You were doing a live [video] and passed out. You woke up to her hitting you and yelling about getting out. Then her sister stole your clothes. You want your phone back so that you can leave. Did I get that right? **SUMMARY** |
| *Interviewee:* | Yeah. |
| *Me:* | Are you hurt? **CLOSED QUESTION** |
| *Interviewee:* | Look, man, I could say some things that wouldn't look good for her, but I'm not trying to do all that. I want my phone and I'm out. I'm not hurt.[23] |

In this conversation, the interviewee did most of the talking. I used encouragers, reflections, and summary to get his statement. After summarizing what he said, I noticed that he mentioned getting hit but not being hurt, so I asked him about it.

The man with the bleached clothes was probably being straightforward with his story (even if he wasn't being straightforward with his girl). Summarizing his statement helps me see what I am missing, but it doesn't cause any great change in his story. It is what it is.

With deceptive people, though, summarizing their statements can shine a light on how unlikely their statements are. This will cause them to modify their statement or double down on unlikely, which puts them in a bad spot. People intuitively know that changing their statement is a red flag for deception, but they also know that unlikely statements sound like lies.

Another benefit to summarizing statements is locking the suspect into the admissions they have made. In a recent interview, a suspect gradually revealed how he provided a weapon to a friend. That weapon was subsequently used in a serious crime. At the start of the interview, he denied knowing the suspect, lending the weapon to anyone, and having any knowledge of the crime. He gradually revealed the truth of the matter of the course of several hours. I summarized all of his admissions back to him. He confirmed that I had it right. He is now locked into a neat statement of his involvement. As a bonus, I noticed areas needing more clarification, and I got those from him.

As with other techniques, summarizing statements is something that you can practice outside of the interview room so that it can be like second nature when you are in the room. When my kids tell me about their days, I summarize what I heard. When my wife asks me to do something, I summarize what I heard. My friends and family feel heard, and I'm getting a rep in for the interview room.

## Summary

This chapter focuses on effective questioning techniques, emphasizing the importance of open-ended questions, active listening, and patience. It introduces the CI method, which significantly enhances information retrieval by encouraging detailed narratives and minimizing interruptions. Don't use memory qualifiers or negative questions, as they can lead to unreliable answers. Ask one question at a time. Use reflections and continuers. Assume nothing. With regular application of these techniques, interviewers can obtain more accurate and comprehensive information.

## Immediately Actionable

*When you hear the question mark, stop.* Today, listen for at least three examples of people (maybe you?) asking two or more questions at a time. Your own conversations, podcasts, audiobooks, etc.

*Use at least one encourager*: At the next opportunity, encourage the person you are speaking with to "go on" or explain themselves more "because?" This takes practice. Never miss a chance to practice.

*Use a reflection:* Try to echo back one or two of the last words your conversation partner says. "Have you watched the movie?" "The movie?" / "We went to the bar." "The bar?"

*Summarize:* Review what the other person said to see how well you understood them. Does it make you think of other questions?

## Notes

1 Brandon, Susan E. and Simon Wells, *Science Based Interviewing*, 1st ed. (BookBaby, 2019), 58.
2 Brandon, Susan E. and Simon Wells, *Science Based Interviewing*, 1st ed. (BookBaby, 2019), 57.
3 Brandon, Susan E. and Simon Wells, *Science Based Interviewing*, 1st ed. (BookBaby, 2019), 58.
4 Brandon, Susan E. and Simon Wells, *Science Based Interviewing*, 1st ed. (BookBaby, 2019), 60–67.
5 Fisher, Ronald P. and Edward R. Geiselman, *Memory-Enhancing Techniques for Investigative Interviewing: The Cognitive Interview* (Springfield, IL: Charles C. Thomas, 1992), 21.
6 Fisher, Ronald P. and Edward R. Geiselman, *Memory-Enhancing Techniques for Investigative Interviewing: The Cognitive Interview* (Springfield, IL: Charles C. Thomas, 1992), 20.
7 Reddington, *The Disciplined Listening Method*, 55.
8 Inbau, Fred Edward, *Essentials of the Reid Technique: Criminal Interrogation and Confessions* (Burlington, MA: Jones & Bartlett Learning, 2015), 57.
9 Nichols, Ralph G., and Leonard A. Stevens. 1957. "Listening to People." Harvard Business Review. September 1957. https://hbr.org/1957/09/listening-to-people
10 "The Aftermath Part 1: Kids, Schools, and the Crime Surge." 2022. Apple Podcasts. January 19, 2022. https://podcasts.apple.com/us/podcast/the-aftermath-part-1-kids-schools-and-the-crime-surge/id1570872415?i=1000548337785
11 BBC News. 2019. "Transcript in Full: Prince Andrew's Interview," November 17, 2019, sec. UK. https://www.bbc.com/news/uk-50449339
12 "What a 15 Year Old Mass Killer Looks Like." n.d. www.youtube.com. https://www.youtube.com/watch?v=MtNASztI83c
13 To be fair, the suspect may have been so mentally ill that even softer interview techniques might not have worked.
14 Youtube. 2025. https://youtu.be/QybphTUd-o0?si=IH8D9JXCM4KczJST
15 Alison, Emily et al., "Observing Rapport-Based Interpersonal Techniques (ORBIT)," *Investigative Interviewing: Research and Practice* 12, no. 1 (2022).
16 A thought from Dr. Graham Hill as gathered during his talks at the Crimes Against Children Conference 2019-2024.
17 "Confession Transcript." n.d. Riverfront Times. https://web.archive.org/web/20240804170123/https://www.riverfronttimes.com/news/confession-transcript-2465504. Note: George Allen confessed to and was convicted for the rape and murder of Mary Bell. He was later exonerated.
18 Purdy, Lewis. 2022. "New Video, Stephanie Lazarus." Substack.com. Interview and Interrogation For Police Detectives. March 29, 2022. https://lewispurdy.substack.com/p/new-video-stephanie-lazarus
19 Inbau, *Essentials of the Reid Technique*, 57.
20 "Confession Transcript." Riverfront Times.
21 Interrogations. 2022. "Michael Bailey - Exposed in Walmart Full Interrogation." YouTube. January 24, 2022. https://www.youtube.com/watch?v=-xjWVahqihk. Note: Starting at 28:45.
22 Brandon and Wells, *Science Based Interviewing*, 65.
23 Based on a real conversation from a January 13, 2024 patrol call.

## References

Alison, Emily et al. 2022. "Observing Rapport-Based Interpersonal Techniques (ORBIT)," *Investigative Interviewing: Research and Practice* 12, no. 1: 33–5.

Brandon, Susan E., and Simon Wells. 2019. *Science Based Interviewing*, 1st ed. Pennsauken, NJ: BookBaby.

"Confession Transcript." n.d. Riverfront Times. https://web.archive.org/web/20240804170123/https://www.riverfronttimes.com/news/confession-transcript-2465504

Fisher, Ronald P., and Edward R. Geiselman. 1992. *Memory-Enhancing Techniques for Investigative Interviewing: The Cognitive Interview*. Springfield, IL: Charles C. Thomas.

Inbau, Fred Edward. 2015. *Essentials of the Reid Technique: Criminal Interrogation and Confessions*. Burlington, MA: Jones & Bartlett Learning.

Interrogations. 2022. "Michael Bailey - Exposed in Walmart Full Interrogation." YouTube. January 24, 2022. https://www.youtube.com/watch?v=-xjWVahqihk

Nichols, Ralph G., and Leonard A. Stevens. 1957. "Listening to People." Harvard Business Review. September 1957. https://hbr.org/1957/09/listening-to-people

Purdy, Lewis. 2022. "New Video, Stephanie Lazarus." Substack.com. Interview and Interrogation For Police Detectives. March 29, 2022. https://lewispurdy.substack.com/p/new-video-stephanie-lazarus

Reddington, Michael. 2022. *The Disciplined Listening Method: How a Certified Forensic Interviewer Unlocks Hidden Value in Every Conversation*. Charlotte, NC: Per Capita.

"The Aftermath Part 1: Kids, Schools, and the Crime Surge." 2022. Apple Podcasts. January 19, 2022. https://podcasts.apple.com/us/podcast/the-aftermath-part-1-kids-schools-and-the-crime-surge/id1570872415?i=1000548337785

"What a 15 Year Old Mass Killer Looks Like." n.d. www.youtube.com. https://www.youtube.com/watch?v=MtNASztI83c

Youtube. 2025. https://youtu.be/QybphTUd-o0?si=IH8D9JXCM4KczJST

Chapter 3

# Detecting Deception

### Key Points

1. *Deception detection is dynamic*: You can detect deception at all levels of interviewing. Work the level you're at. Don't worry about some deception getting away from you.
2. *There is no single definitive indicator of deception*: An indication is not a certainty. Look for it, but be open to the possibility that the indicator has a meaning other than deception.
3. *Vagueness, failing to answer, and redefinitions*: These are some deceptive indicators.
4. *Nonverbals*: Good to know. Should not be prioritized over verbal.

What is a lie? Lies are statements or actions intended to mislead another. Lies can range from inconspicuous, to subtle, to obvious. When the layperson thinks about a lie, they usually think of the obvious: a lie by fabrication. "I'm not cheating on you (but I am)." "My grandma died so I need time away from work (but grandma is alive and well)." In fact, most lies fall into a trickier category of lying. Lies by evasion: omission, distraction, or deliberately misleading statements. These are lies told deliberately in a way that, if caught, the person can theoretically save face by denying that such was not their intent.[1]

You can detect deception at all levels of interviewing, but detecting deception is different at each level. At level 1, we suspect the person is lying because what they say conflicts with previous statements or our case facts. At level 2, we suspect the person is lying based on a careful examination of their words. At level 3, we suspect the person is lying based on what they *do* in the context of what they say. As you level up your game you'll have the ability to detect deception at all of the levels.

Be kind to yourself when it comes to detecting deception. ***You are going to miss lies.*** Be aware that a lot of deception detection discussed in the following sections takes place at level two interviewing when you really start to listen. Because lie detection via careful statement analysis takes place at a level possibly higher than where you are, my recommendation is not to focus on it until you are proficient at level one.

Level one interviewing, remember, is knowing what to say and how you are going to say it. Bad input (poor preparation, sloppy question asking, etc.) equals bad output (hard to interpret responses). Deception detection at this level is relatively easy. As a result of your careful questioning, they say something that conflicts with previous statements or known case facts, and you note the discrepancy. **Your best odds of having positive interview outcomes come from working at the level you are at.**

DOI: 10.4324/9781003663904-4

## Basics of Spotting Lies

Lies have different levels of stress associated with them, correlated with the likelihood of being found out.

*Omission*: low stress, hard to spot
*Evasion*: moderate stress, observable but easy to miss
*Fabrication*: high stress, easy to spot

What should we do when we are lied to? Let's review Don Rabon's writing on lies,[2] which I think answers this well. He says that the easiest lie to tell and the hardest to detect is the lie by omission.

*Omission*: The robber talks all about cruising around town with his friends, but he neglects to mention (omits) that he robbed a convenience store.

The hardest lie to tell and the easiest to detect is by fabrication (making something up entirely).

*Fabrication*: The robber makes up an alibi rife with details of things that never happened.

Between omission and fabrication is what Rabon calls the "portal of refuge." These are three tricky techniques to avoid fabrication if possible. These are:

1 Excessive detail on barely related topics
2 Very short answers
3 Evasiveness

In terms of what to do about being lied to, Rabon recommends maneuvering the deceptive interviewee from the easy lies to the harder lies in order to place them in a more vulnerable position.

The convenience store robber first tells you all about that day, but he omits the robbery. He's pretty safe here because he hasn't really lied yet. Through careful questions about his timeline, the robber opts to take you down a rabbit hole and tell you all about his tough childhood (which you didn't ask about). When you, being the dogged interviewer you are, guide him back to the subject, he becomes evasive.

Example:

*Interviewer:* Were you ever in a convenience store that night?
*Interviewee:* I hardly ever go into convenience stores.

These stratagems draw the attention of the attentive interviewer. The robber is resisting, but he still has a thin layer of plausible deniability because he hasn't exactly lied. That interviewer will continue to direct questions into those topic areas. "Okay, but were you in a convenience store *that* night?" Eventually, the robber will need to provide a specific answer.

Finally, the interviewer leads the robber to where he is forced to declare that, yes he did it or no he didn't do it. Either of these is a falsifiable statement. In order to support it, he will need to fabricate information to provide an alibi or account for evidence. Now the robber is exposed. The cognitive demands of lying are likely to make him contradict himself.

We can see some elements of Rabon's interviewing process in the interview I did with a mother that (accidentally?) smothered her baby. In this case, a wandering homeless person found a backpack on a wooded path. When he opened it, he found a dead (human) newborn baby inside. He carried it to a nearby hotel, and he called the police. When we responded to the scene, other items in the backpack led us back to a woman I'll call Amanda.

A witness told us that Amanda was "flying a sign" (holding a sign for cars to see) on the side of the highway, begging for money. When I approached Amanda as she held her sign, I asked, "Do you know why we're here?" To which she responded, "Because of the sign? I can move." My partner saw how scared Amanda was. She said, "Amanda. Hey. It's ok. It's ok now." Amanda began to cry. She said, "I didn't mean to!"

What was Amanda's reflexive strategy for lying? Omission. She didn't fabricate anything, but she still lied. She knew why we were there. When you had your baby die within the last 48 hours, and you left him in the woods in a backpack, the whole truth when police ask if you know why they are talking to you is, "probably about my baby."

Upon questioning, Amanda told us that she was homeless. A few days before, she fell asleep at a bus stop holding her newborn child. When she woke up, her baby was gone. Her boyfriend told her that it was in the backpack at her feet. When she looked inside the backpack, she saw that her baby was dead. Not knowing what to do, she left the backpack there so she could walk across the street, charge her phone, and look for a place to bury her baby. While they were gone, somebody stole the backpack with her baby inside.

I wanted to explore the possibility that she had been on drugs at the time.

*Me:* Were you using heroin?
*Amanda:* No.
*Me:* Marijuana?
*Amanda:* No.
*Me:* Crack?
*Amanda:* I don't like the smell of crack.
*Me:* (thinking: so it's crack)

Her answer was evasive. I asked if she was using crack at the time her baby died, and she told me that she doesn't like the smell of crack. Those aren't the same things.

So, is Amanda telling the truth about how her baby died? I don't know. The best way to distinguish between truth and a lie is what we know to be true. In Amanda's case, at the time I interviewed her, there were still too many things I didn't know at all. **As a general rule, your first formal interview with a suspect should happen when you know everything you can hope to know about your case.** Sometimes it doesn't happen that way, though. If you find yourself in an earlier-than-ideal interview with a suspect, focus on locking them into a story.

In Amanda's case, I didn't accuse her of anything during this interview. I gathered a careful account. I pointed out discrepancies and asked her to explain them. I suspected that Amanda was lying to me about some things (drugs, leaving the backpack but intending to come back, etc.), but I didn't know which things. If I had chosen to accuse her of purposefully causing the death of her child in this first interview, I would have ruined the chance for a second interview, the interview where I'd actually have evidence to back up my hunches. By the time we finished, I had a detailed story and a good rapport with Amanda. Should we ever need to talk further, I have no doubt that she would agree to speak with me.

How can we spot a lie? If I had a definitive answer for you, I'd be very rich. I have some ideas, though.

Over Christmas break, I asked different people, "Tell me all about what you did last night, but lie about everything." It was surprising how different each person approached this unplanned, forced fabrication. A lie by fabrication is the hardest for the liar to tell. Because they didn't have a chance to plan for it, I think that their natural lying tendencies, which would otherwise be more subtle, were highlighted.

One person gripped the side of the chair, opened her eyes wider than I thought they could go, and stared unblinking at me as she told me her story. Another person made big, illustrative gestures with her hands that she hadn't done at any other time during the evening.

I had a lot of fun acting like an expert in body language, which I am not. I was probably right about the tells on how those people lied, but the way they were forced to lie isn't a realistic scenario you'd encounter. If they really wanted to lie to me about last night, they'd probably choose to omit, evade, and minimize before fabricating a single fact much less all of the facts.

We can still learn from this exercise. For example, people lie differently and unplanned lies of pure fabrication appear to be very stressful. This is an exercise I'll continue to try because I want to see more and more ways that people lie. I think that the more ways we can observe people lying, the better chance we will have to spot the lie in the moment that we are interviewing a suspect.

I think of the movie *Rounders*. This is a movie about underground, high-stakes poker games. The Matt Damon character realizes that the John Malkovich character's "tell" is when he lifts his Oreo cookies to his ear. Once Damon's character knew the tell, he was quick to spot it.

How can we get better at spotting lies? Again, I don't have the final answer, but I'd like to share with you something that I do, which I think helps me get better at spotting lies: I pay attention to how I lie.

Most of us don't want to admit to being liars. But, truthfully? We all do it. All of us are liars. We lie, consistently, in all kinds of ways, for all kinds of reasons. "The *average* adult tells between .59 and 1.56 lies daily."[3] Even if you think of yourself as an honest person, odds are that you lie regularly.

If you don't know how you lie, I recommend that you start paying attention. No matter how often we may suspect others of lying, we rarely know they are lying. Because it is hard to know, we can think lots of things about lying that may be based on bad input (we thought they were lying but they weren't). Ourselves on the other hand? We always know when we are lying. This means that analyzing how we lie pulls from that unicorn of deception research: situations where we know what is actually true.

Aldert Vrij is one of the most cited persons on the topic of detecting deception. He uses the phrase "ground truth" to refer to what is actually true. He writes extensively about how the weakness in many of the attempts to detect deception is that the ground truth isn't known. *In Detecting Lies and Deceit* he writes:

> Establishing the ground truth, however, is crucial in field deception research. Only when ground truth is established can researchers conclude with certainty that all the alleged

> truth tellers in their study were actually telling the truth and that all the alleged liars were actually lying. Certainty about truth status of all the examinees in a study is essential for drawing any conclusions or for being able to trust the outcomes.[4]

Here you are, a walking talking laboratory, lying .59–1.56 times per day and not collecting any of the research. Shame.

Let's look at a situation about which I know the ground truth. I know it because I did it. Recently, I sold a nice watch to a friend. My kids were with me, and they saw the transaction. When my wife came home, she asked me about our day. I listed off all the things we did without mentioning meeting my friend for lunch or selling him the watch. Later, the kids told my wife about daddy selling his watch. She turned to look at me. One of the kids chimed in, "How much did you sell it for, dad?" "None of your business." Then my wife asked. I told her how much I sold it for. She said, "You didn't mention selling the watch." I said, "I didn't *not* mention selling the watch." When the opportunity came up, I gladly switched the subject. I had other plans for the money that might not have been plans we both would have agreed on.

So what strategies did I use here? First, I **omitted** the information when discussing our activities that day. Second, once we started talking about the watch I "**attacked**" the interviewer by saying it was none of their business what I sold it for. Third, I **changed the subject** to avoid talking more about what was going to happen with the money. **Every single one of these strategies is used by people you will be interviewing.**

If you can really tune into yourself, you can also pay attention to nonverbal things that you do when you lie. When I was caught in #watchgate, I felt my heart rate increase, the heat in my face increase, and increased rate of speech. As much as the scientists like Vrij (cited above) hate nonverbals, they are a real thing. They aren't easy to interpret, but maybe as you continue to pay attention to how you lie, you'll be more interested in directing follow-up questions to the topics under discussion when you notice them. I guarantee that I'll be suspicious if those family members from Christmas talk to me all wide-eyed or wavey-handey like they did when they were fabricating their stories.

If you can learn how you lie, you'll be better able to spot how other people lie. How did you approach that omission? How might you gain insight into a suspect doing the same with that knowledge? How could you counteract it? What crafty language do you use when you want to mislead? Is that something you could spot in another person? How do you feel when you are confronted about a lie? If the interviewee felt like you felt, what would be the key to get them to open up?

As a bonus, being real with yourself about misleading statements and other tricky lies might make you wonder if you should just … tell the truth? Until that day of radical honesty comes, though, you might as well learn from yourself.

## Level 1 Interviewer Deception Detection

This foundational level of deception detection has two main components: *questioning technique* and *preparation*. We discussed questioning technique in the previous chapter. Asking questions the right way isn't complicated, but it takes practice. The second component to detecting deception at level 1 is to know your case facts.

This level of deception detection prioritizes noticing conflicting statements and discrepancies, which presupposes a thorough knowledge of your case facts. If you don't know anything, all things are equally likely. What do you know? How do you know it? Are there any other alternative explanations for what you think you know?

If a case comes to my attention via the queue (as opposed to a patrol call), my investigation starts by reading the report. I'm looking for answers to the standard questions: Who? What? Where? When? Why? How? These are the latter types of cases discussed in Chapter 1. In these cases, I have the luxury of conducting a full investigation before contacting the suspect.

After reading the report, I recommend reviewing any footage captured of conversations between officers and the victims, witnesses, and suspects. Officer's reports are summaries of interactions, often made hours after they happened. Many things can be missed. If a suspect makes conflicting statements, for example, the officer may or may not write that in their report. The reports are a good starting point, but you'll want to review the actual footage of the on-scene interviews if time permits.

Look up past reports with all of the involved persons, not just the suspect. Have they reported similar crimes in the past? Do any of the parties have a history of drug use or mental illness? Are there any significant arrests?

Consider your evidence. Your evidence is essential for creating your overall interview strategy. (This is discussed in depth in Chapter 9.) Are there other explanations for the evidence? How can you prompt the interviewee to account for the evidence without telling them everything you have?

Once I have conducted my investigation and identified the suspect, I can start to prepare my questions for the suspect interview. Write more questions than you think you'll need. In general, I organize my questions from least problematic for the interviewee to most problematic. Even though they may be organized like that, I never ask in order, straight from my question list. I follow the conversation and then use my prepared questions to get back on track.

The process for the more urgent Now cases (where patrol has called in the report straight to a detective), is mostly the same, but it happens on a more compressed schedule. You should have access to the officers, witnesses, victims, and sometimes the suspect. Thus, while you may not be able to review the videos of first responders yet, you can do the next best thing, which is to interview the involved parties themselves. You should still prepare questions, even if it is just handwritten on a notepad.

*Once you have your prepared questions, a basic understanding of how to ask your questions, and a thorough knowledge of your case facts, you are well set up for success.* As an investigator, you have the most control over level 1 deception detection. You have plenty of time to practice *how* to ask questions before you ever even get in the room with the suspect. You get to decide how deeply you look into the case, examine the evidence, and question the involved parties. You get to choose how long you spend preparing your questions. This is not so much a skill issue as it is a preparation issue.

## Level 2 Interviewer Deception Detection

Level 2 interviewer deception detection builds on the knowledge generated using level 1 skills. Here, you do level 1 things *and* listen for the finer points of what the suspect says and how they say it. At this level, we are considering paralinguistic elements (how the suspect says what they say), word choice, apparent stress level, and sentence structure.

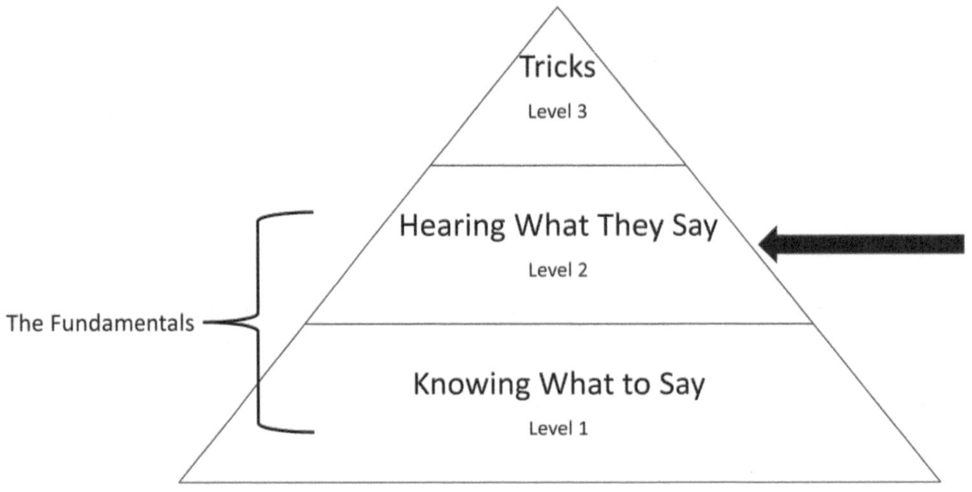


*Image 3.1* Pyramid of Interviewing and Interrogation, emphasizing the second level, Hearing What They Say.

Look to Chapter 12 for an essay on Statement Analysis, which firmly fits within level 2 deception detection.

In this next section, I will discuss several techniques employed by those whose intention is to deceive. Many of these deceptive indicators will go unobserved by level 1 interviewers. If you are a level 1 interviewer, the goal is to know about the techniques and practice spotting them. It is the level 2 interviewers that will benefit the most by prioritizing follow-up on these indicators. When these indicators emerge, push more and more questions into those areas of the story. With some persistence, the deception will be revealed. *Then* you can decide what to do about it.

### *Vagueness*

Much of interviewing is being curious. A lack of specificity around key parts of the story is an indicator of deception. I say it's an indicator not that it is a certainty. Sometimes it's obvious. Sometimes it's much more subtle. Anytime your interviewee engages in vagueness at key moments in the story, you should be curious and follow up.

When Congressman Anthony Weiner got swept up in a controversy over sending nudes to underaged girls, he engaged in a number of deceptive techniques including vagueness. In his ABC interview, the interviewer asked Weiner, "…You can't tell me definitively that is a photo of you or not a photo of you?" To which Weiner replied, "Look here's what…I am reluctant to say to you anything definitive about this." This is laughably vague. Any interviewer would follow up on this lack of specificity.

Sometimes the vagueness is more subtle. This is where the art of noticing and following up comes in. In 2019, police interrogated Grant Amato about his involvement in the murders of his three family members. Amato had spent a quarter million dollars of his father's money to sext with an overseas pay-for-chat model. When it was discovered, he murdered his family. Here is an exchange between him and the police detectives. Look for vagueness.

| | |
|---|---|
| *Interviewer:* | He leaves to go home, and you leave to go where? |
| *Amato:* | I stay in that general area. Just so that…if anything happens somebody like knows where I am. |
| *Interviewer:* | How long did you stay there? |
| *Amato:* | I stayed there for (several seconds of silence) I mean like couple hours I would say. |
| *Interviewers:* | (Talking over one another) In that same area you were talking about? |
| *Amato:* | Like I would go kind of like just up and down that road a little bit just so like my car isn't just like sitting there. But, for the most…Yeah, I would stay in that like general area, and then I decided to go to Publix.[5] |

This answer is about a crucial part of Amato's timeline. This is a time to be as specific as possible and yet he is being completely vague. It is possible that he doesn't remember specifics - human memory is fragile after all - but his vagueness in this portion of the story is a significant indication of deception. The only thing he was specific about at all was having ended up at Publix. Let's look at the excerpt again and highlight where he is vague.

| | |
|---|---|
| *Interviewer:* | He leaves to go home, and you leave to go where? |
| *Amato:* | I stay in that **general area**. Just so that…if **anything** happens **somebody** like knows where I am. |
| *Interviewer:* | How long did you stay there? |
| *Amato:* | I stayed there for (several seconds of silence) I mean like **couple hours** I **would say.** |
| *Interviewers:* | (Talking over one another) In that same area you were talking about? |
| *Amato:* | Like I would go **kind of like** just up and down that road **a little bit** just so like my car isn't just like sitting there. But, for the most…Yeah, I **would stay** in that like **general area,** and then I decided to go to Publix. |

If you were interviewing Amato, you would want to direct questions into all of these vague areas. Here are some questions you might want to ask:

- "You said you stayed in that general area, tell me more about that."
- "Besides that general area, where else did you go?"
- "You said, 'somebody knows where you are.' Who might have been looking for you?"
- "You said, 'a couple hours.' Tell me more about that."
- "You went up and down the road 'a little bit.' What do you mean?"

In order to get the most out of this, do not be overly specific in your questions. For example, you wouldn't want your first follow-up to be, "You said a couple hours, exactly what time did you get there and what time did you leave?" The reason you don't want to do this right away is that it restricts the amount of talking he needs to do. That question could be answered with, "I got there at 1 pm, and I left at 5 pm." That's good, but you could get more by giving him the open-ended prompt of "Tell me more" and *then* be more specific if he doesn't answer.

Here are key questions or prompts that you can direct to the interviewee.

1 What do you mean?
2 Tell me more.
3 Explain that.
4 Describe that.[6]

In casual conversation, vagueness is fine. If you ask your friend what they did yesterday, and they tell you, "Nothing much." Then they either don't want to share with you (and being a good friend you should let it go) or they don't feel like expending the mental energy to recall what happened (and you may or may not let it go depending on your friendship dynamics). In suspect interviews, we have to insist on specificity even if they don't want to provide it. Notice it. Follow up on it.

**Key words to listen for: somebody, somewhere, something, some stuff, about, more or less, I think, generally, a couple, a few.**

### *Failing to answer the question*

*Emily Maitlis:* Are you saying you don't believe her, she's lying?
*Prince Andrew:* That's a very difficult thing to answer because I'm not in a position to know what she's trying to achieve but I can tell you categorically I don't remember meeting her at all. I do not remember a photograph being taken and I've said consistently and frequently that we never had any sort of sexual contact whatever.

Emily Maitlis and Prince Andrew[7]

A question deserves an answer. When the interviewee does anything other than provide an answer to the question you asked, it should draw your attention. Good liars make it seem that they have answered a question when, in fact, they have not.

I have found that evasive answers emerge at moments of high anxiety for the interviewee. At that moment, their defenses are up. If you confront the issue right away, you are fighting against a well-defended position. Rather, consider passing the question up. Typically, the defenses lower as you move into less threatening territory. Later, return to the topic, and ask the question again.

The quotation that started this section is from the Emily Maitlis interview with Prince Andrew about his connection to Jeffrey Epstein, a convicted sex offender. In the excerpt, Prince Andrew refused to answer the question. He talked a lot about other things, but he didn't actually answer. Emily Maitlis asked, "Are you saying you don't believe her, she's lying?" The question, to be fair, is a little convoluted. It's a negative question about his belief in her and a positive question about whether or not she is lying.

What would answer Maitlis' question? Maybe, "Yes. I'm saying that she's lying." That would be clear. Prince Andrew doesn't even try when he says:

> That's a very difficult thing to answer because I'm not in a position to know what she's trying to achieve but I can tell you categorically I don't remember meeting her at all. I do not remember a photograph being taken and I've said consistently and frequently that we never had any sort of sexual contact whatever.

What if your boss said, "Jimmy accused you of stealing from the company. Is he lying?" To which you replied, "Well, boss, it's difficult to say, because I don't know what Jimmy wants." I think you'd be looking for a new job.

> Prince Andrew has a number of other deceptive indicators in this question. Phrases like "I can tell you..." are highly correlated to deception. They are telling you what they can tell you (without getting caught), but not necessarily what happened. Also, "I've said consistently and frequently that we never had any sort of sexual contact whatever." Ok, you've said that, but is it true? Referring to statements you have made does not actually address the truth of the matter.

Here, again, I point to Don Rabon's writing in *Interview and Interrogation*. He correctly points out that a typical interview should follow the pattern of Question: Answer. Question: Answer. But, "Should we move into a phase where the interviewee responds to a question with another question, or with a statement instead of an answer, chances are we are dealing with an individual who is becoming resistant..."[8] So an answer in response to your question is good. A question in response to your question is suspicious. A statement in response to your question is also suspicious.

I reference it elsewhere in this book as well, but I think of a statement from a 2012 rape suspect:

*Detective:* Is that the route you took that night?
*Suspect:* I always go that way.

This is a tricky response because it sounds like he's agreeing that he took that route that night, but our attention is drawn to it because it's a statement. An answer would be "Yes," "No," or "I don't remember." Here, he makes a statement that he always goes that way. The detective spotted it, followed up, and the rapist ultimately admitted that he did not go that way that night.

As with all indicators of deception, failing to answer the question is an indicator, but it is not a certainty. The way you find out is to ask more questions. The non-answer will either resolve itself, or it will reveal itself as more likely to be a lie.

#### *Unexamined Time*

The problem for many questioners is that they believe their job is to identify which part of a story is a lie (fabrication). In fact, *the challenge is usually to find out what the interviewee left out*. Most liars have *omission* as their first line of defense. The deceptive person's story usually contains all of the major, provable elements, but it leaves out the embarrassing or criminal thing. Therefore, the challenge isn't to find out which part of the story they told you is a lie, but rather to question them until they are forced to reveal what they didn't tell you (omitted) or to lie.

A gap in the story sequence is called "missing time." These gaps should always be followed up on. The missing time may be explicit in a statement like "I don't remember what happened next." Or it may be more secretive. For example, the person says they went to sleep and implies they stayed asleep. This leads the questioner to avoid asking questions about that period of time, but in fact they were still active. All missing time, especially surrounding key events, should be examined.

During the 2021 Crimes Against Children (virtual) conference, I attended a presentation on the rape and attempted murder of a young girl in the southwestern United States. When the detective detailed her interview with the suspect, she picked up on missing time in the suspect's statement. This discovery led to the revelation that helped solve the case. According to the suspect, the night before the early morning rape he spent time with his wife and then he went to bed. The detective asked a perfect question of, "And then what happened?" The suspect then admitted that he got back up around 4 am, and went for a walk.

The suspect said he went to sleep, so that should be the end of that right? In fact, I'll admit that the question seemed ridiculous when I first heard it, then my eyes were opened when he responded in that way. I learned something here. Do not be afraid to sound ridiculous. Stories often end with "and then I went to sleep." Consider asking, "and then?" I've had people look at me like I was crazy and say, "and then I woke up the next day." I've had other suspects admit that they went back to the scene of the crime.

Any block of time should be interrogated, particularly if it occurs in an important section of the story. They went to a movie? Ask if they ever left. They were with their girlfriend at home? Ask where else they were. They went to school? That doesn't mean they never left and came back home.

The following two accounts are about the same morning. Let's say the allegation is that the suspect downloaded Child Sexual Abuse Material (CSAM). This is a crime that could happen relatively quickly. Both of the accounts have time gaps that need to be examined.

*Account A*: I woke up at 6:28 am. I lay in bed until 6:35 am when I got up, and I poured myself some coffee. The kids got ready for school. My wife and daughter left at 6:50 am, like they always do. I made my son breakfast, three eggs and toast. He watched YouTube videos on his tablet until he left for the bus at 7:40 am.

*Account B*: I don't know. Woke up. Made breakfast. Everybody left. I watched TV. It was normal!

Account A has a lot of specific times to work with. My first question would be, "What helps you remember the times so well?" Next, we can examine 6:28-6:35. It might make sense to you that nothing much happened in this 7 minutes, but *assumptions like that are when deceptive subjects will slip one by you*. "Tell me everything that happened from the moment you woke up until the moment you got out of bed."

Continuing with Account A: From 6:35 to 6:50 you can examine where everybody was and what devices everybody was using. From 6:50 to 7:40 is the section needing the most examination. You'll want to go step by step through the actions of the interviewee. "You said your son watched YouTube videos, what were you doing?"

Account B has almost no details at all. There is a missing time everywhere. Imagine grabbing each of the provided elements and separating them to reveal the gaps. In your left hand is "Woke up" and in your right hand is "Made breakfast." Pull them away from one another and examine what is in between. Do the same with "made breakfast" and "everybody left." What is in between?

In Account B, "Watched TV" is a different problem. Here, the truthful suspect doesn't think it's of interest to detail their other actions during this time. The deceptive suspect wants you to assume they sat passively and did nothing else. When was the last time you watched TV without being on your phone at all? What about taking a bathroom break or visiting the kitchen? If the suspect is being deceptive, it is probably true they watched TV, but the lie may be in the omission of what they did while they watched. "You said you watched TV, what else did you do during that time?"

Deceptive people usually lie by omission first. This technique is successful because they capitalize on your assumptions. Assume nothing. Examine everything.

### *The Ridiculous*

> I heard…as I was crossing the intersection…I heard "Empire!", and I don't answer to Empire. (Laughs) My name ain't Empire (Laughs).
>
> Jussie Smollett[9]

Sometimes ridiculous things happen, but usually they don't. In interviews, the ridiculous enters in either explicitly (said aloud) or implicitly (described but not named). The explicit version happens when your interviewee says something like, "You're not going to believe this, but…" The implicit happens when they tell you about an event that is highly improbable.

*When an interviewee points out that something they are saying is ridiculous, you should believe them.*

In the quotation from the beginning of this section, I point to a portion of the Jussie Smollett interview with ABC News anchor Robin Roberts. Smollett is an actor from the show *Empire*. He reached new levels of fame when, in January of 2019, he reported having been attacked by Donald Trump MAGA supporters on a snowy night in Chicago. After making the rounds of media interviews, his story began to fall apart. In December of 2021, Smollett was convicted on multiple counts of making false police reports.[10] Looking back at some of his interviews, there are indications of deception.

Note: In November of 2024, an appeals court judge overturned Smollett's conviction based on a finding of double jeopardy. They were explicitly not ruling on the facts of the case. He is presumed innocent.[11]

For example, when Smollett laughs at the idea somebody would call him "Empire," he is communicating to his interviewer that it's ridiculous. In the moment, the interviewer couldn't be expected to *know* it was a hoax. What she could have done is examine the ridiculous. "You said they called you 'Empire', tell me more about that." Anything outside of the norm should be examined reflexively.

Anytime you hear phrases explicitly pointing out that something is ridiculous, you should follow up with more questions, especially if it is at a key point in the interview. Listen for "You're not going to believe this." "It's crazy, but…" "I hardly believe it myself." When you hear those phrases or something similar, use your prompts like "Tell me more." "Explain that to me." "Describe that for me." "What do you mean?"

Sometimes the ridiculous is in a description of a completely unbelievable incident. In these implicit cases, it is the challenge to common sense rather than any one specific word that will draw your attention. Of course, sometimes crazy or ridiculous things happen. Just because it sounds crazy or nonsensical doesn't mean it's a lie, but you'd want them to be able to talk in great specificity about the thing that happened to them. If you come across somebody telling you a story that is both ridiculous *and* vague, you're probably hearing lies.

My partner and I responded to the local hospital in 2019 to investigate a kidnapping of multiple young girls. Patrol had been called to a scene where a 14-year-old girl with a bleeding cut to her head reported that she had been playing ball with her friends when a hand grabbed her from behind, putting a cloth to her mouth. She remembered being dragged backwards into the woods when she blacked out. She woke up hours later not knowing what happened. In fact, her two friends corroborated her story and said that they, too had been dragged into the woods.

All of the department was getting prepared for a national news story. Initial fears were that a predator was raping young girls. Contingency plans were being made for news and media. The problem is that none of the girls outcried to any sort of sexual acts being perpetrated on them. In fact, none of the girls remembered anything about what happened. We had no suspects and no leads.

I immediately recognized some problems with the story. I knew the area the girl said they were playing in. There were no woods, trees, or even shrubbery in that area. Where would they have been dragged into the woods? Next, it was suspicious that there wasn't a single descriptor provided by any of the three girls to aid in identifying a suspect. Finally, the girls seemed to be describing chloroform or some sort of drug being used on them with the ensuing hours of lost time. Maybe this isn't impossible, but it has a dramatic feel to it like something from a movie. On the other hand, the one girl had a bleeding cut to her head that suggested she might have been assaulted. This needed to be explained.

We drove to the hospital. The first question I asked of the nurse, "It sounds like what she's describing is chloroform. I've seen that in the movies, but I've never come across it in real life. Is that a real thing that people use?" She responded, "It's a real thing, but it's not a thing that would cause anybody to lose hours of time." I was still mystified by the cut to the forehead, but I was forming the opinion that these girls might be lying.

My partner and I split up. He talked to one of the girls, and I talked to another. During this interview, I asked open-ended questions in empathetic tones that gave her the chance to explain what happened. As we talked, her story remained just as vague. There were no details to add. She had no idea what happened. The conversation turned to clarification, where I asked her to explain the discrepancies. After a while, she admitted that she and her friends had made the whole thing up.

She said that she was new to the city, and she didn't speak English. She was nervous about going to school. She and her friends decided to stage the event in hopes that her mom would allow them to stay home. Her mom called the police, though, and the medium-sized lie grew into an ever bigger lie. I walked out of the room, just as my partner was walking out of the other room. We met in the middle, I said, "She said she was lying." He said, "So did mine!"

Of course, some people get kidnapped. Some people get drugged. Sometimes ridiculous things happen. It's just that they usually don't. Be open to the possibility that it is true when something ridiculous comes up. Give them the opportunity to talk about it. If the picture becomes clearer, they may be telling the truth. If it remains vague despite lots of questioning, it's a good indicator that they are lying.

### *Redefine and Deny*

*Rauch:* I still feel sabotaged.
*Interviewer:* I'm not trying to sabotage…
*Rauch:* But I still feel sabotaged. Because of…the fact is I'm not out there fucking 13 year olds…and…and…or getting them drunk and taking them up to hotels, as we obviously know from the news. I'm not doing that, and I don't have a desire to do that.[12]

Redefining narrowly is a technique where the interviewee narrows the question, sometimes after redefining the terms themselves, and then denies that narrowed portion. It's a slippery technique that can happen either explicitly or implicitly.

Example of explicit redefinition:

*Interviewer:* Have you ever robbed anyone?
*Interviewee:* If by 'rob' you mean point a gun at a store clerk or something, then no, I've never robbed anyone.

*Explanation*: Robbery is essentially an assault combined with a theft. This is a broad definition. Here, the interviewee redefines robbery to pointing a gun at a store clerk. He then denies ever robbing anyone *under HIS definition.* This masquerades as a denial to the interviewer's question, but it isn't. If any other combination of assault and theft is considered, the interviewee has NOT denied those.

Example of an implicit redefinition:

*Interviewer:* Have you ever robbed anyone?
*Interviewee:* (Thinking to himself: I've never hurt anybody. You have to hurt someone to rob them. All I did was push that man and take his wallet.) Nah.

The implicit redefinition can only be spotted by defining all important terms as they come up. Here, the interviewer should follow up with, "How do you define 'robbery?'"

I've written about Jussie Smollett and his alleged hoax hate crime in the section on ridiculousness as an indicator of deception. He demonstrated the redefine and deny strategy during his sentencing hearing.

*Jussie:* Your honor I would just like to say to you, your honor, that I am uh…I am not suicidal…That's what I would like to say.
*Judge:* Ok.
*Jussie:* I am not suicidal.
*Judge:* Ok.
*Jussie:* I am not suicidal. I am innocent, and I am not suicidal. **If I did this, then it means that I stuffed my fist in the fears of Black Americans in this country for over 400 years, and the fears of the LGBTQ community. Your honor, I respect you and I respect the jury, but I did not do this.** [Emphasis added]

Here, Jussie demonstrated a version of redefine and deny starting with, "If I did this…" We have to follow his logic.

1 If I did this [committed the hate crime hoax of which he was just convicted]
2 Then it means that I stuffed my fist in the fears…
3 I did not do this [stuff my fist in the fears]

He wants the judge and the audience to believe he is denying perpetrating the hoax, but he isn't. He is denying stuffing his fist in the fears of those groups of people. That is something much harder to prove.

James Rauch was a 60-year-old faculty member at a regional college when he solicited sex from a minor. He was arrested, and his interview is well known to fans of *To Catch a Predator*.[13] I use the James Rauch video in our interview classes. If you look back to the quote at the start of the section, he is being confronted after a sting operation caught him soliciting sex from a minor online. The response he provides seems like a denial of being involved in the activities he is accused of, but look what it is he actually denies.

*Rauch:* But I still feel sabotaged. Because of…the fact is I'm not out there **fucking 13 year olds**…and…and…or **getting them drunk** and **taking them up to hotels**, as we obviously know from the news. I'm not doing that, and I don't have a desire to do that.

I've highlighted the key denials here. First, he isn't out there "fucking." What about soliciting? What about sex acts not commonly defined as "fucking?" Second, he narrows the denial to 13-year-olds. What about 12-year-olds? Or what about 14-year-olds? Third, he denies getting them drunk. What about getting them high? Finally, he denies taking "them up to hotels." What about in his car? Or his house?

Rauch does the interviewers a favor by explicitly redefining the question and narrowing it to deny those acts. In order to push back against the explicit version, you have to notice it is happening and then ask questions around the area of resistance. He is denying sex with 13-year-olds? Ask him about nearby ages. Anytime this happens, you are close. It's like a metal detector hit. You've spotted a problem in the general area, and now you have to search the area to find it.

Other deceptive indicators in this response include when Rauch says "I'm not out there." No matter what he said it would be technically true. He isn't out there because he's in here. This is not the same as saying, "I never fucked a 13-year-old," which would actually be a strong (though specific) denial.

Another deceptive point in the response is that he says, "I don't have a desire to do that." Maybe right then in that moment in the police station he didn't have a desire to do that very specific thing he is denying, but what about yesterday? What about tomorrow? Be alert to denials that deny past events in the present tense.

The implicit version of this technique is what I call "definitional ignorance." I've written a longer essay on this in Chapter 12. For now, definitional ignorance is a strategy employed by deceptive interviewees in order to claim they told you the truth based on how they define the words. To prevent definitional ignorance, we must throw out assumptions and clearly define the terms that we are using in our interviews.

**Every time an interviewee denies anything, they are doing so based on the definitions they choose to use at that moment.** Typically, they will choose to use the definition most convenient for them whether or not that is how you meant it. I encourage every interviewer to be crystal clear as to the definitions they are using regarding any term crucial to the case. *If you were not clear in your definition of terms, then you can't know if the interviewee is lying or telling the truth with different definitions.*

I was interviewing a suspect in a sexual assault of a child case, and he was denying convincingly that he ever had sex with the victim. As the questions continued, I remembered that the victim had not been clear if the suspect's penis went in her vagina or her anus. She seemed to be unclear on the separation in parts. I began to list the parts. "Has your penis ever gone inside..." When I got to this question pertaining to the victim's anus, the suspect admitted that he had put his penis inside her anus. He said that wasn't sex by his definition because the victim was still a virgin. I believe this suspect was able to lie convincingly about never "having sex" with the victim because he was implicitly using a definition of sex meaning "penis in vagina." In other words, he was using definitional ignorance against me.

The best defense against Redefine and Deny is to define everything, and insist on sticking to those definitions.

### *Nonverbals*

> However, as a principle, more accurate truth/lie classifications can be made if a cluster of nonverbal cues is examined rather than each of these cues individually.
>
> Aldert Vrij[14]

There are entire books and courses devoted to nonverbal deception detection. This isn't one of them. I have some training on nonverbal deception indicators, but I do not claim to be an expert here. Furthermore, I strongly believe that nonverbal deception detection is most important at higher levels of interviewing than most of us ever reach. This book is on the *fundamentals* of interviewing and interrogation, which doesn't meaningfully include advanced topics. Who cares what his shoulder did if you didn't even hear what he said? Do not *focus* on nonverbal indications of deception until you are proficient at level 1 and 2 interviewing.

Observation and interpretation of nonverbal deceptive indicators is a level 3 skill I am calling Tricks. My recommendation: do *not* prioritize this as a new interviewer. See what you see, but it's what you say and what you hear that will be the bedrock of your success.

With all that being said, nonverbal indicators of deception are an area of which interviewers should be aware. In general, the idea is everyone has a normal way of acting when they respond to questions. During conversation about non-threatening topics (rapport building), you can observe what their normal is. This is called their "baseline." Deviations from their baseline can point to a disturbance of sorts, possibly deceptive

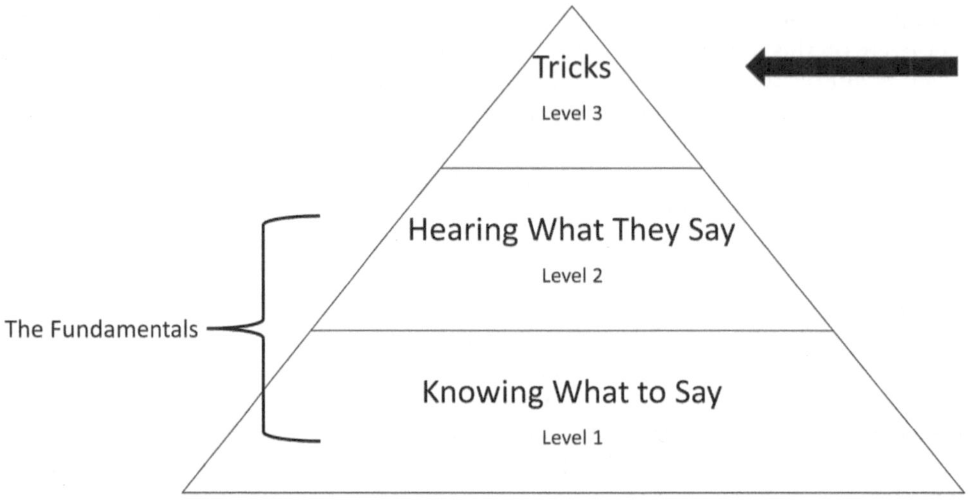


*Image 3.2* Pyramid of Interviewing and Interrogation, emphasizing Tricks as the topmost level.

behavior. If it changed, it changed for a reason. Examples of nonverbal behaviors to look out for would include: eye movements, shoulder shrugs, arms crossing (or uncrossing), legs crossing (or uncrossing), or even the complete and unnatural cessation of movement.

When you spot clusters of changes, there is a good chance that the interviewee has a problem with that particular response. They *may* be lying.

Deviations from the baseline are significant, especially when they occur in and around significant questions. If you ask the person if they want to use the bathroom and they clear their throat to answer, it doesn't tell you anything useful. If you ask a person if they robbed the convenience store last night and they clear their throat before answering, it may be deceptive. You must compare this to the person's baseline responses. Do they clear their throat every few minutes? Or have you talked to the person for an hour and a half and this is the first time? If it's the latter, their nonverbal actions have just given you an *indication* of deception.

When you see these deviations, slow down! If you have identified them correctly and the person is lying directly or by omission, they want to move on to the next topic as quickly as possible. You will do them a favor by asking another question right away. Don't. Write your notes without talking. Notate what caught your attention. Also, if the person starts to chatter on about a topic they are more comfortable addressing, hold your hand up and ask them to wait while you catch up on your notes. This will make them sit on their lie for longer without having directly confronted them. Keep in mind that the full response to a question may last beyond the length of their verbal response.

The nonverbal indicators of deception I've found to be useful are: asymmetrical shoulder shrugs, mouth and eye covering, unusual stillness, and distancing. Of course, there are whole books and courses that cover many more. Remember: clusters and context matter. *Do not observe a single nonverbal action and decide for certain that the person is lying.*

## Asymmetrical Shoulder Shrug

First, let's look at the asymmetrical (unequal) shoulder shrug. This is something introduced to me by Trent Watts. I later read about it in Joe Navarro's work on nonverbal deception.[15] Once it was pointed out to me, I saw it regularly. The body usually acts symmetrically when we shrug. We shrug with both shoulders to indicate that we don't know a thing, for example. When the body acts asymmetrically - one shoulder does something the other doesn't - particularly on the left side, it is associated with a negation of what was just said, which may mean deception. Navarro wrote, "If only one shoulder comes up, or if the shoulders rise nearly to the ears and the person's head seems to disappear, it is a sign of high discomfort and sometimes seen in an individual preparing to answer a question deceptively."[16]

I noticed a distinct asymmetrical shoulder shrug in an interview with WNBA star Brittney Griner on the topic of transgender inclusion in women's sports.[17]

*Brittney Griner:* Everyone deserves the right to play. Everyone deserves the right to come here, sit in these seats, and feel safe and not feel like there's a threat and not be who they are. I definitely will be speaking up against ASYMMETRICAL LEFT SHOULDER SHRUG against those, that legislation and those laws that are trying to be passed for sure.

If you watch the video, you'll see a very distinct lifting of the left shoulder that does not happen on the right side. What does it mean? This is where nonverbals get very tricky. We know in context Brittney Griner is an outspoken member of the LGBTQ community. We also know it's possible to be a member of the community without necessarily thinking trans women should be included in women's sports.

Her asymmetrical shoulder shrug *might* mean she doesn't think trans women should be in women's sports and doesn't *really* intend to speak out against laws banning their inclusion (despite what she said). That's possible. It's also possible she feels strongly about laws she regards as bigoted against members of her community and she rejects those laws. That's possible. It's also possible that it means nothing at all!

If I were interviewing Griner, and it was important to me how she felt about this topic, I would observe the nonverbal, asymmetrical shoulder shrug, and I would ask more questions on the topic. "You said you intend to speak up against certain laws, what do you mean?" "Regarding trans women, what policies do you think the WNBA should support?" I'm not a mind reader. I don't know what the shoulder shrug meant. What I do know is, having observed it, I may need to ask more questions on the topic.

## Eye/Mouth Covering

As to the covering of the mouth or eyes, this can mean something as simple as closing our eyes or compressing our lips. It can also mean physically covering them with our hands, arms, or clothing. The theory behind these actions being associated with deception is that lying exposes the person to a threat of consequences, and they may reflexively cover their eyes so as not to see the "threat." The threat in this sense would be the interviewer analyzing them or expressing doubt.

Navarro writes, "While eye-blocking behaviors are usually associated with seeing or hearing something negative that causes us discomfort, they can also be an indication of low confidence."[18] If the eye blocking or mouth covering happens right after they deny involvement in the incident, what does it mean that they are indicating low confidence in that statement? It means they are possibly being deceptive.

These coverings of the mouth or eyes are actions that are often masked by a purported display of emotion. I remember speaking to a mom who was suspected of breaking her child's arm. At every single moment of intense questioning, she would cover her eyes or mouth and make sobbing sounds. When I asked, "Did you break his arm?" She put her hand to her brow and lowered her hand so it covered her eyes. When I asked, "Do you know why his arm is broken?" she covered her mouth and shrunk her shoulders inwards while saying that she didn't know. This happened a half dozen times in the interview and all around the topic of the arm break.

Is she lying in her responses to my questions? I don't know, because I don't know the ground truth of the matter. Nonverbals are hard to interpret without knowing the ground truth. Maybe she did it. Maybe she feels like it's her fault it happened. Maybe she's worried about CPS taking her baby. I don't *know* why she is having problems with her answer. However, I definitely asked more questions about the topics she was discussing when she displayed the deceptive nonverbal gestures.

### Unusual Stillness

I have seen several instances of unusual stillness that I believe are likely associated with deception. I watched my partner, Val De Los Santos, interview a dad accused of using his daughter's hands to masturbate his penis. The interview was so bizarre to watch because the subject responded almost robotically. He hardly moved at all. At one point, I watched my partner walk out of the room to take a break. *Immediately* after he left, the interviewee stood up and engaged in a series of active, full-body stretches. As soon as my partner walked back in, the man was reseated in his robot posture.

Anybody who is a fan of the Jim Can't Swim YouTube channel will recognize "The Bizarre Case of Stephen McDaniel."[19] McDaniel is being interrogated in reference to the murder of a neighbor of his. Before her body was discovered, McDaniel was all over the news talking about what he was doing to help look for her. Once she was discovered, the investigation led to him as the prime suspect in the killing.

Stephen McDaniel, like my partner's suspect, was unusually still and robotic. He spoke slowly and stared weirdly throughout the interview. I believe that actions like this are exaggerated attempts to control their nonverbal behavior, which is almost certainly more correlated with deception.

### Distancing Behaviors

Distancing behaviors are also associated with deception. When you are interviewing a person, and the question you ask causes them to cross their arms, lean back, and thrust their feet out between you, for example, this is a person that is engaging in actions that distance themselves from you. Distance equals deception. This is part of the fight or flight response that we all have. In this case, they are effectively choosing "flight."

These distancing actions are notable when they deviate from the baseline. If you are talking to the person freely during the rapport stage, you may see them sitting naturally. When you ask them if they stabbed their wife, and all of a sudden they lean back and away from you, it suggests that particular question causes them fear. Of course, it is possible they are fearful they will be arrested for the crime when they didn't do it. That is possible. My experience has been that most honest people expect to be believed. As a result, they don't *tend* to display fear responses around even the most direct of questions. For this reason, my study and experience suggest to me distancing behaviors are indicators of deception.

We cannot *know* what the person is thinking when we observe these nonverbal actions. Rather, our job is to observe them in the context that they happen, and continue to ask questions about those topics. These are hints that something may be amiss. They are not certainties.

I was presenting at one of the round table discussions on interview and interrogation, which I run for my department. I had some SWAT guys in attendance. I asked:

*Me:* If you were searching a room for a suspect, and you saw a human-sized lump on the bed under a blanket, what would you do?
*SWAT:* Point guns and yank the blanket back.
*Me:* And will the person be there?
*SWAT:* I don't know
*Me:* But you're going to check?
*SWAT:* For sure!
*Me:* That's what its like to observe words or actions that might be deceptive. They create a lump on the bed. Your job is to check that human-sized lump (ask questions). If it's a human (a lie), take appropriate action. If it's nothing (appears not to be a lie), move on.

Any of these nonverbals is like the human-sized lump during a building search. You would be insane not to check it, but you have to understand that it might be nothing. I think that some of the literature on nonverbals being bad science is negative on the subject because they seem to say "the human-sized lump isn't always a human, so therefore don't even check." My middle ground is: observe it, check it, realize it may be nothing.

### Final Note on Handling Deception:

When you detect deception in the interview, *don't point out the deceptive actions to the interviewee.* There are two good reasons for this. First, the deceptive interviewee is almost sure to change what they are doing, robbing you of the clue. Second, in my experience, this leads to arguments. You point out the deceptive indicator, they say why it isn't what you think it is. *The key is to ask more questions in the section of the story where you observed the deceptive indicators.*

Pointing out deceptive indicators may be useful during the interrogation. At that point, questioning has largely stopped. Discussing the deceptive indicators may help demonstrate the futility of lying about what happened, which would be particularly useful with rational types. On the other hand, it gives the interviewee something to argue about. Many of them will.

### Summary

The best indicator of deception is what you know to be true. Lies come in various forms, such as omissions and fabrications. Omissions are the hardest to detect and the easiest to tell. Fabrications are the hardest to tell and the easiest to detect. Some common deceptive indicators include: vagueness, failing to answer the question, missing time, and redefining narrowly. Nonverbal cues can be helpful in identifying deception, especially in clusters, but they are of secondary importance. As a rule, don't point out deceptive indicators you've noticed during the interview.

## Immediately Actionable

*Listen for a vague response:* Key in on words like "someone," "something," "somewhere," and the like. Ask questions about those topics. "Someone like who?" "Somewhere like where?"

*Listen for failing to answer the question:* See if you can spot a time when a question is answered with a statement or another question. What was the context? What will you do about it?

*Listen for the ridiculous:* See if you can find a time when the interviewee doesn't seem to believe their own story. "You're not gonna believe this…" "This never happens, but…"

## Notes

1 Our court system knows a thing or two about how people lie, which is why, when we are sworn in, we are usually asked to swear, "To tell the truth, the whole truth, and nothing but the truth." Demanding that we swear to tell the truth addresses those that might have ideas of lying by fabrication. To tell the whole truth addresses those that might have ideas of lying by omission. To tell nothing but the truth addresses those that might have ideas of lying by distractions and other stratagems. It's a well-crafted oath that anticipates all of the varied ways people lie.

2 To include: Rabon and Chapman, *Interviewing and Interrogation*, 31–37.
3 Lembke, Anna, *Dopamine Nation: Finding Balance in the Age of Indulgence* (New York: Dutton, 2021), 171.
4 Vrij, Aldert, *Detecting Lies and Deceit: Pitfalls and Opportunities* (Chichester: Wiley, 2008), 196.
5 2025. Youtube. 2025. https://youtu.be/Cwtk97dWSJQ?si=Ms3JDhoUIVgMXvmS
6 Credit to Federal Law Enforcement Training Center (FLETC) instructors for first pointing me to this Tell, Explain, Describe (TED) series of questions.
7 BBC News. 2019. "Transcript in Full: Prince Andrew's Interview," November 17, 2019, sec. UK. https://www.bbc.com/news/uk-50449339
8 Rabon and Chapman, *Interviewing and Interrogation*, 77.
9 "Jussie Smollett FULL Interview on Alleged Attack | ABC News Exclusive." 2019. YouTube Video. *YouTube*. https://www.youtube.com/watch?v=pXLx5OY21Bk
10 "Jussie Smollett Hate Crime Hoax." 2023. Wikipedia. March 28, 2023. https://en.wikipedia.org/wiki/Jussie_Smollett_hate_crime_hoax
11 O'CONNOR, JOHN, and SOPHIA TAREEN. 2024. "Jussie Smollett's Conviction Overturned in 2019 Attack on Himself." AP News. November 21, 2024. https://apnews.com/article/jussie-smollett-conviction-overturned-chicago-91178cf27f6ef0aec8a5eef67a3a6125
12 The Cappening Channel. 2016. "Music Professor Caught on to Catch a Predator James Rauch (Audio Boost!)." YouTube. August 14, 2016. https://www.youtube.com/watch?v=nuX6kgww1Is. Note: go to 46:40 into recording.
13 Various Contributors. 2019. "Jim Rauch." To Catch a Predator Wiki. Fandom, Inc. 2019. https://to-catch-a-predator.fandom.com/wiki/Jim_Rauch
14 Vrij, *Detecting Lies and Deceit*, 66.
15 Navarro and Karlins, *What Every BODY Is Saying*, 230.
16 Navarro and Karlins, *What Every BODY Is Saying*, 230.
17 "WNBA Star Brittney Griner on Legislation Targeting Transgender Athletes #Shorts." n.d. Www.youtube.com. Accessed May 14, 2025. https://www.youtube.com/shorts/CPHc5yJMa9Q
18 Navarro and Karlins, *What Every BODY Is Saying*, 178.
19 JCS - Criminal Psychology. 2020. "The Bizarre Case of Stephen McDaniel." *YouTube*. https://www.youtube.com/watch?v=HkRjIq8Cp2A

## References

Youtube. 2025. https://youtu.be/Cwtk97dWSJQ?si=Ms3JDhoUIVgMXvmS

*BBC News*. 2019. “Transcript in Full: Prince Andrew’s Interview,” November 17, 2019, sec. UK. https://www.bbc.com/news/uk-50449339

JCS - Criminal Psychology. 2020. “The Bizarre Case of Stephen McDaniel.” *YouTube*. https://www.youtube.com/watch?v=HkRjIq8Cp2A

“Jussie Smollett FULL Interview on Alleged Attack | ABC News Exclusive.” 2019. YouTube Video. *YouTube*. https://www.youtube.com/watch?v=pXLx5OY21Bk

“Jussie Smollett Hate Crime Hoax.” 2023. Wikipedia. March 28, 2023. https://en.wikipedia.org/wiki/Jussie_Smollett_hate_crime_hoax

Lembke, Anna. 2021. *Dopamine Nation: Finding Balance in the Age of Indulgence*. New York: Dutton.

Navarro, Joe, and Marvin Karlins. 2008. *What Every BODY Is Saying: An Ex-FBI Agent’s Guide to Speed-Reading People*. New York, NY: Harper Collins.

O’Connor, John, and Sophia Tareen. 2024. “Jussie Smollett’s Conviction Overturned in 2019 Attack on Himself.” AP News. November 21, 2024. https://apnews.com/article/jussie-smollett-conviction-overturned-chicago-91178cf27f6ef0aec8a5eef67a3a6125

Rabon, Don, and Tanya Chapman. 2019. *Interviewing and Interrogation: Questioning, Detecting Deception and Gaining Compliance*. Durham, NC: Carolina Academic Press.

The Cappening Channel. 2016. “Music Professor Caught on to Catch a Predator James Rauch (Audio Boost!).” YouTube. August 14, 2016. https://www.youtube.com/watch?v=nuX6kgww1Is

Various Contributors. 2019. “Jim Rauch.” To Catch a Predator Wiki. Fandom, Inc. 2019. https://to-catch-a-predator.fandom.com/wiki/Jim_Rauch

Vrij, Aldert. 2008. *Detecting Lies and Deceit: Pitfalls and Opportunities*. Chichester: Wiley.

“WNBA Star Brittney Griner on Legislation Targeting Transgender Athletes #Shorts.” n.d. www.youtube.com. Accessed May 14, 2025. https://www.youtube.com/shorts/CPHc5yJMa9Q

Chapter 4

# Contact with the Suspect

## Key Points

1 *Importance of non-custodial interviews*: Custodial interviews are the default for many investigative units. I make the case for non-custodial interviews being part of your overall strategy.
2 *Effective scheduling techniques*: Strategies for making phone calls to the suspect which are more likely to bring them in. "I'm available tomorrow at 1 pm or next Tuesday at 9 am, which can I put you down for? Tomorrow?"
3 *Handling legal requests*: The chapter provides advice on how to respond when a suspect asks for a lawyer, emphasizing the importance of remaining neutral and managing the case effectively.
4 *In custodial situations, interview first*: Just because they are in custody does not mean you have to start with accusations. In fact, you shouldn't.

## Non-custodial Cases

The first step to a successful suspect interview is getting them in the room in the first place. Although it's true some investigative units have most of their people brought in as a custodial event (robbery and aggravated assault, for example), for many investigative units, this process begins when the investigator calls the suspect to schedule a non-custodial interview.

Check the section on Now and Later Interviews in Chapter 1 for more thoughts on how to approach these interviews differently.

Most investigators need improvement in how they call the suspect. This makes sense as it's not a subject on which investigators train. It's considered as basic as typing. You do it the way you do it, and that will be good enough. Just like typing, though, small improvements in this seemingly basic skill can have an outsized impact on your effectiveness.

When it comes to making phone calls to suspects, the errors are common and, thankfully, easy to fix. For example, most detectives hesitate to directly identify the issue being investigated. This leads to ridiculous situations where the suspect asks what they are being investigated for, and the detective says they'll talk about it when the suspect comes into the station. *You absolutely should identify the crime being investigated on these calls.* **Always remember: if the suspect did it, they know they did it. Refusing to identify the issue will only serve to confuse innocent people.**

I know I have felt anxious about making these calls, and I bet you have, too. I've found myself taking a long lunch break or volunteering for a patrol call that just came

DOI: 10.4324/9781003663904-5

across the line instead of picking up the phone. Why am I so helpful today? Oh. Right. It's because the time has come to confront a suspect, and I don't know how it's going to turn out.

I have seen detectives twist themselves into knots to justify why they aren't calling a suspect. "He's a flight risk." "I don't speak Spanish." "I think the case facts speak for themselves." "Nobody would criticize me for suspending this case without taking that extra step." Don't be this detective! If the suspect is guilty, you've missed a chance to get justice for your victim. If the suspect is innocent, you've bypassed an important safety mechanism to prevent them from being charged.

So you are going to be the detective that calls a suspect in for an interview. Great. What's his number? I have done a number of investigations where I got to this point, and I couldn't believe that I failed to actually ask the family this question when I should have. When you have access to the victim or their family, always ask if they have contact information for the suspect (if the suspect is known). Ask them for a phone number, a girlfriend's phone number, email, WhatsApp, Snapchat, Facebook, or anything else they may use to communicate.

You've done everything right up to this point. You identified a suspect, you have their phone number, and you decided to call them. Something is still holding you back. At this point, stop thinking about it. Pick up the phone and call them. If you have to, set a time like 10:30 am and no matter what, you have to pick up the phone and make that call.

I know these delay tactics are used because I have used them, and I have seen them used. What is it about calling a suspect we avoid? I think it's that you just can't predict what they are going to say. The result of your conversation could have a momentous impact on the course of your investigation. Anything could happen, and how quickly you respond to these random possibilities will make a big difference. It can be hard to think on your feet in these situations, so there is often extra pressure to get it right.

I've laid out steps that you can follow to increase your likelihood for success when scheduling suspects for interviews. Following these steps will lead to smoother and more successful interactions with suspects. Here is the list of steps and the reasoning behind them:

1 Record, record, record.
2 Identify yourself and ask them to identify themselves.
3 Be direct about what you are investigating, but use soft words.
4 Listen to what they say.
5 Sell them the car.
6 Set the appointment, and follow up.
7 If they ask for a lawyer, have a response.
8 If they refuse to come in, interview them on the phone.

**1. Record, record, record:** This is fundamental. You need to record the call to the suspect every single time. The suspect may admit to something on the phone, which will be useful in your investigation. The suspect may decide to confess on the phone. The suspect may complain about you later (and you'll be wanting an accurate account of what happened). Whatever he does, you'll have a record of it. These days people need recordings and video to believe events. Give them that.

**2. Identify yourself and ask them to identify themselves:** My typical introduction goes like this, "Brian? This is Detective Lambert with the Police Department. How are you doing today? Listen, I have something I need to discuss with you, but I need to make sure I'm talking to the right person. Can you spell your last name for me? Can you tell me your date of birth? Ok, great..."

Why is it so important that the suspect identify themselves? Because if they don't, it gives the defense something to argue about that might lead to suppressing any statements they make. "Yes, you called my client's number. Yes, a male answered the phone. Yes, he spoke knowledgeably about the situation, but did you know he has a twin brother that hates him and sometimes impersonates him?" They might not win the argument, but every chance you give them to argue is another chance you might lose.

If you forget to have the suspect identify themselves at the beginning, have them do it at the end. One time, I called a man on the phone that was accused of hitting a person on the head with a baseball bat. When I called, I delivered my introduction. I asked him to come in, but I forgot to ask him to identify himself. He said, "I'm not gonna come in, but I'll tell you what happened on the phone." I thought this sounded like the second best thing to him coming in person.

Within a few minutes, he told me a not-so-believable story about feeling threatened and responding with the bat. About this time, I realized I had an unidentified man on tape confessing to an aggravated assault. Great. I hurriedly blurted out, "How do you spell your last name again?" and then, "So your date of birth makes you...Oh that's right. I have it written down somewhere, but can you remind me of your birthday?" Then I had what I needed. I thanked him for his time, added the recording to the digital case file, and I promptly cut a warrant for him for aggravated assault.

**3. Be direct about what you are investigating, but use soft words.** Give them the information they need to make an informed decision about speaking with you by correctly identifying what it is you are investigating, but use soft words. Instead of, "I'm investigating the aggravated sexual assault of a child." You could say:

> Susie says you put your finger in her butt. I work these cases all of the time. I haven't made any final decisions on the case. I'd really like to talk to you so I can understand why it is that Susie would say such a thing. When would you be available to come to my office so that we can clear this situation up? Would next Tuesday afternoon work?

Aggravated Sexual Assault of a Child sounds scary. Both my description and the literal charge describe what happened. Only one gives the suspect the sense that maybe what they did was wrong but not, like, prison-wrong.

I ran into a newly promoted detective that I knew from a day of taking calls with him on patrol earlier that year. I asked him how detective life was treating him. He told me about a case he was working on. It was a stranger rape case where the suspect had been identified through good police work. Then it took a turn. He said, "The guy wouldn't come in for an interview, look." He showed me text messages with the suspect after explaining he had called numerous times without an answer. I read through the text messages. After I read them, I understood why he hadn't come in!

The message thread read something like this:

*Detective:* Mr X. I need you to come to the police station and talk to me.
*Suspect:* Sure. What's it about?
*Detective:* Are you going to meet me or not?

*Suspect:* Yeah, but I don't understand why.
*Detective:* If you aren't going to meet me then I'm going to have to see this as an act of non-compliance...

You get the picture. This is not verbatim, but it definitely captures the tone of the messages.

I believe this approach comes from some misguided belief that the big secret to interrogation is springing the accusation on the person with no prior warning in order to gauge their response. Maybe there's a fear that telling them about being investigated for a felony will rush them into the arms of a lawyer and you'll miss your chance. This is wrong. *The advantage over a guilty suspect is not surprise – they know they did it – the advantage is in anxiety over how they will perform while trying to convince the detective of a bunch of lies.*

Given the chance, an innocent suspect may be able to provide an alibi or defense you didn't know about beforehand. If you don't clearly explain the issue under investigation, an innocent suspect may face unfair scrutiny. What if the suspect is guilty of a robbery but innocent of the rape you are investigating? If you told them, I suspect you hit a woman and stole her money, he may say, "I'd like you to call my lawyer please." If you told them, I suspect you hit a woman and raped her in an alleyway, he may say, "I've never raped anyone in my life. When can we meet?" If you want to increase your chances for a successful interview, tell the suspect why you want to talk to them.

**4. Listen to what they say.** When you say, "Little Susie says that you put your finger in her butt," there are a lot of ways that conversation can go. Some signs you have the right guy might come in the form of objections. If you hear, "Why would I do that?" You're hearing an objection, not a denial. If you hear, "I always knew something like this would happen," you're hearing an attempt at getting sympathy. If you hear, "Wow, what kind of prison sentence does something like that carry?" you're hearing a person bargaining rather than denying. These are not typically the hallmarks of innocent people.

In my opinion, the most reliable indicator of innocence is a direct denial of the specific action, especially when it starts specific and then broadens. You might hear, "I did not put my finger in Susie's butt. I have never had any sexual contact with Susie at all."

As in all things, there is no single magical indicator that will let you know if the person is lying or not.

**5. Sell them the car.** By this I mean get them to agree to an interview with all the techniques we know our friendly neighborhood car salespeople use. After all, you're calling to get them into the interview room not to actually interview them on the phone. Let's look at two different interview scheduling techniques. I've heard them both. You decide which is more likely to bring a person into a police station.

> Hi Brian, thanks for taking my call. My name is Detective Lambert with the Police Department. How are you doing? Listen, the reason I'm calling today is that I got assigned this case. Hold on, let me pull it up. Okay here it is. So here it says that a guy named Andy is saying you cut him a little bit with a knife. We get these types of cases all the time. Do you know Andy? Okay right, I get the sense that there is more to the story. Would you like to come in and make a statement?

This isn't a bad call. This call gets through the introduction. It identifies the issue at hand but with soft language. It lets the person know maybe you're not all the way sold on what

Andy has to say. But where it could improve is on closing the deal to make the sale. Let's try it again, picking up towards the end.

> ...I get the sense there is more to the story. I want to make sure you get heard so we can find out what really happened. I'm available either tomorrow at 1 pm or next Tuesday at 9 am. Which day can I put you down for? Tomorrow or Tuesday?

Now we're talking. This one makes it clear you want to hear his side of the story and it provides two options for time slots. It is possible but much more mentally challenging to say, "I don't want to talk at all" or to choose any sort of option that involves not coming in for the interview.

Some sales just aren't that hard. Some people are ready to buy the car. I've made calls and had the suspect say, "I can be there in an hour. I can't wait to clear this up." When you hear this tactic, I recommend remaining neutral as to interpreting this development. It is possible that it is the mark of an innocent person who is anxious to clear their name. It is also possible you are dealing with an aggressive personality type who thinks they can overwhelm you or get to you when you aren't prepared.

**6. Set the appointment and follow up.** Suspects tend to find better things to do around the time of their interview appointments. Follow up with them at least once before the appointment. By treating the interview appointment like a doctor's visit, you'll make it seem routine instead of momentous. If a suspect is on the fence about coming in, they will be reassured by a text message that says, "Robert, thanks for taking my call the other day. This is really going to help clear this issue up. See you tomorrow at 9 am. Call me if you need directions." A message like this is reminiscent of the dentist confirming an appointment. You are making yourself available in a way that may encourage the suspect to soften their expectations. I believe many suspects view a police interview like a battle of sorts. If you're expecting a fight but all you get is helpfulness, it will be hard to maintain the hard outer shell.

**7. If they ask for a lawyer, have a response.** I used to really worry about this development. I don't anymore. You want to talk to a suspect for two reasons: in the interest of fairness and to get the truth. But let's be clear: a good case should be able to stand whether or not the suspect confesses to the crime. If your entire case relies on getting a confession, it's not that good of a case. I find that I am successful in having suspects come in by staying neutral with this development. Do not get angry. It's not personal.

There are legitimate reasons to want to retain counsel before making statements to police detectives. I have had suspects say, "You'll be hearing from my lawyer!" When I respond, "Great! What is your lawyer's name? I'll reach out to them." They often seem put off by this. Their big gun was LAWYER and I didn't flinch or worry about it. I've had this turn out two ways. One, they say, I'll make some calls and let you know. I've also had a person relent and say that they didn't do anything wrong and they'd rather just come in and talk about it.

Let's look at these two outcomes. Outcome 1: "I'll make some calls and let you know." I don't know about you, but I don't have enough hours in my work days to wait indefinitely to hear from a lawyer that may or may not be retained by this suspect. If this happens, I say, "Sure. That makes sense. One thing, though: I have a lot of cases and I want to get this case resolved as quickly as possible. Some lawyers will advise you to come in with them and make a statement and other lawyers will tell you not to make a statement. In order to wrap this case up, I really need to know if there will be a statement or not be a statement.

Either is fine of course. Will you have your lawyer contact me or should I follow up with you tomorrow to get their name?"

This is a case management technique more than a getting-the-person-into-the-interview technique. When a person definitely expresses a desire to have counsel, you have no idea if they are going to actually call a lawyer or if what they are really saying is they don't want to make a statement, and also they aren't calling anybody. If "I want a lawyer" really means, "I'm not talking to you, do what you need to do," then I want to know that! If they are really getting a lawyer, then you want their name so you can ask them if they want to have their client make a statement. If they aren't getting a lawyer and just don't want to talk, the box is checked and you can move on to next steps.

Outcome 2: The person is upset you aren't impressed with lawyers and says they'll just come in and make a statement. In this scenario, move in and make the sale like we discussed before. You might consider reading Miranda when they come in, but in my opinion it would not be necessary because you will, of course, follow best practices when it comes to non-custodial statements.

**8. If they refuse to come in, interview them on the phone.** In-person interviews are always best, but sometimes the suspect isn't willing to come in for one. I've listened to detectives plead and cajole the person on the other end of the line to come in for an interview. I've listened to detectives call a suspect three or four times to try for the interview. This is where you need to be flexible. There will come a time when it is obvious that the suspect is unlikely to come in for an interview. When this becomes clear to you, pivot, and interview them on the phone. In no particular order, I've had suspects confess over the phone to the Continuous Sexual Abuse of a Young Child, Aggravated Assault, Aggravated Sexual Assault of a Child, and Injury to the Elderly.

Practicing the skills discussed in this section will increase your chances of achieving the first and most important step of interview and interrogation: getting the suspect in the room. There will always be suspects who refuse to come in for an interview. Don't worry about them. Your mission is to persuade the undecided suspect to show up for an interview. Once they come in, you can get down to the business of the interview and interrogation.

### Making Contact with the Suspect in Custodial Cases

The other side to making contact with a suspect is in custodial situations. This happens a lot in robbery, aggravated assault, and murder. Many of these suspects are not people with stable lives. They move about. Their phone numbers change a lot. They often have extensive history with the police. Some people are legitimate flight risks. All of these things make calling the suspect and scheduling a time for them to come in and talk harder. Compounding all of these problems is the likelihood that these suspects may be a danger to the public, which will make your bosses want them arrested sooner rather than later. Typically, the investigation results in a warrant being issued. When they are arrested, officers bring them in for a custodial interview.

I recognize the reality of the situation described above. A lot of these people aren't answering the phone or volunteering to come into the police station. However, before I move into a few pointers on managing your first contact with the suspect in custody, I'd like to make a plug for attempting a non-custodial when possible.

One common argument I hear for why an investigator issues a warrant before trying to call the suspect in is that the person is such a bad dude that there's no way he's going to ever cooperate. I have found this assessment to be wrong as often as not. Personally, I've had documented gang members, people covered in face tattoos, and others with previous convictions for murder come in and be cooperative and pleasant. Of course, I've had the opposite experience, but the point is that history does not tell you what the present will be like. You'll be surprised how often your predictions of uncooperativeness are wrong.

Additionally, sometimes people are innocent. If you don't attempt to interview the suspect before issuing a warrant, you have removed one safety valve from the system that prevents innocent people from being charged with crimes. Getting charged with a crime is a serious event which shouldn't happen early just out of convenience for the investigator. How good is your evidence? How urgent is the need to remove the threat posed by their continued freedom?

Even if you have grade A evidence that the person did it, when you issue a warrant before attempting to talk to the suspect, you give a point to the defense. Investigations are like sports: you want to take as many points as possible while giving up as few as possible. The highest score wins. When you don't attempt to contact a suspect, the defense may choose to take the point, which is, "You did a rushed investigation. You didn't even give my client the chance to give their side before issuing a warrant." It's just a point, but you want to give as few away as possible in order to win.

With all of that said, contacting the suspect in a custodial situation is a little bit different. First, **there will have been things that happened between the suspect and the arresting officers which are outside of your control or knowledge**. You need to learn what those are, which will involve careful questioning of the officer to understand what the situation is. For example, the officer may have accused the suspect, read them their Miranda warnings, or taken other actions that could impact your ability to interview the suspect successfully. Ask the officer if they read the person their rights. Ask them to characterize their conversation with the suspect.

Most of the time the officer will have done the right thing. If there is a problem, however, you want to know up front. What if, unbeknownst to you, the officer read the suspect his Miranda warning, and the suspect demanded to speak to a lawyer? That officer passes your suspect off to the next guy to bring in, and that guy doesn't communicate to you the Miranda issue. If you were to Mirandize the suspect, they waived their rights, and proceeded to confess to everything, that interview could be suppressed. While you can't control what happened before the suspect got to you, you can take steps to get that information and adjust accordingly.

As another example, I've had the experience of my suspects being brought in after being tased or shot with beanbag rounds. One guy I interviewed kept wincing in pain as he reached down to feel his shins, where he seemed to have caught the beanbag rounds. The discomfort he felt for sure affected our communication. I was starting the interview with an injured and angry person, which is not the best foundation on which to build a rapport-based interview.

Next, in these custodial interview events, you'll want to manage your first meeting with the suspect. Ideally, you want your first meeting to be similar to how it would look in a non-custodial setting: they are sitting in the room un-handcuffed when you walk in to shake their hand and give them a bottle of water. I instruct the officers in advance to take the person to the bathroom (or at least offer it to them) and leave them in the locked room without handcuffs. That sets me up for my preferred style of greeting.

Some detectives like to make a show of walking in, appearing surprised to find the person in handcuffs, and ordering the officer to take the handcuffs off. "This guy's still in handcuffs! That's ridiculous! Take them off!" The theory is that the suspect now sees you as somebody who's on their side. If that's your style, It's cool with me. I don't use it, because I prefer to be as genuine as possible without all the play-acting.

*Once you hear officers are coming, go ahead and set up the room the way you want it.* Be purposeful in how you have your room setup. I write more about this in Chapter 5. Rooms have a tendency to get moved around. I had two interviews at the main police station in mid-2024. When I walked in for the first one, the room was set up with four chairs and a table. The suspect chair was so deep in the corner that the cameras couldn't capture all of his body. I rearranged the room. When I went in the very next day for the second interview, the room had been rearranged all over again to a setup with three chairs and a table. Don't assume the room will be set up the way you prefer.

It's ok to have your arrested suspect sit in the locked interview room for a period of time before you make contact with them. You do not have to rush in. Use this time to talk to the officers. Find out what new information they have discovered. Find out the circumstances of the person's arrest. **My opinion is you shouldn't leave the suspect inside the room without anything happening for more than 45 minutes.** If I have to have them in there longer than that, I'll check on them and bring them water, coffee, or snacks. During a check-in like this, I'll provide them a reason for the delay. In my experience, arrested suspects get bored, sleepy, or angry with very extended waits.

If you have not prepared for the interview, use this wait time to prepare. Sometimes these wait times turn into purposeless hangout sessions. If you care about your case, you should be preparing. Re-read your report. List out major topics you need to explore. Familiarize yourself with your evidence. Use the Strategic Use of Evidence (SUE) process described in this book to come up with a plan for how to use the evidence you have (I write about SUE in detail in Chapter 9). Write or type out your questions so that you will have them in the interview room.

From there, the only difference between my custodial versus non-custodial interviews is the pre-Miranda monologue for the custodial interviews. This monologue is a few minutes long, and it seeks to inspire curiosity (what does the investigator know?), and hope (maybe I can talk my way out of this), while reducing fear (you'll be treated with respect). See Chapter 7 for more information on pre-Miranda monologues.

Even if the person is in custody, I recommend attempting to interview them before interrogating them. Too many people rush to the interrogation because, after all, they are under arrest. What questions could you possibly have? This is a silly mindset to have. No matter how airtight a case may be, there are always more questions. If the person has any exculpatory evidence that can show they didn't have anything to do with it, you want to know about it.

## Summary

This chapter provides practical guidance for investigators on conducting non-custodial and custodial interviews with suspects. It highlights the importance of effective communication when calling the suspect. The chapter also addresses common anxieties investigators may face when contacting suspects and offers strategies to overcome these hesitations. Additionally, it provides advice on managing situations where suspects request a lawyer, ensuring that the investigation continues smoothly regardless of the suspect's response. Finally, this chapter provides ideas for managing custodial situations such as minimizing the amount of time the person sits alone in the room. Even in custodial situations, attempt to build rapport and interview them before accusing them of anything. The chapter aims to enhance the chances of conducting a productive interview with the suspect.

### Immediately Actionable

When scheduling, use the line, "I'm available tomorrow at 1 pm or next Tuesday at 9 am. Which can I put you down for? Tomorrow?"

Do not be afraid to tell the suspect what the investigation is about. If they did it, they know they did it.

In custodial cases, make sure you ask detailed questions of the officer bringing the suspect in. Were rights read? If so, what did they say?

Chapter 5

# Interview Room Setup

## Key Points

1. *Two-investigator rule*: With two investigators, the secondary interviewer should remain silent unless prompted by the lead investigator to avoid disrupting the flow and effectiveness of the interrogation.
2. *Room setup*: The layout and environment of the interview room significantly impact the outcome of the interrogation. A cramped or intimidating room can create resistance and anxiety in the suspect, while a more neutral, comfortable setup facilitates cooperation.
3. *Flexibility and comfort*: The ideal interview room is flexible, spacious, and comfortable, without clutter or intimidating features, to promote a productive interview environment.

## Number of Investigators: 1 v 2

Two investigator suspect interviews have a lot of potential *if* you lay one essential ground rule: the secondary interviewer stays quiet until prompted by the lead interviewer. You can't ballroom dance with two leaders. You can't interview with two talking investigators either. With two talking investigators, it is inevitable that they will interfere with one another. When I go into the room with someone I haven't worked with before, I ask them to stay quiet until I prompt them, take notes, look for holes in the story, and look for deception.

On January 24, 2019, in Seminole County, Florida, Grant Amato murdered his family. He was questioned by two detectives for approximately four hours. During this interrogation, the detectives interfered with one another in ways that probably negatively affected the outcome of the interview.

Note: In the following section, I criticize a very narrow portion of a four-hour interview. I don't mean to put down the interviewers themselves. This would have been a very stressful interview. The purpose of my criticism is to highlight an area of interviewing that is commonly mishandled and easy to fix.

I have a video clip you can watch linked in my blog.[1] I'll provide a transcript of that clip below.[2]

(Grant Amato sits on one side of the table. He has two investigators on the opposite side of the table from him)

*Female:* We got called to the house because Cody didn't show up to work. So law enforcement comes over there and…can you tell us what we found?

DOI: 10.4324/9781003663904-6

(11 seconds of silence)
(Male investigator's phone dings. He looks at it then turns it face down and lifts his hands towards Grant. Grant looks at him)
(21 seconds of silence)
*Female:* What do you think we found?

<part 1 of the clip ends>

<second clip starts>

*Female:* What are you not telling us?
(Male investigator's phone dings. He looks at his phone for several seconds)
*Amato:* Umm…
*Female:* What happened at that home that you know?
(Approximately 10 seconds of silence. Then male and female speak at the same time)
*Male:* It's on the tip of your…
*Female:* Grant I know you're not telling…
*Male:* It's on the tip of your tongue. It's right there. It's that bad taste you want to get out. To get it off your chest and out of your head. But you gotta do it. I can't make you say it.

Ok, what happened there? It is two clips I extracted from a Red Circle Interrogation YouTube channel post on the Grant Amato killing. Grant has been convicted of killing his brother and their parents. The first clip shows how the second investigator thinks, "I'm not leading, I'll just check this text message." This clip is taken from perhaps the most important point in that interrogation. It is where the female investigator announces what they are actually doing there: "We got called to the house because Cody didn't show up for work today."

There has been almost two hours of buildup to this point. They are about to talk about the bodies that Grant left in the house. Then the male investigator's phone dings with a message, and he checks it. It is impossible to check phone messages while conveying a deep sense of interest in what your interviewee is saying. You need maximum credibility at these pivotal interview moments.

If you are watching a murder interrogation – or any interrogation for that matter – and hear your messages making that investigator's phone ding in the room, STOP IT! As an investigator, you may need to explain this to your chain of command. "I won't be answering any messages in there." If you are the investigator, put it on silent and put the phone away.

If your case is high profile or actively being investigated, consider taking breaks to check in with your team rather than having your phone dinging at you during the interview.

The second clip shows another instance of the male investigator's phone distracting from the interview. It also shows the two investigators talking over one another. The female investigator asks, "What happened at that home that you know?" I like this question. She seemed ready to wait for an answer, which would be a good use of forced silence. Unfortunately, the male detective broke the silence with another statement.

A common instance of forced silence is maybe 10 seconds to 2 minutes. Forced silence puts the suspect under immense pressure to talk. It is uncomfortable. It CAN be done with two investigators IF you establish the rule – the lead investigator talks and the backup says nothing until prompted, no matter what – and both follow it.

In the Grant Amato clip, the male investigator speaks, interrupting the silence that follows the female investigator's question before it can achieve its intended effect. Then the suspect gets to look between the investigators and decide who he wants to talk to. This creates a plausible delay for Grant, and it gives him more time to think of his response.

If you haven't experienced forced silence, practice it with a friend. Prep your friend by telling them not to say anything for as long as possible. Then ask them, "What did you do last night?" while you continue to look at them and they continue to be silent. It's awkward. It will make your friend want to talk. It will also make *you* want to talk.

Let's discuss another negative aspect of two investigator suspect interviews: if one of you is less committed to getting the truth, it is likely that they will demonstrate this in a way that destroys momentum and rapport. A friend of mine in sex crimes asked me to watch a suspect interview she was going to do with a partner. I did, and they were doing great. I was on the edge of my seat watching the suspect struggle to answer their questions. He was definitely lying, and my friend had him on the ropes.

Then, out of absolutely nowhere, the second investigator thanked the suspect for coming in and shut the interview down. I immediately texted my friend, "What was that?!?" She said her partner wanted to wait for DNA and call the suspect back. I looked at my watch, saw it was noon, and I suspected the second investigator just got hungry and didn't care enough to keep going.

### If You Go in with a Second Interrogator: Lay. The. Ground. Rules.

There ARE some positives to having two investigators in a suspect room. You have a built-in backup for safety, and there is another person watching without having to think of questions. The backup investigator can watch for non-verbals and can think about larger picture issues like "Did they ever actually answer the question?" That can be a great way to maintain the focus.

Also, you can work with another investigator who complements your skills. If you're a good-enough personality type, work with a perfectionist. If you're a rational type, work with somebody who is more emotional. If you're an introvert, find yourself an extrovert. These alternate ways of thinking can diversify your strengths and help ensure a better outcome. No matter how much you know about the person, it's hard to predict what approach is going to open them up. Having another person can give you more tools in your tool belt to approach the problem.

I worked an Aggravated Sexual Assault of a Child case once with a senior detective in the unit. The suspect spoke Spanish, and the other investigator didn't (although he knew enough to have an idea of what was being said). We arranged in advance that I would lead the interview, and I would turn to him if I needed help. I prefer this to translating just for the lead investigator. I made a lot of progress in the interview, but I ran out of things to say.

I passed the lead for questioning to the other detective. He had been engaged and undistracted throughout. He immediately guided the interview to sections I had overlooked. Within a few minutes, I was ready to take back over with a new direction. While I got a full confession on a very difficult interview, I am almost certain I would not have had the same good result without a 2nd interviewer who did his job as well as he did. When done well, two detective interviews are almost certainly superior.

Doing a two-detective interview well takes ground rules and discipline. If you work with the same people a lot, you won't have to spend much time on the ground rules. The discipline is always an issue. I worked with a different detective to interview a man that groped a child at a bus stop. This time I was in the second chair. It took a lot of discipline to let the other investigator run the interview in different directions and with different methods than I would have. This is something that requires self-knowledge. If you can't play well with others, you may be better served by solo interviews no matter what benefits a two-detective interview may serve.

A benefit to having one investigator in the room is that there is a greater feeling of intimacy. We are often asking people to admit to sexual felonies or felonies of violence in some other way. It's easier to admit to something one-on-one than in a group setting. Would you want to admit to being a screwup for the first time to one person in an intimate setting or two people? I think it's pretty obviously one person.

If you have a unit or department policy of using two investigators, follow the policy. Establish the "no talk til I say so rule," and go forth to do good things.

If you are a patrol cop, the issue is the same out there on the streets. Let your partners know what you expect from them if you are the lead. If you are the backup, pay attention, but don't talk until the lead asks you to and don't cause any undue distraction with your radios and cellphones.

### Furniture Layout

The second part of room setup is where the furniture goes. We have about 10 suspect interview rooms across my department's various buildings. Every single one of them is set up differently. The oldest ones are small, decrepit things with soundproofing material and bad carpeting. The newer ones are twice as big with comfy chairs and white paint. I much prefer the newer rooms.

First, from a practical standpoint, there isn't enough space in the older rooms. It is very difficult to position a table (if you choose to use one) and three chairs (for one suspect and two detectives) without being noticeably cramped. What about four chairs and a table? This would happen if there were two detectives, a translator, and a suspect. This could also happen with two detectives, a suspect, and his lawyer. With that many people the video camera can't capture everything that is going on, and the room gets hot.

I think small, cramped rooms with dingy carpeting are both impractical and counterproductive. The same would go for the classic movie interrogation rooms with the steel table, a couple of hard chairs, and a swinging bare light bulb overhead. Any room that is likely to cause anxiety in the subject by its very setup is impacting the interview in negative ways. Bad interview room setups create friction. You can overcome friction, but it's harder than it would be without it. Remember the first rule: don't do anything to make your job harder.

At about the ten-year mark in my career, I was notified internal affairs wanted to talk to me as a witness officer in an unspecified incident which had occurred five years before. I had nothing to hide and no fear of speaking to any of IA's investigators. When I arrived, I was shown into a cramped room with three chairs and a long table. My chair was on the side furthest from the door and wedged into the corner. Two sergeants from internal affairs sat opposite me in the other chairs. It was obvious to me that their objective was to intimidate me. As I sat there, I fumed in anger at the pointless tactics they were using on me. I was there to tell the truth! The room setup and their questioning style made me want to resist simply because they were pushing me. This is a personal anecdote of mine, but I suspect it has broader application to other cases as well.

In early 2024, another detective and I flew up to the northeastern United States to conduct a suspect interview. The local department was kind enough to allow us to use their rooms. You never know what you're going to find in a room. This is what I saw:

This layout was not ideal for my purposes. There is clutter. A table entirely blocks my view of the lower half of the suspect's body. I am placed between the suspect and the door.

I set to moving things about. I dragged the table to the right-hand side of the room. I put myself at the head of the table with my back to the door. I put the suspect chair so that her left arm would rest on the table. I placed my partner in the bottom left corner (as looking at the room from the picture) so that he did not block the door.

Funnily enough, after I re-organized the room, a ranking officer walked into the room while we were down the hall waiting for our suspect to arrive. I heard him yell that somebody had screwed his room up. I hustled down the hall to smooth it all over and ask him to humor me, promising I would put it back the way he had it afterwards.

What is the best interview room setup? The ideal interview room should be about 12′ X 12′ and flexible. You should be able to modify it by adding chairs and moving tables. There shouldn't be clocks on the wall or clutter. Nothing should be bolted to the ground.

*Image 5.1* A picture of an actual police interrogation room provided to the author.

A good interview room setup has a chair for the suspect, a chair for the detective, and a desk of some sort to write on. The chair for the suspect should be facing the door without anything between the suspect and the door. The desk should be oriented so that it is on the right side of right-handed detectives or the left side of left-handed detectives. If you have a second interviewer, they should sit next to the lead detective. If you have a translator, see if you can put them behind the detective. If you put them next to the detective, the suspect will spend the interview looking back and forth between the two of you in a way that creates friction. Unless it's dictated by the policy of your department, there is no reason to have any desktop computers, TVs, handcuffs, or other detritus in the interview room.

I believe all efforts should be made to make the room as equitable as possible. If you get the cushy swivel chair and they get the uncomfortable plastic chair, I think it creates a sense of unfairness, which leads to resistance. **In fact, my preferred setup is a big room with two equal, opposing, comfortable chairs, offset slightly, and 3-4' apart. I have a small card table I can pull to whichever chair I end up in.** That's it!

## Summary

This chapter discusses the importance of the lead interviewer maintaining control in two-investigator interrogations and how the room's setup can influence the suspect's cooperation. It advocates for using a flexible, comfortable, and non-intimidating interview environment to optimize outcomes. The investigator should be sure to review the room prior to introducing the interviewee to it, even if he or she saw it the day before.

## Immediately Actionable

*Look at your interview room with fresh eyes*: Is it cluttered? Are tables blocking your view of the suspect? Is the suspect chair in the corner?

*Look for other furniture*: The best rooms are flexible. You should be able to add a chair for a lawyer or a partner. Do you know where furniture is you can add? Could the table be smaller?

## Notes

1 Purdy, Lewis. 2025 "Two Investigator Suspect Interviews," Substack.com, https://lewispurdy.substack.com/p/two-investigator-suspect-interviews.
2 This is a clip I made for my post. It puts several moments from the interview side by side.

## Reference

Purdy, Lewis. 2025 "Two Investigator Suspect Interviews," Substack.com, https://lewispurdy.substack.com/p/two-investigator-suspect-interviews.

Chapter 6

# Greeting

### Key Point

1 *A good greeting is persuasive*: Certain easy-to-replicate actions during the greeting play on well-known persuasive principles. These include eye contact, a handshake, and a bottle of water.

A good greeting is a foundational skill. If you read this book and can't think of where you want to start, I recommend starting with the greeting. In this section, I discuss what the psychological principles are behind a good greeting, but I want to be clear: *you don't have to know why it works to start benefiting from it today*. Nothing sets the tone for your interview success like a greeting done well.

No matter if the interview is custodial or non-custodial, do the following steps for an excellent greeting.

1 Enter the room
2 Find the suspect's eyes right away
3 Smile and shake their hand
4 Introduce yourself with first and last name followed by your title
5 Give them a bottle of water or a business card
6 Ask them how they are doing

The goal is to communicate warmth, professionalism, and attentiveness. I'll explain why as this section goes on, but that's the takeaway. This is true even if the suspect is accused of doing something vile, if they are smelly, or if any number of other unpleasant aspects are present.

By now, it is common knowledge that first impressions happen quickly and are hard to shake. Why, then, are we wasting this opportunity with suspects? Most police interviews I see on YouTube show officers enter, sigh deeply, and keep their eyes off of the suspect while they settle into their chairs. Then the officer will say, "I'm Detective So and So with the So and So Police Department."

What message does this communicate to the suspect? It communicates they are in trouble, which is sure to bring up their defensiveness. If I have one rule of interview and interrogation, it's this: Don't do anything to make your job harder. Increasing defensiveness for no reason is making your job harder.

Have you ever had your significant other say, "We need to talk"? What do you immediately do? Think about everything you ever did wrong and start preparing defenses for each

DOI: 10.4324/9781003663904-7

of those things. By the time the next word is said, you're ready to fight. The same is true for bad greetings in the interview room.

There's an interview I show in training. It shows police in New Mexico interviewing Robert Mondrian Powell on suspicion of the murder of Elvira Segura.[1] Once the door first opens, it is approximately 7 seconds before the detective makes any sound at all. It is approximately 10 seconds before the detective begins to speak. The detective doesn't make eye contact with Robert until about the 10-second mark when he starts to speak. Robert, on the other hand, is looking at the detective the whole time. If "We Need to Talk" were an interrogation introduction, this would be it.[2]

This is a typical entrance into the interview room. Everything about this entrance communicated that Robert was in trouble, the subject matter was weighty, and maybe a lawyer would be a good idea. I think it could be improved upon with just a little effort. We want to start the interview with as much goodwill as possible.

In this next section of greeting, I will be talking about persuasion. Dr. Robert B. Cialdini wrote a book called Influence in 1984, which identified several persuasive principles. Cialdini's book has sold over 5 million copies, and its impact is likely greater than those sales numbers suggest. In brief, Cialdini identified several principles of persuasion including:

1 Reciprocity
2 Commitment and consistency
3 Liking
4 Scarcity
5 Authority

These principles are persuasive to people at an almost primordial level. When something is advertised as scarce, we want it. When somebody gives us something, we want to give them something back (reciprocity). Interestingly, these principles are persuasive *even when we know they are being used.*

Let me tell you about how Rob Thomas, a detective in Canada, used Cialdini's principles to create the best interrogation introduction I have ever seen. Thomas was a police investigator in Toronto when Alek Minassian plowed a rented van into a crowd of people, killing 11 and injuring 15. Just 9 hours after Alek is taken into custody, Thomas walks in and delivers this amazing performance.[3] I can imagine the amount of pressure he would have been under to get this one right, and he nailed it. I, for one, immediately shifted to using introductions based on this interview. Let me tell you why.

Thomas uses principles of persuasion[4] combined with rapport-based interviewing to engage with and motivate a person that many would have sneered at. There is never a single moment in this interview where Thomas is other than pleasant, but neither is there a single moment where it looks like Alek is running the show. Rather, Thomas methodically works him through the crime to a full confession.

Here is a transcript of Rob Thomas' introduction to Alek Minassian:

*Rob Thomas (RT):* Alek?
*Alek Minassian (AM):* Hello
*RT:* Hi how are you?
*AM:* I'm doing good. How are you?

| | |
|---|---|
| *RT:* | Good good. Do you drink water? |
| *AM:* | Sure |
| *RT:* | (Hands him bottle of water) Thanks so much. How you feeling? |
| *AM:* | I'm good. |
| *RT:* | You feeling okay? My name is Rob Thomas (shakes Alek's hand) how are you? How are you? You doing ok? |
| *AM:* | Yeah yeah. |
| *RT:* | Yeah, you probably have better days than this I guess eh? |
| *AM:* | Yeah I am a little shaken to be honest. |
| *RT:* | A little shaken |
| *AM:* | Like it's not my usual day, obviously. |
| *RT:* | Yeah yeah well I can appreciate that. Alek - mind if I call you Alek? |
| *AM:* | Yeah sure. |
| *RT:* | Use it? What do your friends normally call you? |
| *AM:* | Alek. |
| *RT:* | Alek, my name's Rob Thomas. I want you to call me Rob from here on in, okay? |
| *AM:* | Okay |
| *RT:* | Is that okay? |
| *AM:* | Ok |
| *RT:* | Alek I want you to understand something. I'm a senior detective with the Toronto Police, you understand what that means? |
| *AM:* | Uh, yes. |
| *RT:* | You know I'm a police officer? |
| *AM:* | Yes. |
| *RT:* | Okay. I don't wear a uniform. I wear a suit and tie because of the type of work that I do. But although I'm in a suit and tie, I'm an actual police officer, okay? And I'm one of the senior investigators on this case. Okay? I got called in for this...this specific case because of what's happened and the involvement and everything else that's been going on, okay? Before we get started, I want you to know that we're being videotaped and audio taped. |
| *AM:* | Mmhmm |
| *RT:* | Okay? Do you know what I mean by that? |
| *AM:* | Yes, everything I say and do is being captured. |
| *RT:* | Exactly. Yeah on audio and video, okay? |
| *AM:* | Yeah. |
| *RT:* | You know, here's what I want to do Alek: I want to talk to you okay? We're gonna spend a good deal of time together. Ok? |
| *AM:* | Ok. |
| *RT:* | It's important that I talk to you, alright? I'm gonna ask you questions okay? Gonna ask you questions about your background, your education, your relationships with your family and friends. Work, travel. And I'm gonna ask you questions about what happened today, okay? You don't have to answer those questions if you don't want, okay? You understand that? |
| *AM:* | Yes. |

*RT:* But if you do decide to answer my questions, okay, I just ask that you do two things for me, okay? First thing is, I ask that you treat with respect, okay? I promise to treat you with respect throughout the entire night, okay? All I ask is you do the same for me. Is that okay?

*AM:* Yes.

*RT:* Okay, and the other thing I ask, Alek, and I've been doing this a long time, okay? And I typically never have any problems for the people or anything like that. I don't expect to have a problem with you today, but if you do decide to answer my questions, would you do me the favor and just speak from the heart, okay? And just be truthful. That's all I ask. Does that sound fair?

*AM:* Yes

*RT:* Is that okay?

*AM:* Yes.

*(Begins interview)*

The first thing that jumps out at me is that Thomas hands Alek a bottle of water, and then looks him in the eye, shakes his hand, and says, "You feeling okay? My name is Rob Thomas (shakes Alek's hand) how are you? How are you? You doing ok?" Followed shortly by, "Yeah yeah well I can appreciate that. Alek - mind if I call you Alek?" and then, "Alek, my name's Rob Thomas. I want you to call me Rob from here on in, okay?...Alek I want you to understand something. I'm a senior detective with the Toronto Police, you understand what that means?"

The very first thing that Thomas does is hand Alek a bottle of water. This is an example of Cialdini's principle of Reciprocity. Basically, when we give people things, they want to give us things back. You can generate this automatic response in people by handing them objects, but, maybe more importantly, by handing them intangible things like information or respect. I recommend that you get the ball rolling with a bottle of water or a business card, and then continue the reciprocity with respect and sharing on your part too.

> Cialdini points out that the principle of reciprocity creates an urge to respond that can stretch across time. I experienced this in 2024.
>
> After I presented at the Crimes Against Children Conference in 2023, I gave one of the attendees a challenge coin. He didn't have anything to give me in return. When I was presenting again in 2024, I had forgotten all about it, but the same man found me and put a challenge coin in my hand. I looked at him quizzically. He reminded me of the gift, and he told me he had waited all year to return the gift.

**Note:** While it is good to share some information about yourself or the case, don't overshare. The flow of information should be asymmetrical in your favor (more coming to you than going to them). Important information about your case should always be held back so that it can be verified later.

Michael Reddington writes about Cialdini's principles in his book *The Disciplined Listening Method*. He writes, "For our purposes, one of the most effective ways to ethically leverage reciprocity is to share information and demonstrate vulnerability prior to asking your counterparts to do the same."[5] I was speaking to a witness to a child endangerment case recently. She told me about her addiction to drugs. I told her about my personal and professional experience with addiction, and I included anecdotes specific to what somebody with that experience would know. This was an hour after the "rapport building phase" was done. Shortly afterwards, she told me everything about what she had seen, including a lot of details that she could have been expected to keep private (like her own drug use). When I was willing to share with her, she was willing to share with me.

Now, how about that handshake and introduction? "My name is Rob Thomas (shakes Alek's hand) how are you?" It's so simple it feels revolutionary. Most of us introduce ourselves as "I'm Detective... with the ....Police Department." Most introductions I see involve heading to the desk without looking at the subject, putting our stuff down, sighing, then just looking at them from 6 feet away. This is a cold reality shower right when we are best served by warmth. Thomas gets it right when he shakes Alek's hand and uses his first and last name followed shortly after by his title. People who aren't cops might not understand how ingrained it is in us to lead with the title and a wall of skeptical assessment. In this setting, we have to let it go.

Think about how you introduce yourself to subjects in the room, then contrast that with walking straight up to them, looking them in the eye, and introducing yourself by first and last name followed by "I'm a senior detective with the Police Department." Which is better?

I think, as cops, we get used to being a little paranoid with our information. We hide behind Officer X or Detective Y because we don't want to provide more information for people to type into Facebook. It occurred to me the other day, however, that I had gotten used to introducing myself by title and last name as an outcropping of a sort of standard issue standoffishness. I then realized I avoided saying my first name while handing people my business card with my first name and email (which has my first name) and multiple phone numbers to call me, and then later filing warrants with my first and last name all over them. I know I'm not the only one who does this.

If they are going to know your name anyway, use it to your advantage to build some good will between the two of you. Be a person first, a title second. People will be less likely to view you as playing for the other team and more likely to engage in a reciprocal exchange of information.

Just after introducing himself the right way, Thomas creates his first social contract with Alek. He says, "Alek - mind if I call you Alek?" To which Alek, replies, "Yeah, sure." This is related to Cialdini's Consistency and Commitment principle. Basically, humans want to appear consistent. If we take a stance, we want to follow through on it even if our thoughts might change. When we get somebody to commit to letting us call them a certain informal name, we are laying the groundwork for other, larger commitments (like talking about mass murder).

Then Thomas tells Alek that he is a "senior investigator for the Toronto Police Department." This is a take on Cialdini's principle of Authority. Basically, we tend to listen to people in authority and take them more seriously. By citing his own authority, he gets the benefit of it even while never being asked to prove or back it up. I was talking to one of the newer detectives in a class I taught, and I told her, "You are now a senior detective with the police department! I grant you the title." The one caveat to this is that you must look serious, professional and prepared. If your actions say you're a rookie, they'll believe those more than your assertions.

Thomas goes on to create at least two more social contracts to build on his consistency progress with Alek. Namely: "First thing is, I ask that you treat with respect, okay? I promise to treat you with respect throughout the entire night okay? All I ask is you do the same for me. Is that okay?" This is so good. For a while now I've looked to include promises like this in my talks with suspects. "I promise I'll get this right." "You can trust me to get this right." Promises as a word carries a lot of weight. Making promises like this can go a long way towards establishing consistency.[6]

The next social contract is this: "...if you do decide to answer my questions, would you do me the favor and just speak from the heart, okay? And just be truthful. That's all I ask. Does that sound fair?" Alek agrees to all of them, which creates a bedrock of consistency that should be easy to build on.

Finally, Thomas uses Cialdini's concept of Social Proof when he says "Alek...I've been doing this a long time, okay? And I typically never have any problems for the people or anything like that. I don't expect to have a problem with you today..."[7] This is Thomas saying that everybody else voted to work with me (so my reviews are 5 stars favorable!).

Investigator Rob Thomas absolutely nails this interview and, particularly, the introduction. I hope that when my name is called to do the big interview that I'll be as prepared as he was that day. I hope that you all are able to use these techniques in your interviews.

Is it making sense how much more Rob Thomas set himself up for success from the jump than did the Robert Mondrian Powell interrogators? The best news is, unlike other techniques in interview and interrogation, this one can be learned in a few minutes and applied with very little effort. Once you do that, you'll immediately benefit from the half dozen persuasive principles it touches upon such as reciprocity, consistency, commitment, and liking.

I attended a lecture during the 2023 Crimes Against Children Conference by Dr. Michael Bourke. He interviews sex offenders in prisons as part of his work. On one occasion, he walked into the room, and he shook the offender's hand. They sat and talked. The offender confessed to many things he had not previously admitted to. Dr. Bourke was curious. He asked the offender why he shared so much with him. The offender said, "Because after you shook my hand, you didn't wipe your hand on your pants. I could tell you weren't judging me."

These greetings set the stage for your interview. Enter the room. Find the suspect's eyes right away. Smile and shake their hand. Introduce yourself with first and last name followed by your title. Give them a bottle of water or a business card. Ask them how they are doing. The goal is to communicate warmth, professionalism, and attentiveness. Do not waste the opportunity.

## Summary

This chapter highlights the critical role of a well-executed greeting in interviews, explaining how to automate persuasive principles. It uses real-world examples to illustrate how these techniques can lead to increased cooperation from criminal suspects. At a minimum, you should: establish eye contact immediately, shake hands, use your first and last name followed by your title, and provide them a bottle of water.

## Immediately Actionable

*Practice your greeting:* Get used to introducing yourself by first and last name followed by your title. Have business cards or water bottles handy to give the other person something. This may take some practice to unlearn previous habits.

## Notes

1 Red Circle Interrogations and Confessions. 2020. "Robert Mondrian Powell - Full Murder Confession - Police Interrogation." YouTube. September 24, 2020. https://www.youtube.com/watch?v=vE5hSlXEFOc.

2 I don't want to pick on the detective at all. He got a court-admissible murder confession, so we could all learn something from how he conducted himself. If you read this, well done, sir!

3 Finkle, Jim, and Anna Mehler Paperny. 2018. "Shoes, Bodies Strewn on Toronto Street after van Attack." *Reuters*, April 24, 2018. https://www.reuters.com/article/world/shoes-bodies-strewn-on-toronto-street-after-van-attack-idUSKBN1HV065/.
"Police Interrogation of Toronto van Attack Suspect 'Textbook,' Experts Say | Globalnews.ca." n.d. Global News. https://globalnews.ca/news/5961942/alek-minassian-interrogation-reaction/.

4 Identified and popularized by Dr. Robert Cialdini in his book: Cialdini, Robert B. (1984) 2008. *Influence: Science and Practice.* 5th ed. Harlow: Pearson Education.

5 Reddington, *The Disciplined Listening Method*, 271.

6 One of the prohibited activities in the interview room is a promise of leniency. If you do X, I'll make sure you get a lighter sentence. This has been shown to create an increased chance of false confessions. Promising to listen, not to judge, or get things right are NOT the same, and any prosecutor or defense attorney that suggests it is being dishonest.

7 This is something J. Schanke (instructor of interrogation for FLETC) pointed out, along with other uses of Cialdini during this introduction.

## References

Cialdini, Robert B. 2021. *Influence: Science and Practice.* 5th ed. Harlow: Pearson Education.

Finkle, Jim, and Anna Mehler Paperny. 2018. "Shoes, Bodies Strewn on Toronto Street after van Attack." *Reuters*, April 24, 2018. https://www.reuters.com/article/world/shoes-bodies-strewn-on-toronto-street-after-van-attack-idUSKBN1HV065/

"Police Interrogation of Toronto van Attack Suspect 'Textbook,' Experts Say | Globalnews.ca." n.d. Global News. https://globalnews.ca/news/5961942/alek-minassian-interrogation-reaction/

Red Circle Interrogations and Confessions. 2020. "Robert Mondrian Powell - Full Murder Confession - Police Interrogation." YouTube. September 24, 2020. https://www.youtube.com/watch?v=vE5hSlXEFOc

Reddington, Michael. 2022. *The Disciplined Listening Method: How a Certified Forensic Interviewer Unlocks Hidden Value in Every Conversation.* Charlotte, NC: Per Capita.

Chapter 7

# Custodial Issues

### Key Points

1. *Complexity of custodial issues*: Determining whether or not a suspect is in custody can be highly complex, involving factors like the suspect's freedom to leave and the nuances of police conduct, making it challenging even for experienced judges.
2. *Miranda rights*: Miranda warnings must be given when a suspect is (a) in custody, (b) by police, and (c) being questioned, but the specifics of what constitutes "custody" can vary significantly.
3. *Pre-Miranda monologue*: I suggest using a pre-Miranda monologue to reduce the suspect's fear and increase their curiosity and hope, making them more likely to talk voluntarily.
4. *Non-custodial interviews*: These interviews do not require Miranda warnings, but officers must ensure the suspect understands they are free to leave and are not under arrest.

A solid understanding of custodial issues is fundamental to being successful in the interview room. There are so many variations of custody events that even experienced judges can come to different conclusions with the same case facts. Most of my readers will be working cops, so it is unreasonable to expect they can be as knowledgeable as a judge. In this section, I discuss custodial issues from the perspective of a working cop.

It's unlikely you will always have the answer to complex custodial issues when they arise. Sometimes, you have to make your best decision, and move forward. Things start going off the rails when investigators get ideas for creative ways to circumvent Miranda. If you are acting from a place of integrity, with a sincere desire to do the right thing, you'll be okay.

### Custodial Cases

If a suspect is in custody, by police, and being questioned, they must be advised of their Miranda rights. Although Miranda rights are straightforward on the surface, the nuances of custody and Miranda are complex. For example, I've read case law that referenced the detective's facial expression and tone of voice when determining custody. If legal scholars can't reduce it to a few bright line rules, what's the average working detective to do?

Of course, the primary case law for custodial interrogations is Miranda v. Arizona (1966).[1] Ernesto Miranda was accused of rape. He was interrogated for two hours, and he confessed to the rape. He signed a confession that acknowledged his rights, but he hadn't been told his rights. His attorney argued that Miranda's confession should be thrown out because he

DOI: 10.4324/9781003663904-8

wasn't provided an attorney or notified of his rights.[2] The Supreme Court changed the way policing was done when they ruled in favor of Miranda.

As a result, police are required to read a suspect their Miranda "rights" when they are in custody, by police, and being questioned. I put rights in quotes because they are more appropriately referred to as warnings. Your rights don't come from the Miranda decision but rather from the 5th and 6th amendments to the US Constitution.

The Miranda warnings vary subtly. The exact wording was not prescribed by the Miranda ruling. In Texas, we are guided by the Code of Criminal Procedures 38.22:

Sec. 2. No written statement made by an accused as a result of custodial interrogation is admissible as evidence against him in any criminal proceeding unless it is shown on the face of the statement that:

a the accused, prior to making the statement, either received from a magistrate the warning provided in Article 15.17 of this code or received from the person to whom the statement is made a warning that:

  1 he has the right to remain silent and not make any statement at all and that any statement he makes may be used against him at his trial;
  2 any statement he makes may be used as evidence against him in court;
  3 he has the right to have a lawyer present to advise him prior to and during any questioning;
  4 if he is unable to employ a lawyer, he has the right to have a lawyer appointed to advise him prior to and during any questioning; and
  5 he has the right to terminate the interview at any time; and

b the accused, prior to and during the making of the statement, knowingly, intelligently, and voluntarily waived the rights set out in the warning prescribed by Subsection (a) of this section.[3]

Innumerable books, research papers, and court opinions have been written on this topic. This book is not the place to rehash all of what has been said elsewhere. Below, I've reduced the complex issues around custody to a few quick answers. I'm not a lawyer, and this is not legal advice. Consult policy and your county or district attorneys if you are in doubt. These are good, working definitions and considerations I use based on my training and experience, presented here in question and answer form.

*Q: Is the suspect really in custody?*

A: If the suspect is free to go and could reasonably know that, they are not in custody. If the suspect is not free to go or could reasonably infer that they weren't, they are in custody.

Quick test: If the suspect said, "I want to leave." Would you let them? If the answer is "yes," they aren't in custody. If they answer is "no," they are in custody.

*Q: If the suspect is detained but not under arrest, does Miranda apply?*

A: The safest answer is, "Yes." The distinction between detention and arrest is significant to working cops, but it isn't significant in a legal sense. For a working cop, a detention is a status in which the person is not free to leave, but isn't necessarily going to jail. An arrest is when the person is definitely going to jail. Remember, though, Miranda applies when the person is in custody, by police, and being questioned. Being detained is being in custody. I hedge my yes answer because I believe there are court cases where – detention status notwithstanding – the decision came down to whether or not suspicion had become particularized to that specific person.

***Q: If I am conducting a non-custodial interview, and the suspect begins to incriminate himself, do I have to stop and Mirandize him?***

A: No. As long as he is still free to leave after the interview, he isn't in custody, so Miranda doesn't apply.

***Q: Do I have to Mirandize the suspect on a phone interview?***

A: No. They aren't in custody.

***Q: If I give the suspect a ride to the police station for a non-custodial interview, do I have to Mirandize them?***

A: It depends. In order for it not to be custodial, you should tell the person clearly and on camera they are not under arrest and you'll take them back anytime they want to go. Vocalize you are giving them a ride because they requested one and not because they are in custody. Of course, if they tell you they want to leave or end the interview, you need to actually take them back.

***Q: What if the suspect invokes their rights but then re-engages and says they want to talk?***

A: Whether the suspect invokes the right to silence or to counsel, it is acceptable to interview them again under three circumstances: (1) As long as the suspect initiated the contact (rather than being re-approached by police); (2) it was "freely" initiated (not a result of prodding or coercion); and (3) the re-initiation opened a general discussion about the case (rather than, say, a question about a jail call they might get).[4] An example I had: a suspect invoked his right to counsel. I left. Later, he started pacing about and grabbing his stomach. He knocked on the door to the room. I opened and asked what he needed. He said he felt sick because he was in there and the other guy was out there. I read him his Miranda warnings again, and he agreed to be interviewed.

***Q: If the suspect invokes their right to counsel, does that mean that police can never attempt to question him again except through an attorney?***

A: No. Maryland v. Shatzer 559 U.S. 98 (2010)[5] gave a rare bright line rule. The court determined police have to wait 14 days after the suspect invokes before re-approaching him and attempting to interview him again. Of course, there is some nuance to this that may require deeper reading on the topic.

***Q: What if the suspect's request for an attorney is ambiguous? Such as, "I wonder if I should talk to a lawyer?"***

A: An explicit request for an attorney requires all questioning to cease. That might be, "I'm not saying anything else without an attorney present" or something similar. On the other hand, if the suspect makes an ambiguous or equivocal statement concerning the right to legal counsel, the officer does not need to stop and ask clarifying questions.[6] This comes from Davis v. United States. For example, some suspects will say, "Maybe I should talk to a lawyer" as Davis did. This request is ambiguous. You are not required to clarify and ask, "Do you want a lawyer present right now?" Here, you'll need to make some in-the-moment decisions as to whether or not the request is ambiguous. Many detectives will address the ambiguous request by saying, "You have every right to consult with a lawyer" and then keep on asking questions. Personally, I prefer to err on the side of caution. I've ended interviews others may have continued on with.

Again, these issues are so complex. Be able to articulate what you are doing and why. If the person isn't in custody, you should feel comfortable telling them so. If they *are* in custody, read them Miranda. *If you aren't sure, read them Miranda.*

### *Pre-Miranda monologue*

Miranda is three pronged. It applies when the subject is (1) in custody, (2) by police, and (3) being questioned. If you are talking to them without questioning them, Miranda doesn't apply. You have some leeway here to talk to them about why you want to ask them questions.

Guilty suspects talk to the police when they are under arrest for two main reasons: they want to know what you know, and they want to see if they can talk themselves out of it. The first reason is based on curiosity and fear; the second is based on hope. If you do a proper pre-Miranda monologue, you can trigger their curiosity, reduce their fears, and give them hope, which will make them want to talk.

Imagine we are strangers and we walk up to a wall together at the same time. The wall is tall, rough, and covered in concertina wire up top. You don't want anything to do with this wall, so you are on the verge of leaving. I say, "Let's climb this wall. You don't have to. You can definitely have a climbing coach with you before we start. Seriously, it's cool if you don't. In fact, it's kinda dangerous if you do." You are going to walk away from that wall more often than not. This is walking in, waving at a person, and reading them Miranda.

Now, imagine the same situation. This time, I say, "Whoa. That wall looks terrible. You seeing this thing? Ugh. Have you ever heard the story of why they made it look so bad, though? Deal is, it's got some sites you'd like to see. If you ever saw them you'd be really interested in them. In fact, if you're the right kind of person, it might be just what you need. I've been over this wall lots of times, but it's cool if you want to wait for a climbing coach. Wanna climb with me?" This is gonna work more often than not. It's the same with using a pre-Miranda monologue.

I'd estimate, without going back and watching them all again, that I was 50/50 or 60/40 against reading arrested people Miranda right away and having them talk in my interviews. Since I started using a pre-Miranda monologue, I'd bet it's closer to 80/20 in favor of talking. Once I realized curiosity and hope were behind the phenomenon, I became more effective at using it. Labeling things is a superpower.

Here is an example of how I craft my pre-Miranda monologue invoking the motivating factors of reducing fear and increasing curiosity and hope:

> I'm going to be straight with you. You're under arrest. I can't change anything about that now. This situation led me to a point where my bosses wanted to know where I was at,

and I told them it was more likely than not that you were the one. They're impatient, and they wanted me to put a warrant out, and I did. I wish I'd have had time to talk to you first, of course.

While we talk today, I promise to treat you with respect. I will listen to what you have to say. If you need water, coffee, bathroom breaks, or snacks, just tell me. I'll make sure you have those things. **REDUCING FEAR**

I can't tell you how many times I've talked to people that were also in the tough position of having it be more likely than not that they were involved, but then they explained their side of things, and I saw it all differently. These conversations always change my view on the situation. No matter what happens while we talk today, I promise that I will treat you with respect. I just ask that you do the same for me. **HOPE**

While we talk, if you have anything at all that can show that you weren't involved, point me in the direction so that I can find it. I promise you that if you can show me evidence that proves you didn't do it is, I will go and find it. That's my job. When I find it, I will make sure that all of the decision makers involved know about it. **HOPE**

Luckily, we still have time to talk so you can help me understand. I've got some evidence I'd like to show you. When I looked at it, it seemed to point to you, but I want your opinion on those things. We can look at that evidence together, and maybe you can help me see how it isn't what it seems. **CURIOSITY**

Before we get started, I want to make sure you understand your rights...[Miranda]

However you craft your pre-Miranda monologue, if you successfully convey the selling points of reducing fear and increasing curiosity and hope, you have made Miranda seem much less scary. It becomes an afterthought rather than the elephant in the room.

When you come up with your pre-Miranda monologue, make it sound like you. Use your words. There was a student in a recent class that had a great delivery, totally different from mine. She would have sounded silly using my exact words. I would sound ridiculous talking like her. It's the elements that matter. Remember: curiosity, hope, and reducing fear are the keys.

Make sure you don't make any threats or promises of leniency. If you look up at mine, I tell the person I promise I'll search out their exonerating evidence. That is not a promise of leniency, so it does not violate that guideline.

I've been asked by a previous student if I was serious about looking for exonerating evidence they pointed me towards. That answer is: absolutely. I want the truth. As long as it is a legitimate lead, I'll go look. If he says, "Come by my place and look at my laptop, I'll show you ..." I would absolutely make a time to go review that laptop. If he says, "I think there was a dark shadowy guy I don't know standing in the corner. Go find him. He would have seen everything." I'm not going to look for that "witness." If I talk to other witnesses, sure, I'll ask if there was anybody else around.

The pre-Miranda monologue only takes a minute or two to say, and its impact is enormous. It reduces fear, "I promise that I will treat you with respect..." It triggers hope. If they have something that can show they weren't involved, they should just point me in the direction. It turns on curiosity. I'm telling you I have the evidence, I'll share, and we can look over it together. Who wouldn't want to know what evidence the police have implicating them in a crime?

What I like most about this technique is that it is fully consistent with respecting the rights of innocent people. It is absolutely possible to have evidence point at you and you be totally innocent. Innocent people are probably just as likely as guilty people to invoke Miranda, especially with aggressive cops who don't tell them why they want to talk to them. While innocent people may be understandably shy about talking, we definitely want to hear from them. I've had the experience of a very guilty-seeming person turn out to be innocent. If you show an innocent person the evidence against them, there is a good chance they will be able to explain it in a way that changes how you think about the case.

Using a pre-Miranda monologue to encourage people to talk is not just about getting a confession. It is about getting people to talk so you can get to the truth. Even if that person already has a warrant out for them, you should want to interview them. A warrant is based on probable cause. A verdict is won on "beyond a reasonable doubt." That suspect's statement is a big piece of getting innocent people freed and guilty people convicted. You should want to get it.

## Non-custodial Cases

A non-custodial suspect interview happens between a police detective and a suspect under circumstances when the suspect has not been charged, is not in custody, and is free to leave at any time. The biggest distinction between custodial and non-custodial interviews is that a non-custodial interview does not require the detective to read the suspect their Miranda warnings. Miranda applies only in instances when a suspect is (1) in custody, (2) by police, and (3) being questioned.

As you'll see in this section, a lot of thought is given to how to question a criminal suspect without reading them their Miranda rights. I'll say the quiet part out loud: the basic presumption is reading a suspect their rights makes them more likely to invoke either their right to counsel or their right to remain silent. Either of these invocations makes it less likely you will be getting a statement from the suspect.

Non-custodial interviews were given shape by a case known as California v. Beheler.[7] In that case, a homicide suspect was brought in for a voluntary interview in which he was not read his Miranda warnings. He was allowed to leave after the interview. Five days later, he was arrested, read his Miranda warnings, and he confessed to the crime. The courts allowed both interviews into evidence because, as they explain, the suspect was not in custody during the first interview. Therefore, police were not required to have read him his Miranda warnings.

When you testify in the suppression hearing or in open court about your non-custodial interview, you should expect questions from the defense to center on custodial issues. If they can create doubt as to whether or not the exact situation you were in was actually custodial, they may be able to convince a judge to suppress the interview. Some questions I have gotten include:

- Were you in uniform?
- Were you armed?

- My client said that they wanted to go, but you kept asking her questions. Was she free to go?
- Did you meet my client's biological needs?
- Did you lock the door to the room?
- Were they free to go?
- Did you have probable cause to arrest my client? If so, wouldn't that mean that they were in custody?
- My client denied it, but you kept accusing them. Why?

Think about a recent suspect interview. What would your responses be to these questions?

Something to consider is most of the conversation around non-custodial suspect interviews is generated by the fact that you usually don't read them their Miranda warnings. Remember that nothing is preventing you from reading them their Miranda warnings in a non-custodial setting. In fact, some jurisdictions make it so their officers have to read Miranda before both non-custodial and custodial interviews. If you live in a jurisdiction where reading Miranda is optional in a non-custodial setting, and you think the interview could possibly be custodial, read them Miranda. Alternatively, if you are certain it isn't custodial but just don't want to give the defense ammunition to attack the interview, you can read them Miranda.

At the end of the day, any statement you gather is supposed to be voluntary. In a non-custodial situation, the suspect is supposed to understand they are not under arrest and they are free to go at any time. It is not required to tell them explicitly they have the right to have an attorney present to advise them during any questioning, *but the premise is they should know this and feel able to request it at any time with or without the explicit warning*.

My standard non-custodial warning to the suspect goes like this:

> You are not under arrest. You know that right? That means you are free to go at any time. If you decide to leave, you don't need my permission to leave. Just get up and walk out. I haven't filed any charges against you, and I haven't made any final decisions on this case. While we talk today, if you need water or coffee, I'll bring them to you. If you need a bathroom break, I'll show you were the bathroom is. Do you have any questions about that?

There are slight variations when I present it, but it should always include the following elements:

1 You are not under arrest
2 You are free to go at any time
3 Your biological needs will be met

These make for a strong non-custodial statement. Since I've been asked on the stand in several trials whether or not I had already made my decision on what to do (in an effort to argue that they were *actually* in custody), I usually include the line that I haven't made any final decisions in the case. This is obviously true if the conversation is non-custodial.

I got a call one time in the child abuse unit. The officer told me that he had a guy detained on suspicion of sexual assault of a child. I was indecisive on whether or not I had enough to arrest the suspect. While it was probable he did it, I typically authorize arrests on much more than merely probable cause. I asked the officer to ask the suspect if he wanted to come in and voluntarily make a statement. The officer relayed back that the suspect agreed. Relieved that I didn't have to make the call, I asked him to bring the suspect in.

Now, a voluntary interview is non-custodial, which means you'd be willing to give the suspect directions to the police station and trust him to get there without an escort. Any indication of being in custody is going to be a strong point for the defense to point at and say the suspect was actually in custody. Those indications of being in custody could be as small as a stern tone and as significant as pointing a gun at the suspect and giving them commands. I hadn't given this officer any directions on how to get the guy to the station.

When the officer arrived with the suspect, I gasped in surprise. The suspect was wrapped in a yellow EMS blanket, handcuffed, and wearing only his boxers. I'm no legal expert, but I'd say that the guy was in custody. If you choose to go the route of inviting a suspect in for a non-custodial interview, you may need to give very clear instructions on how you'd like to have that accomplished.

I've heard complaints from defense attorneys and academics that there is a coercive nature to interviewing, whether custodial or non-custodial which brings into question the voluntariness of the statement. I've had an attorney protest that their client denied the allegations, yet I kept asking them. Why was that? I responded to the effect, "If I told you something that conflicted with other facts you had, and you suspected I was lying, would you just let me get away with it, or would you keep asking questions?" The attorney let it go and moved on, but I know the answer.

The majority of my interviews in child abuse were non-custodial. That means the subject was free to leave at any time, they were not under arrest, they could end the interview at any time, and, at a minimum, I would meet their biological needs. I would ensure they have bathroom breaks and water. If the person I had in the interview room got up and left, I wouldn't stop them.

That doesn't necessarily mean I need to facilitate their leaving. I've had people say things like, "So I could walk out of here if I wanted to?" I've responded, "Of course, that door is open. When you are done talking, just open the door and head to your left." Then I kept talking. In my training and experience, this is consistent with a non-custodial interview. They were free to go. They knew how to. They chose not to. As I said, it isn't my job to facilitate an ambiguous exploration of whether or not they could leave if they wanted to. Of course, the defense may move to suppress by articulating a different view. Check with your local prosecutors or bosses to make sure this is the same where you are.

As case in point, a friend of mine, Katy Conner, interviewed Kaitlin Armstrong, who was accused of murdering her boyfriend's love interest.[8] This was a case that captured national attention after Armstrong fled the country, got a nose job, and hid out as a yoga instructor in Costa Rica. Early in the investigation, Armstrong was invited in for a non-custodial interview. Detective Conner informed her she was free to leave at any time, and other associated non-custodial warnings. As they reference in this news clip you can watch,[9] Armstrong said several times she wanted to go, to which Connor replied she was free to do so, but Armstrong didn't make any move to actually leave. This interview survived the suppression hearing.

Like I said at the beginning of this section, the variations are endless in police interactions with suspects. In fact, any two different judges might rule differently on whether or not your actions violated the suspect's rights. You may not have a bright line rule for how to handle the situation. Get training when you can. Consult with your bosses, co-workers, and attorneys as needed. When in doubt, use doing the right thing as your guiding principle.

## FAQ

*Q: If I accuse the suspect, do I have to stop and read them Miranda?*

A: No. Look back at the holding from California V. Beheler cited earlier in this section, "Miranda warnings are not required simply because the questioning takes place in a coercive environment in the station house or because the questioned person is one whom the police suspect."

*Q: Can an interview in jail be non-custodial?*

A: I've heard this argued both ways. On the one hand, it seems obvious because the person is in jail. What could be more in custody than that? The source of the confusion is whether a person is in custody for an unrelated charge and being questioned about an entirely different charge. Since they aren't in custody for your charge, then maybe ... For me, the simplest answer is to treat them as in custody and read them Miranda.

## Summary

This chapter explores the intricacies of custodial issues in law enforcement, emphasizing the challenges officers face in determining when a suspect is in custody and how Miranda rights apply. I provide insight on handling custodial and non-custodial interviews, including the use of a pre-Miranda monologue to encourage suspect cooperation. Legal nuances, such as the distinction between detention and arrest and the implications of ambiguous requests for counsel, are highlighted. The chapter underscores the importance of acting with integrity and understanding the complexities involved in custodial situations.

## Immediately Actionable

*Practice Your Pre-Miranda Monologue*: A good pre-Miranda monologue increases curiosity and hope while reducing fear. Look at the script in this chapter for ideas on basic structure. This monologue should be about 3 minutes long. Practice it out loud in the car or on a run. Sincerity is key.

*Practice Your Non-custodial Monologue*: You don't want to leave it up to chance to remember the key components. You are not under arrest. You are free to go at any time. Your biological needs will be met. Again, it's best to practice this out loud.

## Notes

1 U.S. Supreme Court. 1966. "Miranda v. Arizona." Justia. June 13, 1966. https://supreme.justia.com/cases/federal/us/384/436/.
2 Partida, Maria Guadalupe. 2022. "1966: Miranda v. Arizona." Library of Congress. 2022. https://guides.loc.gov/latinx-civil-rights/miranda-v-arizona. Important to remember that Miranda was later convicted of rape even without the confession. He is not exactly the hero that some think of him as. The same link above notes, "Four years after his release on parole, a killer, who did receive his Miranda rights, stabbed Miranda to death."
3 "CODE of CRIMINAL PROCEDURE CHAPTER 38. EVIDENCE in CRIMINAL ACTIONS." n.d. Statutes.capitol.texas.gov. https://statutes.capitol.texas.gov/Docs/CR/htm/CR.38.htm.
4 "Miranda: Post-Invocation Questioning." n.d. https://le.alcoda.org/publications/files/MIRANDAPOSTINVOCATION.pdf.
5 U.S. Supreme Court. 2010. "Maryland v. Shatzer." Justia. February 24, 2010. https://supreme.justia.com/cases/federal/us/559/98/.supreme.justia.com.
6 "Davis v. United States, 512 U.S. 452 (1994)." n.d. Justia Law. https://supreme.justia.com/cases/federal/us/512/452/.
7 It's worth reading this syllabus and holding from California v. Beheler:
"California v. Beheler, 463 U.S. 1121 (1983)." n.d. Justia Law. https://supreme.justia.com/cases/federal/us/463/1121/.
California v. Beheler, 463 U.S. 1121 (1983)
"After respondent called the police to report a homicide in which he was involved, he voluntarily accompanied them to the station house, having been told that he was not under arrest. At the station house, the police did not advise respondent of his rights under Miranda v. Arizona, 384 U. S. 436, and after an interview that lasted less than 30 minutes, he was allowed to leave. He was arrested five days later and, after receiving Miranda warnings, gave a second confession during which he admitted that his earlier interview had been given voluntarily. Subsequently, respondent was convicted in a California state court for aiding and abetting first-degree murder, the court having admitted into evidence respondent's statements at both interviews. The California Court of Appeal reversed, holding that the first police interview constituted custodial interrogation, which activated the need for Miranda warnings.
Held: Miranda warnings were not required at respondent's first interview with the police. For Miranda purposes, "custodial interrogation" means questioning initiated by law enforcement officers after a person has been taken into custody or otherwise deprived of his freedom of action in any significant way. Respondent was neither taken into custody for the first interview nor significantly deprived of his freedom of action. Although the circumstances of each case must influence a determination of whether a suspect is "in custody," the ultimate inquiry is merely whether there is a formal arrest or restraint on freedom of movement of the degree associated with a formal arrest. Miranda warnings are not required simply because the questioning takes place in a coercive environment in the station house or because the questioned person is one whom the police suspect. Cf. Oregon v. Mathiason, 429 U. S. 492."
8 "Fueled by Jealousy, Kaitlin Armstrong Fatally Shot an Elite Cyclist and Then Led Officials on an International Manhunt." 2024. NBC News. April 5, 2024. https://www.nbcnews.com/news/us-news/kaitlin-armstrong-killed-cyclist-mo-wilson-fit-jealousy-led-officials-rcna146267.
9 KVUE. 2023. "Detective and Deputy Testify in Day 6 of Kaitlin Armstrong Trial." YouTube. November 9, 2023. https://www.youtube.com/watch?v=Wi7gtZFyI8Q.

## References

"California v. Beheler, 463 U.S. 1121 (1983)." n.d. Justia Law. https://supreme.justia.com/cases/federal/us/463/1121/
"CODE of CRIMINAL PROCEDURE CHAPTER 38. EVIDENCE in CRIMINAL ACTIONS." n.d. Statutes.capitol.texas.gov. https://statutes.capitol.texas.gov/Docs/CR/htm/CR.38.htm
"Davis v. United States, 512 U.S. 452 (1994)." n.d. Justia Law. https://supreme.justia.com/cases/federal/us/512/452/

"Fueled by Jealousy, Kaitlin Armstrong Fatally Shot an Elite Cyclist and Then Led Officials on an International Manhunt." 2024. NBC News. April 5, 2024. https://www.nbcnews.com/news/us-news/kaitlin-armstrong-killed-cyclist-mo-wilson-fit-jealousy-led-officials-rcna146267
KVUE. 2023. "Detective and Deputy Testify in Day 6 of Kaitlin Armstrong Trial." YouTube. November 9, 2023. https://www.youtube.com/watch?v=Wi7gtZFyI8Q.
"Miranda: Post-Invocation Questioning." n.d. https://le.alcoda.org/publications/files/MIRANDA-POSTINVOCATION.pdf.
Partida, Maria Guadalupe. 2022. "1966: Miranda v. Arizona." Library of Congress. 2022. https://guides.loc.gov/latinx-civil-rights/miranda-v-arizona.
U.S. Supreme Court. 1966. "Miranda v. Arizona." Justia. June 13, 1966. https://supreme.justia.com/cases/federal/us/384/436/.
U.S. Supreme Court. 2010. "Maryland v. Shatzer." Justia. February 24, 2010. https://supreme.justia.com/cases/federal/us/559/98/.supreme.justia.com.

Chapter 8

# Rapport Building

## Key Points

1 *Importance of Rapport:* Building and maintaining rapport is essential in interviews, significantly increasing the likelihood of obtaining satisfactory outcomes.
2 *Motivational Interviewing Principles*: Techniques such as autonomy, adaptation, acceptance, empathy, and evocation are key strategies in building rapport with suspects during interviews.
3 *Challenges for Law Enforcement*: Patrol officers and violent crime detectives often resist rapport-building, either due to time constraints or the perception that it won't work on hardened criminals.
4 *Effective Communication*: Using non-judgmental, empathetic, and curious approaches can prevent conflict and encourage suspects to share information.
5 *Safety Considerations*: While building rapport is crucial, it should not compromise officer or suspect safety, especially in high-risk situations.

According to training materials put out by the Federal Law Enforcement Training Center (FLETC), the purpose of rapport building is twofold. First, we talk to people we like. Second, we want to establish a baseline for the interviewee. In order to get the most out of rapport building, we must achieve both of these goals. Rapport is without a doubt a level one, fundamental part of interviewing. Don't even think about trying to read body language (a level three skill) until you have a plan for building rapport.

In 2012, Dave Walsh and Ray Bull published a study on the effectiveness of rapport building in achieving positive outcomes for suspect interviews. In the study, they reviewed 142 suspect interviews. The researchers broke down rapport building into a series of measurable tasks. They concluded, in part, that "interviewers rated as at or above [the interview style] standard in both their rapport building and maintenance skills were over five times more likely to obtain satisfactory outcomes (42% vs. 8%)."[1] That's a number that should raise eyebrows.

They point out something in their study I haven't seen talked about elsewhere: rapport is not just a thing to be accomplished at the beginning and then forgotten. Rather, it must be built and *sustained* in order to achieve the best results. There are a few techniques that can possibly purport to yield results as profound as "five times more likely to obtain satisfactory outcomes." It may come as a surprise, then, how resistant police officers are to building rapport. In my experience, this is particularly true for patrol officers.

We want the benefits of rapport-based interviewing. How do you actually build rapport, though? Is it just being cool? Or is it something else?

DOI: 10.4324/9781003663904-9

### Practical Ways to Build Rapport

This section of the interview should take 15-30 minutes. The basic goal is to get to know the interviewee on a personal level. What do they care about? What do they want? How do they spend their days? I generally start this section with a prompt. For example, *"Before we get started, I don't know you. What can you tell me about yourself?"*

Choose a prompt that works for you. Ideally, it lets the other person choose what to talk about as opposed to you picking a topic like sports or work. Try to focus on positive topics. Keep your prompt simple. Say it and wait until the other person responds. This will feel awkward for a few moments, but it almost always results in the person saying something you can work with. Be ok with the awkwardness.

Talking about preferred topics relaxes the other person. It allows you to observe their baseline speech and behavior patterns. Often, the person will say something vague like, "I work. I spend time in the house with my kids. That's pretty much it." Typically, the things people bring up after this first prompt will give you direction to explore topics the person cares about. After all, they listed those things first. Follow up with, "You said that you work. Tell me about that." Otherwise, you might prompt, "Tell me about spending time with your kids." Be interested in the other person. Ask follow up questions that make sense. The more you spend time on a topic the person cares about, the more likely they are to relax and share about themselves. Note how long their responses tend to be. Observe how expressive they are with their bodies. I typically stay in the rapport-building phase until the interviewee and I are able to share a laugh or some other moment of connection. That lets me know we have rapport with one another.

Some people readily talk about themselves. Others require prompting. Some will resist you. In a recent case at my department, a social media influencer was arrested. A partner of mine went to talk to him. My partner used a tactic that is also effective at building rapport: talking about himself. Talking about yourself can increase rapport because it builds on the principle of reciprocity. You share something about yourself. It often prompts the other person to share about themselves. My partner led off with something like, "Before we get started, I'd like to share a little about myself. I…" The influencer almost immediately cut him off. "I don't give a fuck about you. We're here to talk about me." What can you do with a person like this?

Quite a few suspects you interview will resist your efforts to build rapport. On numerous occasions, I've had the interviewee say, "Why don't we get to the point? What are we actually here to talk about?" If you happen to be the type that would also prefer to get to the point, resist the temptation to skip rapport building with this suspect. We know that the best interviews are built on rapport. There are two strategies I've found to counteract this. First, I ask them to reconsider. I might say, "I understand wanting to get to the point. I want to do that too. The reason I ask you to talk about yourself is because it helps me be more fair to you. Right now, all I know about you is what I've read in reports and been told by others." This usually works. If they insist on getting to the point, you can say something like, "You're a straight-talker. I like that. Let's get to it. Tell me your name and date of birth." Gather their basic details, then look for places to build connections with them. Maybe you patrolled the place they grew up. Maybe you worked in the food service industry too. Agree to walk the direct path with them, but try to take them on detours.

### Advanced Concepts in Rapport Building

The FLETC course I attended in 2022 – Advanced Interviewing for Law Enforcement – was the most modern interviewing course I had been to up until that time. They were recommending science-based strategies, and they had the research to back it. One of the strategies they recommended to build and maintain rapport was based on the principles of Motivational Interviewing. Strategies for building and maintaining rapport included:

- **Autonomy,** Consciously acknowledge others' right to decide
- **Adaptation,** Demonstrate respect for others' autonomy
- **Acceptance,** To convey it, be non-judgmental
- **Empathy,** Communication of one's understanding
- **Evocation,** Listening actively to get what's beneath the surface[2]

What are some realistic scenarios in which a working cop might use these Motivational Interviewing principles to build and maintain rapport?

One might encourage Autonomy by saying, "would you like to talk here or over there?" "Is it okay if I call you Ben?" Or maybe, "Can we talk?" This gives them power within reason and in a way consistent with small concessions an officer could make (without letting the suspect walk all over you).

> Physical safety for the officers and the subject always has to trump the use of autonomy to build rapport. A friend of mine was on scene in 2023 when a rookie cop allowed a suspect to gather a few things from his home before being placed in handcuffs. Instead, the man walked into the kitchen and attempted to kill himself.
>
> He survived. Barely. What makes this such an important example is that letting the man walk into the kitchen is completely consistent with a scientific, modern usage of autonomy to build and maintain rapport. The problem is that the need to build rapport is in tension with the realities of dealing with desperate people. While there are ways to encourage autonomy in small ways, be careful to keep safety in the forefront of what you are doing.

You'll demonstrate Adaptation by adjusting to their response to your offers for autonomy. For example, if you ask, "Is it okay if I call you Ben?" And they say, "Actually, I go by Benjamin." You'll demonstrate adaptation by saying, "Okay Benjamin, I'd like to ask you about..."

Acceptance is a powerful tool which Motivational Interviewing takes to such an extreme it takes some getting used to. This is non-judgment, no matter what they say. At no point are you trying to fix the person. In an interaction I think about a lot, a person told me they tried to castrate themselves like a farm animal. My face never varied its pleasantly neutral expression when I replied, "Like with rubber bands?" I didn't endorse or condemn his statement. Acceptance is not approval.

Empathy is a hard one for people who aren't naturally empathic. The tactic of using Empathy with a capital E is to communicate to the other person that you understand. If they say, "I stabbed her because she mouthed off to me." You might say, "You must have been pretty mad" even while you might be thinking, "That's an awful thing to do." Identifying how the person is feeling demonstrates attentiveness, which is always good for rapport.

Evocation in the Motivational Interviewing realm is a form of questioning like what police officers and other investigators will be used to, but without a pre-determined goal. Instead of asking, "Why did you hit her?" You might ask, "What did you hope to gain by hitting her?" Or "What did you think would happen when you hit her?" Of course, "Why did you hit her?" is a perfectly good question, but the other two are in the vein of this technique which helps build and maintain rapport.

My experience in teaching is the two groups of officers most resistant to building rapport are patrol officers and violent crime detectives (robbery and aggravated assault). Patrol officers say they don't have enough time. Violent crime detectives say that touchy-feely stuff doesn't work on their suspects. I agree that patrol officers have limited time, and violent crime offenders often are pretty hard, but with the outsized benefits from rapport building, maybe we could find a way to make it work?

## Why Patrol Officers Should Build Rapport

On patrol, building rapport only takes a few moments. Officers will typically approach stressful situations by taking control. This is appropriate when the situation starts *out* of control. Once the situation has calmed down, though, you can usually let go of some of that control and give it back to the suspect. You may not be able to take them out of handcuffs, but you can explain the situation to them, explain why things happened the way they did, set expectations for what will happen, and check on their well-being. All of this could happen in less than a minute.

I don't think I ever consciously built rapport with anyone as a patrol officer. Looking back on it now, I think I missed a lot of opportunities. On a tactical level, I missed opportunities to gather good information. On a human level, I missed opportunities to minimize negative impacts officers are sure to have. It is common to see your role on the scene as adversarial to the suspect. They have been accused of a crime, you are there to keep the peace and make arrests. What if you took a moment to let them see you as a fair and reasonable person who cared about their side of the story?

Most patrol investigations, particularly arrests, start with a power imbalance. You have come on the scene with your shiny badge, ordered people around, and put the main aggressor in handcuffs. This is good for safety, but it isn't good for having people divulge secrets. If you interview this suspect while maintaining the imbalance, they will feel bullied. When people feel bullied, they don't offer up secrets.

So after it's all safe and arrests have been made, try moving the suspect to the side and saying something like this,

*Officer:* "I hate that this situation had to start like this. I have some basic protocols I have to follow. If I don't process the scene like this, my bosses ask questions. It's nothing personal. Are you hurt at all?"
*Suspect:* (Shakes his head no)
*Officer:* "My name is Officer ___. I want to make sure I get this call right. Right now I've heard her side of the story, but I want to hear yours. I promise I'll hear what you have to say and report it the right way. How are you feeling about this situation?"

Ok, the gruffer of y'all may be wondering if I've become a crisis counselor instead of a cop. Fair enough. I might have asked the same thing ten years ago. To see the difference, let's look at how these situation usually go:

*Officer:* "You're under arrest! You understand? Sit down! Cross your ankles. Look away from me. <to the dispatcher> Baker 123? Start EMS to my location. <end radio chatter>"

*Suspect:* "You're arresting me?!? What about her? She hit me too!"
*Officer:* "Right. That's why she's bleeding from the face. I said sit down! Alright. Here's your Miranda warning. You wanna say something about this?"

Which of these two approaches is likely to encourage the suspect to talk? Obviously the first one. Furthermore, which one of these approaches is likely to have the suspect feeling like they were treated fairly even if the outcome is them going to jail? Obviously, again, the first one.

Some officers make the mistake of letting their feelings get involved in the arrest. They start high on the stress charts ordering people around and then fail to regulate back to normal once the scene is under control. Remember, if the suspect hit his wife, it isn't personal. If the suspect raped his daughter, it isn't personal. If the suspect did literally anything at all, it isn't personal (if it is personal for some reason, you need to have somebody else investigating). Don't make it personal. By building rapport you increase your chances of getting a good statement. Take a minute or two to do that.

## Why Violent Crimes Investigators Should Build Rapport

No matter how many felony arrests a person has, no matter how hard the person may look, everyone wants to be treated fairly. Some people think that felons will think you are weak if you don't speak in short, harsh sentences full of veiled threats. I think this is wrong. I'm not asking you to talk to them like a therapist. I'm asking you to convey strength through calm.

For example, in an interaction I find very silly (removing from thought the very serious crime under investigation), a pair of Palm Beach Florida detectives interrogate Robert Alvarez. Robert is accused of killing two people in a Circle K gas station during a robbery.[3] Prior to this segment, the investigators have asked for a sample of the suspect's DNA (saliva).

*Interviewer 1:* You ain't got no charges on you.
*Robert:* Ok I know that. But shit, I'm fucked up. I wanna take a shower now. I can't jump in the shower? While y'all doing the saliva thing?
*Interviewer 1:* Where the fuck you gonna get a shower 'round here?
*Robert:* Ain't no...shit there's a fucking shower over here.
*Interviewer 2:* Ain't no shower.
*Robert:* Let me get naked and go fucking shower somewhere.
*Interviewer 1:* What are you? Fucking crazy?

This is an example of a suspect in a very serious crime being completely unreasonable. For the record, I like the detectives in it. They come across as movie-worthy, tough street cops. I think, though, their interaction leads to conflict. I think conflict is what Robert Alvarez wants. The conflict makes it easier to resist and lie to the person you are dealing with. We resist people we don't like. We cooperate with people we like.

Why is Robert being difficult? Well, one possibility is they are about to take DNA swabs from him to compare to the crime scene. Maybe he thinks a quick rinse in the shower will improve his chances. Maybe he has drugs hidden in secret parts of his body he wants to get rid of. Maybe he just wants to delay. It could be anything.

The investigators chose a judgmental approach that ridicules Robert. It's funny, but it might not be the best at building and maintaining rapport. After all, the purpose of interviewing Robert is to get the truth about a double homicide. That's a serious investigation, and you'll want to use whatever methods are the most likely to yield positive results.

Let's see what a more rapport-based approach might look like.

*Interviewer 1:* You ain't got no charges on you.
*Robert:* Ok I know that. But shit, I'm fucked up. I wanna take a shower now. I can't jump in the shower? While y'all doing the saliva thing?
*Interviewer 1:* You want a shower. How am I supposed to do that right now?

Or maybe:

*Interviewer 1:* Maybe you're worried about the DNA test. Do you want me to explain what's going to happen?

When Robert says:

*Robert:* Let me get naked and go fucking shower somewhere.

They might have said:

*Interviewer 1:* You're wanting to get out of your clothes. What would that do for you?

Or:

*Interviewer 1:* What is it about showering right now that has you so spun up?

In the original excerpt, Robert and the investigators are clashing like for like. I've watched the whole interview. They don't gather much information from Robert. In the more rapport-based options I'm suggesting, there's no clash between the two. If the original interaction is a tug of war, the new interaction is just Robert running with the rope. Eventually, he's going to get tired. At that point, he's likely to re-engage and talk about the things you want to talk about.

How do you think Robert might respond to the more rapport-based prompts? We see what they receive from the prompt "Where the fuck you gonna get a shower round here?" What might Robert say to, "What would that do for you?" (Said, of course, in a non-judgmental way). "What is it about showering right now that has you so spun up?" Although it's impossible to guess what Robert would say in response to the more rapport-based prompts, *it's near certain that he will be giving you information rather than just arguing.*

I think you can sustain rapport with an attitude of curiosity. Don't get mad when they belittle you or talk trash. Instead, think of ways to refuse them what they want, which is you being mad. Try to push the responsibility of talking back onto them in a way that makes them think and talk. I think you can do that even with the hardest of criminals.

## Residual Rapport

If you build rapport well, you may find yourself making decisions that inappropriately favor the interviewee. This goes against the correct stance of neutrality. When this happens, you avoid asking the interviewee difficult questions. Perhaps you give them the benefit of the doubt on suspicious responses. You may resolve to present their case in a more favorable light to your supervisor or a prosecutor. I call this *residual rapport.*

Building and maintaining rapport is necessary to achieve the best possible outcome, but you have to monitor your attitude towards the interviewee as the interview continues. If you find yourself genuinely liking the person, remind yourself that likable people commit crimes all the time. If you find yourself sympathizing with their position, remember that unlucky people commit crimes too. You must continue to ask the interviewee tough questions.

I'll give you two examples. In one case, a man came in on suspicion of having had sexual contact with a niece of his. The allegations were old and not particularly strong. During the rapport-building phase, I found out he was a local photographer. I mentioned to him that I had just come from visiting a photographer acquaintance of mine, a man who had photographed my wedding. The interviewee told me he was friends with the same person! As we talked, I found him to be funny and a good conversationalist. Needless to say, we quickly built rapport with one another.

As the interview continued, I found myself avoiding the topic of sexual abuse. When I did ask questions, I was asking them in a way easiest to deny. "You didn't have anything to do with that child did you?" Every time he told me his version of events, I found myself accepting them uncritically. After all, he's such a nice guy. This was residual rapport affecting my judgment.

In another case, I found my co-worker in the lobby of our building walking away from the suspect interview room. I asked her how the interview went. She said, "He did it. He said he did, and I believe him. I don't know if he deserves the full punishment, though. I'm going to talk to the prosecutor about it." As we talked more, she admitted she liked the suspect as a person.

I told her, "You're affected by residual rapport." I explained, "The reason you want the prosecutor to go easy on him is because you like him." I encouraged her to present the case in a neutral way, following the facts.

Investigators should be fact finders. We aren't out to get the person. We aren't out to let them off either. Yes, build and maintain rapport. Also, monitor your attitude towards the interviewee. If you find yourself giving them the benefit of the doubt, reorient yourself. Make sure you ask the hard questions you came to ask.

## Summary

This chapter emphasizes the critical role of rapport-building in law enforcement interviews, highlighting that effective rapport significantly improves interview outcomes. It introduces motivational interviewing techniques, such as empathy and autonomy, and addresses common challenges faced by patrol officers and violent crime detectives in applying these methods. The chapter advises on using non-judgmental communication to encourage cooperation while maintaining safety. By fostering a respectful and empathetic environment, officers can better engage suspects thereby increasing the amount of valuable information gathered.

## Notes

1 Walsh, Dave and Ray Bull, "Examining Rapport in Investigative Interviews with Suspects: Does Its Building and Maintenance Work?," *Journal of Police and Criminal Psychology* 27 (2012), https://doi.org/10.1007/s11896-011-9087-x.
2 Quoted verbatim from a business card sized laminated handout they provided at the class.
3 Law&Crime Network. 2023. "Florida Deputies Interrogate Circle K Gas Station Killer - the Case Uncovered." YouTube. February 4, 2023. https://www.youtube.com/watch?v=bxkOBBTET6U.

## References

Law&Crime Network. 2023. "Florida Deputies Interrogate Circle K Gas Station Killer - the Case Uncovered." YouTube. February 4, 2023. https://www.youtube.com/watch?v=bxkOBBTET6U.

Walsh, Dave, and Ray Bull, "Examining Rapport in Investigative Interviews With Suspects: Does Its Building and Maintenance Work?" *Journal of Police and Criminal Psychology* 27 (2012), https://doi.org/10.1007/s11896-011-9087-x.

Chapter 9

# Evidence Presentation

### Key Points

1. *No Matter How Good Your Evidence Is, The Suspect Can Still Lie About It*: Learn the Strategic Use of Evidence (SUE) technique, and make it your default way to use evidence.
2. *The SUE Technique Has Four Phases*: (1) Rate and analyze your evidence; (2) Contact the suspect; (3) Give the suspect a chance to volunteer it; and (4) Present the evidence going from vague to specific.
3. *When You Have the Goods, SUE / When You Don't, Bait*: SUE technique generates the most information from your evidence, but it should only be used when you actually have the evidence. If you don't have the evidence (or not yet), bait questions are useful.

Having solid evidence is a wonderful thing for a suspect interview, but it tends to make investigators overconfident. I have seen time and again that investigators going into an interview with DNA, video, eyewitness testimony, or video surveillance, for example, build their whole strategy around confronting the suspect with this evidence as quickly as possible.

*Sometimes* early evidence presentation works. The guilty suspect relents, and they tell you everything. As often as not, though, the suspect denies even the strongest evidence. In this scenario, the investigator is left with no plan. Worse yet, they have launched into what amounts to an accusatory interrogation before gathering any case facts at all. There is no rapport, no backup plan, and nothing to show for the interview. This should be avoided at all costs.

When you have the goods, you should employ the SUE method outlined in the following section. This is a method scientifically shown to gather more intelligence. I know of no better way to use evidence. I hope you will consider employing this technique.

A typical interview follows the pattern we have discussed in this book. Preparation followed by a thorough, rapport-based interview. After you have greeted the person, covered custodial issues, and built rapport, you enter into the interview stage. In the interview stage, you give the suspect a chance to explain themselves in a non-judgmental and non-accusatory way.

Throughout this interview, you clarify issues that aren't lining up the way they should. "You said this, but you also said this. Help me understand." Or you might ask, "You said this, but I've received information that contradicts that. How can you explain the difference?"

Eventually, the interview and clarification stage comes to an end. This is where you will present your evidence. The evidence presentation happens in a non-accusatory way.

DOI: 10.4324/9781003663904-10

The presumption is that the suspect may have a way of explaining themselves, and they should be given the opportunity to do so.

There are times when you don't have the evidence yet, but you may reasonably expect to have it before the investigation is complete. This might occur when teams are canvassing for video, but they haven't uncovered it yet. Or perhaps a rape victim has undergone a sexual assault exam, but the DNA results are not back yet. Perhaps you have filed search warrants with different providers (cellphone companies, social media companies, etc.), but you either haven't received the returns back yet or you haven't processed through them yet. In this instance, I recommend you use a bait question.

A bait question is formulated in a way that makes it difficult for a guilty suspect to stick to their story. For example, you might ask, "When the video canvas is done, is there any chance that you will be seen doing something you haven't told me about?" Or, "When the DNA results come back, is there any chance that your DNA will be on the victim / the weapon / etc.?" You might say, "You've told me that you haven't had any contact with the victim on social media. Is there any way that the search warrants for your social media accounts will show something different?" A bait question is not an accusation. It is a question the innocent should be able to answer without issue and the guilty have to think about in ways that increase their cognitive load and make it more difficult to lie.

A bait question is *not* a bluff. A bluff is a lie. For example, if you said, "The DNA results have come back, and they show that your DNA is on the victim / weapon / etc." If you don't have those results, then you are lying to the suspect. As of this writing, you are legally allowed to lie to the suspect about having evidence, an outcropping of the Frazier V. Cupp decision from the late 1960s. I write about considerations for lying to suspects in an essay at the end of the book. At this point, I'll point out that you *can* do it, but that doesn't mean you should. I think you can gather just as much (or at least nearly as much) information using the SUE method and bait questions without exposing yourself to the negatives of lying about evidence.[1]

So the interview has come to an end, and you still have evidence that the suspect hasn't been able to explain away. In comes the evidence presentation phase of the SUE technique, which should happen *before* moving into an interrogation.

## Strategic Use of Evidence[2]

"An interview with a suspect has more structural similarities with that of a game in the sense that it relies on the mutual use of strategies to obtain the objective. These strategies and goals that the suspect, particularly the guilty suspect, have…they're in conflict with the interrogator's goals." – Maria Hartwig[3]

SUE principles

- Liars want to be judged as truthful.
- Liars will try to figure out what evidence the interviewer has.
- Liars will develop strategies to convince the interviewer that they are truthful.
- Truth tellers will generally openly report everything with significant details and cooperate with requests for information. They will readily provide a plausible explanation.
- Know your evidence and evaluate it. Resolve to disclose it late if at all.

Every detective should be using the SUE technique. This technique, identified by Drs. Maria Hartwig, Pär Anders Granhag, and Timothy Luke, is immediately intuitive, science-based, and its use extracts the maximum amount of information out of the evidence at hand. Any working detective who hasn't received training in the SUE technique will have had the experience of presenting fool-proof evidence to your suspect only to have them say, "It wasn't me" or something similar. If you want to avoid repeating that experience, read on.

The problem with having great evidence is that it can make you lazy. "I'll show him this photo I have, and he'll have to tell me what happened." No matter how good your evidence is, *the capacity of people to lie is infinite*. Never make the mistake of believing your evidence is so good that it will make your guy talk. I don't care if you have video of him shooting the victim, he's still capable of denying any involvement whatsoever. You were so excited to get to the evidence presentation that you skipped building rapport, gathering basic facts, and now you've accused him and the illusion of cooperation is gone.

With the SUE technique, you still get to show him that piece of evidence you're so excited about, but you have a few extra steps to take. At each step along the way you are almost certain to gather more information. The more information you gather the more likely it is deceptive suspects will reveal themselves. For the SUE technique to work, you need to have at least one piece of evidence. The evidence you use should be the piece the suspect is least likely to be aware of.

There are four phases of the SUE. First, prepare for the SUE. Note the origin or source of each piece of evidence and identify the strongest pieces. Not all evidence is created equal. An eyewitness and a partial fingerprint are not the same. Consider the plausible explanations for the pieces of evidence you will use. I've found this step to be the most eye-opening for me, causing me to rethink what I think I know about the crime.

**In phase one of the SUE technique**, you'll select your best evidence and think of the plausible explanations for it. I think of this as "thinking of the most innocent explanation." It is actually part of the exercise to think of ways the evidence might be in the suspect's favor, even when those explanations seem ludicrous. This seems like a funny thing to do when you have something like DNA from a sexual assault exam or some other surefire piece of evidence, but it is essential to the successful conduct of your interview.

Look back at the quote that I started this section with: you have strategies and the interviewee has counterstrategies. Unless he plans to engage in total denial, the deceptive interviewee is sure to have employed the counterstrategy of thinking of an innocent explanation for their actions. When you have employed the same strategy, you are likely to come up with the same excuses that they came up with. Another important aspect of this step is that it opens your mind to the possibility that the suspect IS innocent. Once you think of a few innocent explanations, you may find yourself wondering how strong your case really is. This is a good thing.

Continuing on with this first phase, develop your initial open-ended questions. These will tend to be along the lines of, "In as much detail as possible please tell me about…" Consider other open-ended and specific questions that allow you to narrow your focus and exhaust alternative explanations for the evidence without disclosing the evidence. The creators of SUE describe this narrowing of questions as a funnel model where the top of the funnel is vague questions and the narrowing of the funnel is the increasingly specific questions. Question 1 may be "Tell me all about the issue.." Then the final question might be the very specific, "Were you at the warehouse at 1401 Airport Rd this past Saturday at 8pm?"

The final step of phase one is to plan how you will disclose the evidence. The creators of the SUE discuss using the Evidence Framing Matrix (EFM): start vague about the evidence's source, providing low specificity and end by identifying its source precisely with greater specificity. If this seems like a lot of information, don't give up! This process quickly becomes second nature. Besides, anything is better than simply walking in the room and showing the suspect what you've got.

**Phase two of the SUE is to inform the suspect of the investigation and get them in the room.** Note how this comes after you've done all the groundwork. Although I've had numerous instances where suspects refused to come in and my preparation didn't have the payoff I'd hoped for, I saw each of those times as getting a rep in so I'd be stronger for the next one. I've had other instances where the suspect demands to come in immediately. If you have done the groundwork in phase one, you'll be happy to say, "Sure, I'm available now!" If you haven't, well, you'll have however long it takes the suspect to get from where they are to where you are to prepare. I cover my approach to contacting the suspect in Chapter 4. I'll skip phase two in the exercises below.

**Phase three of the SUE is the strategic questioning phase.** Here you gather the suspect's story providing them as many opportunities as possible to admit to the evidence you have and provide their own explanation for it. Start by asking your initial open-ended question; explicitly request details. Ask other open-ended and specific questions (funnel-type questioning model) and continue explicitly requesting detailed responses. These commit the interviewee to their answers. If the interviewee has come with the intention to deceive, this drilling down into their story will increase their cognitive load, which is where mistakes get made. Be listening for evidence of those mistakes like lies of omission, avoiding the issue, and direct denials.

**Phase four of the SUE is where you use the EFM** to incrementally introduce the evidence. Phase four of the SUE is where it all pays off. Begin by disclosing your evidence only vaguely, with low specificity. I think of this as phase four, move one. Then disclose the evidence less vaguely with a higher level of specificity. This would be phase four, move two. The final disclosure should be precise with high specificity. This is phase four, move three. Move one is vague. Move two is more specific. Move three is very specific. The explanation you receive may yield more information or a denial which your evidence contradicts.

Let's look at some scenarios. Read through these. Below the scenarios, I go into great detail on how to apply the SUE technique to them. Then, I provide a scenario you can do the work on.

### Scenario – Sexual Assault (Adult)

On Sunday, May 15th, Margie called the City Police from her hotel room downtown. Margie reported to officers that she thinks she was sexually assaulted the night before. After finishing up at her conference on Saturday, she hit the hotel bar with her coworker. While at the bar, she struck up a conversation with the bartender, Will. Much later, around 1:45 am, as the bar closed, Margie was fading in and out. Margie remembered Will and her coworker Angela helping her walk up to her hotel room. When they got to the door, Angela left. Margie remembers Will walking her inside and helping her to sit on the bed. Margie reported she remembered staring at her shoes wondering how she'd get them off of her feet when she felt Will rubbing her vagina from on top of her pants. Margie told him "no." Margie didn't remember anything else. When she woke up that morning, she saw her pants were neatly folded on the ground in a way she would never have placed them.

Margie was uncomfortable about Will rubbing her vagina, but she was more concerned that maybe Will raped her.

As the detective, you gathered video surveillance and receipts from Saturday. The receipts showed Margie settled her tab around 1 am. The tab showed Margie ordered a half dozen beers and two shots. The video showed Margie talked exclusively with Will and her coworker Angela. On one occasion, you can see Margie touches Will's hand as she leans across the bar and appears to whisper something in Will's ear. They both laugh. This is about 1:30 am. On the video you can see when the trio left the bar, Margie was stumbling as Will and Angela alternately lifted her from under her arms and pulled on her shirt to keep her moving forward. The video showed them getting on the elevator together, getting off the elevator on Margie's floor, and going all together to Margie's door. Angela left right away. Will left about 20 minutes later.

You interview Angela. Angela remembered Margie whispering in Will's ear, because she felt self-conscious as though they were laughing at her. She didn't know what Margie said to Will. Angela stated she left the room because Margie was much bigger than her, and Will was plenty strong enough to get her inside. She had a lot to drink Saturday night, too. When she left Margie's, Angela went straight to her room and to sleep.

### Scenario – Aggravated Assault

On Wednesday, January 7th, City Police received a call for assistance at 701 Overby Street. Jamal, the caller, found his neighbor Martin crumpled up in a puddle of blood inside Martin's house. Jamal reported that he had been passing by Martin's house when he saw the door ajar. This was unusual, so he went to check on Martin. At the door, he could see inside where Martin lay. Jamal checked to make sure that Martin was alive, which he was, and he called the police. While waiting for police, Jamal noticed that Martin's left eye was black and his nose appeared to be broken. Jamal put Martin in the rescue position. Looking about, Jamal was surprised to see how messy Martin's house was. There were dirty clothes and empty vodka bottles everywhere.

Martin was transported to the hospital. You started out at the crime scene. While there, you noticed there was a broken shovel in front of the porch. There was a blood trail leading from the porch into the house. While asking follow-up questions, Jamal reveals he and Martin have the same landlord, Julian. A few days before, on Sunday, Jamal heard Julian yelling at Martin for not paying his rent. The argument got more and more heated until Jamal heard Julian shout, "You'll have your shit out by tomorrow, or you'll regret it."

At the hospital the next day (Thursday), you find Martin has a broken skull on his left side and a broken nose. Martin is groggy. He says he doesn't remember anything from Wednesday. He said he is out of work at the moment. Without a regular schedule, he usually has a few mixed drinks before noon. He remembered the argument with Julian. He also remembered he had an appointment to see Julian on Wednesday, but he couldn't say whether or not Julian ever came over.

### Thinking through the Evidence, Sexual Assault

Refer back to the adult sexual assault scenario. In that scenario you have two pieces of evidence we will consider here. You have video surveillance showing Will the bartender helping Angela the friend carry Margie up to her room. You have Margie remembering

Will rubbing her vagina from on top of her pants. If you're Will, and you agree to talk, you have four main strategies: (1) total denial; (2) I helped her to her room, and then I left; (3) "I thought she was into me, and I shot my shot (made my move). She said 'no,' and I left"; and (4) "We had sex, and it was totally consensual."

As to the video surveillance, the most innocent explanation is that he helped a drunk patron up to her room. Maybe Margie invited him up for an after party. Otherwise, Margie might have invited Will upstairs to hook up.

As to Margie remembering Will rubbing her vagina, what are some innocent explanations for this? Maybe Margie is lying. Maybe Will thought Margie was interested in hooking up. Possibly Will helped Margie get her pants off so that she could be comfortable, and the rubbing was just a misunderstanding.

Now come up with questions that allow you to anticipate these innocent explanations. Deceptive suspects tend to change their game plan once their first plan falls apart. Let's say Will's first plan is total denial. Then, when he realizes you have him on surveillance video, he may decide to switch to a consensual hook-up. However, if you place questions early in the interview that anticipate later defenses, you will make it either impossible or, at the very least, implausible when they switch their strategies.

For example, the surveillance footage explanations hinge on what Will's thoughts are regarding Margie. When you plan your questions out, you might include, "Were you ever under the impression that Margie was hitting on you?" "Were you attracted to Margie?" "How did Margie get up to her room?"

As to the vagina rubbing, you might plan some questions like, "Were your hands ever in contact with Margie's vagina?" "How did Margie get undressed?" "What did you do while you were in the room?" "Would Margie have any reason to want to see you get in trouble? (This anticipates the "Margie is lying" defense)" You'll include these anticipatory questions in your question list for use in your interview with Will.

Phase three of the SUE technique is to gather the suspect's narrative. This should take place with open-ended questions, continuers, reflections, and summations. Your question to Will might be, "If you could, in as much detail as possible, please tell me all about Saturday, May 14th from beginning to end without leaving anything out." Once he starts talking, be quiet until he finishes. Do not interrupt no matter how much you want clarification. Prompt him to continue talking with continuers like "go on" and "and then?" You might then ask, "What else happened?" Then, "you said that you served several different customers?" Keep prompting him to add more until he appears to have nothing else to add.

If Will hasn't mentioned walking with Margie up to her room or rubbing her vagina, you'll use the funnel strategy of vague questions leading to specific questions to address that. You might ask, "Where did you go immediately after work?" If he doesn't mention Margie, you might ask, "Did you spend time with any customers after work that day?" Then, "Did you spend time with Margie after work that day?" Pick one or two major parts of the story to funnel down into in this way. If Will had a consensual sexual encounter with Margie, he should readily admit to spending time with her after work. If Will chooses not to disclose spending time with Margie, it won't be because you failed to give him the chance.

Then summarize the suspect's story. "Correct me where I'm wrong. You said ... and ... you said you spoke to... and then after work you... what did I miss?" He will likely add a few details. If anything he says conflicts with what you know, do not rush to present him with the evidence. That will come later.

Once you've gathered the suspect's story, now is a good time to use those questions you came up with in the preparatory stage. If the suspect didn't already address them, ask him those questions now. For example, if Will didn't say anything about Margie hitting on him, you're going to want to ask if she did or not. If Will says Margie hit on him, you'll have more to talk about. If he denies it, you'll have put him in a very difficult position later on should he attempt to swivel to, "Margie and I hooked up and had consensual sex."

Now we come to phase four of the SUE technique. This is where your hard work pays off with a lot of information. You'll ask about your evidence starting with vague assertions and moving onto the ever more specific reveal of evidence. This will usually take place in three moves, which we will look at by considering the video surveillance showing Will taking Margie into her room. You would follow this process if Will has denied or omitted that he went into Margie's room.

SUE technique, phase four, move one: "I have some evidence that you went into Margie's room that night. Tell me why that would be." Here we come to a fork of possibilities. Either he denies that such is the case or he provides more information. If he adds information, he might say something like, "Maybe I went into her room for a minute, I hardly remember." If he is adding information, take the time to explore that. Once he has stopped adding new information, move on to the next step.

SUE technique, phase four, move two: "In fact, I have a witness who saw you take Margie into her room that night. Why would that be?" This requires some flexibility because Will might have admitted after step one he went into Margie's room for a few minutes. You might adjust your question to say, "In fact, I have a witness that saw you go into Margie's room and stay in there for almost 20 minutes. Why?" Even if you didn't adjust the question, you'll create anxiety in a deceitful Will by introducing a witness. Again, you have reached the fork. Either he continues to deny or he adds more information.

SUE technique, phase four, move three: "Actually I have surveillance video that shows you carrying Margie into her room and then staying there for almost 20 minutes. Can we talk about that?" Here you have reached the most specific point. This is the point where untrained detectives start. The untrained detective might start the interview by saying, "Here's surveillance footage of you carrying Margie into her room. Do you deny it?"

It's important to point out that your interviewee may have freely admitted to the events described by the evidence you have. If that happens, just skip that piece of evidence. You can't squeeze blood from a stone. Carry on with the other evidence you have.

Can you see how much more information is likely to be gathered from the same evidence by using the SUE technique? Have you, like me, ever walked into a room, presented your best evidence, and been surprised at the continued denials? If you're like me, you'll be sold on this process immediately.

What I like most about the SUE technique is that it is devastatingly effective against deceptive subjects while also providing the maximum opportunity for innocent subjects to provide evidence of their innocence. I have had cases where the guilt of the suspect seemed certain when I walked into the room, but, because I provided them a fair opportunity to explain themselves, they were able to provide evidence that led to their exoneration. We are in the business of investigating. We should not be anxious to convict or to exonerate. We should be diligent in seeking the truth, whatever that may be. The SUE technique is an important tool for us to use.

## SUE Technique, Aggravated Assault

Let's process through the SUE technique for the aggravated assault scenario. If you'll look back at that case, you'll see that there are a few pieces of evidence that stand out. Let's focus on one of them. There was an argument between Julian and Martin that Jamal overheard. In that argument, Jamal heard Julian yell, "You'll have your shit out by tomorrow, or you'll regret it." In this case, Martin doesn't remember what happened that led to his having a skull fracture and a broken nose. A quick consideration of the case suggests either Julian met up with Martin and assaulted him or Martin, a likely alcoholic, fell and injured himself. The assault is more likely, but the accidental injury isn't impossible. Your interview with Julian will be a major part of the investigation.

SUE technique step one. What is the most innocent explanation of the argument (or what are other plausible explanations)? Perhaps Jamal is lying about Julian. Or maybe it happened, but Julian never intended to follow through on the threat. Maybe Jamal misheard. Could it be it was actually Martin threatening Julian?

Develop anticipatory questions to ask Julian. "Is there any reason that Jamal would want to see you get in trouble?" "Are there any problems between you and Jamal?" "Describe any arguments you've had with Martin." "Any others?" "Have you ever caused injury to Martin?" "How would you describe your relationship with Martin?" "Has Martin ever threatened you?"

SUE technique phase three. Gather the suspect's narrative. "In as much detail as possible, without leaving anything out, please describe your activities on Wednesday, January 7th." Whatever he tells you, you'll follow up with questions to get more.

- What else happened?
- Where else did you go?
- Who else did you talk to?

If he doesn't mention being at Martin's, then you'll summarize, "Correct me where I'm wrong. I heard you say that...What did I miss?" Finally, you'll ask him directly, "Did you cause injury to Martin?" At this point, you have the full narrative. Time for phase four.

SUE technique phase four, move one: "I have some evidence that you argued with and threatened Martin a few days before he was injured. Tell me about that." Here Julian will either deny that it happened, or he will add additional information. If he adds information – even if it is to say somebody must be lying on him – develop that information until you know all he is willing to tell you.

SUE technique phase four, move two: "In fact, the evidence I have is very strong. Can we talk about that?" He will deny or add information. If he adds information, explore it.

SUE technique phase four, move three: "Jamal, Martin's neighbor, has provided a sworn statement that you argued with and threatened Martin. Let's talk about that." Julian will either deny or add information.

**Use the following (brief) scenario to practice the SUE technique:** a woman is stabbed at the local homeless shelter. Jeremy and Jenny, two eyewitnesses, have indicated that Raven stabbed the victim. Further, you have video surveillance showing Raven fleeing the scene after the stabbing happened. You have collected a bloody knife in the path that Raven is known to have fled along.

*Phase one:*

What evidence do you have?
Rank the evidence from best to worst.
Choose your best piece of evidence. What is it?
With your best evidence, what are plausible explanations of that item (don't hesitate to list explanations that rule Raven out as the suspect)?
If Raven wanted to deceive you about that item, what might she leave out?
What question will you ask to prompt Raven's accounting for her actions that night?

Look back at your list of plausible explanations. What anticipatory questions might you ask that would allow Raven to invoke that defense (or, alternately deny it)?

How will you disclose the evidence in phase four during the EFM? What is move one (the broadest question)? What is move two (the narrowed question)? What is move three (the most specific question)?

*Phase two is contacting the suspect.*

*Phase three is gathering the suspect's narrative.*

What question will you ask to prompt Raven's recall of that night?
If Raven doesn't bring up being at the homeless shelter, what questions will you ask to funnel down to the point where you ask her directly?
If Raven doesn't mention stabbing the victim, how will you funnel down towards that?
If Raven doesn't mention Jeremy and Jenny, the two eyewitnesses, how might you prompt her to discuss them?
If Raven doesn't mention running away from the homeless shelter, how might you prompt her to bring that up?
Phase four is using the EFM to present your evidence.
Using the piece of evidence you selected, what is your move one question?
What is your move two question?
What is your move three question?

If you are more of a visual learner, watch this video of detectives interviewing Ralph Shortey, an Oklahoma politician accused of soliciting a minor for sex. The clip starts at about 6:28 seconds into the interview.[4] You'll see the detectives lay out all of their evidence for free. Now that you know what the SUE technique is, how much of a wasted opportunity does this seem to be? How might you approach that evidence knowing what you know now?

## Summary

This chapter discusses the pitfalls of disclosing evidence too quickly during suspect interviews and introduces the SUE technique. The SUE technique involves four phases: preparation, suspect engagement, narrative gathering, and incremental evidence disclosure. By delaying evidence presentation, investigators can gather more information and better assess the truthfulness of a suspect's statements. The SUE technique should happen at the end of your non-accusatory interview. Typically, this will conclude your interview with the suspect. At this point, you'll need to decide if you believe it is reasonably certain that the suspect did the crime. If not, I recommend that you end the interview. If it IS reasonably certain that the suspect is guilty, it's time to move into the interrogation.

## Immediately Actionable

*Do the work*: Select at least one of your cases with evidence. Rate and analyze the evidence. Think of alternate explanations for it. Develop questions to address those alternate possibilities. Think how you would question the suspect to have them volunteer the evidence. Present the evidence. "I have some evidence..." "In fact, it's strong evidence..." "I have you on video..."

*Look out for your partners*: Check in with your partners. See what cases they are working. Ask them what their plan is to present their evidence.

## Notes

1 Juries hate it. It figures prominently in false confessions. It puts you in an awkward position of having to say in court that, yes, you were lying about that, but also you are telling the truth about everything else in your investigation.
2 The steps of the SUE technique were taught to me by instructors for the Federal Law Enforcement Training Center (FLETC).
3 2025. Youtube. 2025. https://youtu.be/BTJPW4Lu74c.
4 News, KOCO 5. 2018. "Watch: Moore Police Interrogate Former State Sen. Ralph Shortey after Being Found in Motel with Teen." YouTube Video. *YouTube*. https://www.youtube.com/watch?v=WJQ6_khlxnc.

## References

2025. Youtube. 2025. https://youtu.be/BTJPW4Lu74c
News, KOCO 5. 2018. "Watch: Moore Police Interrogate Former State Sen. Ralph Shortey after Being Found in Motel with Teen." YouTube Video. *YouTube*. https://www.youtube.com/watch?v=WJQ6_khlxnc

Chapter 10

# Interrogation

### Key Points

1 *Purpose of Interrogation*: Interrogations are accusatory and confrontational, aimed at testing a suspect's assertions of innocence and potentially obtaining a confession if they are guilty.
2 *Importance of a Thorough Interview*: An interrogation should only follow a thorough, neutral, and non-judgmental interview, ensuring all relevant information is gathered before accusations are made.
3 *Strategic Theme Development*: Developing a theme based on likely justifications for the crime helps minimize a suspect's moral culpability while guiding the interrogation effectively.
4 *Avoiding False Confessions*: To reduce the likelihood of false confessions, interrogators should avoid threats, promises of leniency, and anything that might shock the conscience.

*An interrogation is an accusatory, confrontational method for testing the suspect's assertions of innocence. If they are innocent, you hope to gain confidence in their innocence. If they are guilty, you hope to get a confession from them.*

Interrogations are among the most unique activities associated with being a police officer. They capture the public imagination. Movies are made about them. Court cases are fought over them. When they go well, you don't hear much about them. The defendant pleas out in court. When they go badly, everybody hears about them in the press conference in front of the main police station. Here you are in the middle: a hardworking police officer trying to do your best with whatever training you've been given. It can be terrifying, exhilarating, and disgusting, sometimes in the same event. The person you are interviewing has not admitted to involvement in the crime, and you think they did it. What are you going to do about it?

If my experience is any indication, the training you receive is haphazard. Maybe you read a book, got some tips from the senior detective, or, if you were lucky, got sent to a week long training. Then you are given the awesome responsibility of searching for the truth in a tangle of case law, water cooler wisdom, and on-the-job experience. Many never receive updated training after whatever they are given in the first year or so.

An interrogation is distinct from an interview in that it switches into a series of accusations. The purpose of an interrogation is *not* just to get a confession. In fact, it is highly likely you will interrogate an innocent suspect at some point in your career. Obviously no

DOI: 10.4324/9781003663904-11

investigator wants a confession from an innocent person. Knowing interrogating an innocent suspect is likely, then, the goal of interrogation *cannot* be simply to get a confession. Rather, an interrogation is an accusatory, confrontational method for testing the suspect's assertions of innocence. If they are innocent, you hope to gain confidence in their innocence. If they are guilty, you hope to get a confession from them.

In all cases, it is my recommendation the interrogation follow a thorough, neutral, non-judgmental interview. Even if the suspect is under arrest, you should still give them an opportunity to account for and respond to the evidence that led to them being arrested. In situations where the suspect has been unable or unwilling to account for the evidence that led to them being indicated as a suspect, you may reach the conclusion it is more likely than not the suspect did in fact commit the crime they are accused of. In this case, you should consider entering into an accusatory interrogation.

An interrogation should only be entered into when the guilt of the suspect is reasonably certain. That may arise from the evidence against the suspect being so strong and as yet unaccounted for that their protestations of innocence seem unlikely. On the other hand, it may happen that you have relatively weak case facts, and the suspect (possibly only a witness at the outset) engages in a pattern of deceptive responses that lead you to believe that they are being dishonest. In these situations, an accusatory interrogation would be appropriate.

If, however, the suspect's responses in the interview provide plausible explanations for the evidence against them, you should be prepared to walk away without interrogating them. This is true even if they are under arrest.

On one extreme, if you uncover exculpatory information in the interview, you should be scrupulous in reporting that evidence to the prosecuting attorneys. Just because you or another investigator issued an arrest warrant for the person does not mean you stay the course no matter what. Many of the worst abuses of interrogations happen in the context of custodial interrogations when the investigator insists past all reason on getting a confession. The Amanda Knox case, for example, involved 53 hours of interrogation.[1]

At the other extreme, you may have weak case facts, find there were a few deceptive responses, but generally come to the conclusion the suspect's guilt is uncertain. Think of this part like gathering votes. Maybe they answered evasively twice (two votes for guilty), but they appeared straightforward and credible on ten other answers related to the core issues under investigation (ten votes for innocent). Here you have possible deception, but the balance is tipped towards innocent. Again, you have weak case facts in this scenario. If this were a non-custodial interview, I would not move forward with an interrogation.

If it were a custodial interview and they were under arrest for a warrant, I would usually move forward with a guilty knowledge confrontation. "It's clear you know more than what you are sharing with me." This will test their assertions without entering into accusatory conflict you feel less certain about. Be thorough and honest in your reports on what they did and did not say. Let the prosecutor know if there is significant evidence of their innocence.

The reader should know I see a possible future where accusatory interrogations become a thing of the past. In Europe and Canada, for example, they have moved away from accusatory interrogations. In fact, when I spoke to British professor Dave Walsh and Norwegian professor (and ex-cop) Ivar Fahsing in March of 2023, they expressed dismay that we still use accusatory interrogations in our suspect interviews. It was like I told the Jetsons we still used a horse and buggy to get around.

The fact of the matter is accusatory interrogations are very much a part of the American judicial system. I have been to court a half dozen or more times on cases involving accusatory interrogations that produced confessions or at least admissions. The judge and jury looked at the interrogations, admitted them into evidence, and used them in their judgments related to the suspect's guilt or innocence.

My contention is this: *as long as accusatory interrogations are a part of the American judicial system, it behooves the investigators working within that system to know how to conduct them in a legal and ethical manner.*

As far as I know, it was the Reid Institute that popularized the distinction between "interview" and "interrogation." They have a lot to say about it, but the essential distinction is an interview is non-accusatory and an interrogation is accusatory. As a word, "interrogation" carries a lot of baggage. It brings up images of dark rooms, metal tables bolted to the floor, and a lot of yelling. As a result, there is a fun game that happens in the courtroom where the defense will insist on calling your interaction with their client an interrogation and the investigator insists that it was an interview.[2]

One simply cannot talk about interview and interrogation without discussing the Reid Technique. Its presence looms large over the field. As a quick overview, the technique advocates for an initial non-accusatory Behavioral Analysis Interview (BAI)[3] followed by an accusatory interrogation, which they break down into 9 steps. The technique has been popular for at least 50 years.

There are plenty of articles about the Reid Technique describing its history, applications, and misuses. I do not intend to replicate them here. Suffice to say the Reid Technique has been the most-widespread training on interview and interrogation in America, and probably the world. As the most well-known technique there is a cottage industry of experts who will testify against it as yielding false confessions. From what I've read, their main complaints are investigators form too high an opinion of their ability to detect deception through their Behavioral Analysis Interview, and their unrelenting accusations lead to innocent people breaking down and confessing to crimes they didn't commit.

I neither advocate for nor against the Reid Technique. On the one hand, it's easy to learn and implement, which is good for working police officers that need solutions now. On the other hand, its use provides opposing counsel an easy opportunity to undermine your interview and interrogation with expert witnesses. I'll say I think it's purported evils are often misattributed to the technique instead of to the officers that use it incorrectly. Scholarly articles never seem to cite cases which have full video of the interrogation. What really happened in that room? Was it actually the Reid Technique that was used?

In April of 2025, my partner Val and I presented at the Southern New Mexico Conference on Child Abuse and Neglect. After the first part, a retired cop approached us. He told us his career started in the early 1980s. Early in his career, if the suspect asked for a lawyer, the detective would roll up the phone book, smack them with it, and tell them the number for their lawyer was in there somewhere. This was the first time I had ever had a person tell me directly about physical violence in the room as a standard practice.

If you read briefs filed by The Innocence Project, the complaints of physical violence and intimidation used to extract false confessions are many and numerous. With so many old cases being scrutinized for false confessions leading to conviction, the physical violence used to extract those confessions seems to be attributed to the interrogation technique. This is true even if the technique does not espouse or condone violence in any way.

It is my opinion that false confessions don't come from any one technique. They come from the three poison pills of threats or violence, promises of leniency, or actions that shock the conscience.

In a 2024 trial, the defense attorney asked if I had been to training on the Reid technique. I told him that I had. He asked if I was a human lie detector. I told him that I wasn't. He then did everything he could to tie me to the Reid technique. This led to loggerheads at several points where he was pushing for yes or no answers, and I had to tell him that a truthful answer required context. The contextualized answer is that I've been trained in the technique, I sometimes use elements of the technique, but I don't employ The Reid Technique. This appeared to frustrate him, but it was and is the truth.

In order to provide credit to the source, I use two main elements popularized by the Reid Technique in my approach to interrogation. First, I employ the use of a theme that minimizes the suspect's moral culpability. Second, I employ the alternative question that, as far as I know, they came up with. See the end of this chapter for more information on both of themes and alternative questions.

## Before We Proceed

Before you even think about interrogating a suspect, ask yourself if you are done with your interview. Your interview is complete when you have learned all of the information pertaining to the case that the suspect is likely to tell you. Have you provided a chance for them to tell you their alibi? Did you present evidence to them in a non-accusatory way? Is there anything you want to know about the case that you haven't learned yet? *Did you ask them if they did it?*

Once you accuse a person of committing the crime, the interview stage is done. If you propose to tell somebody that there is no doubt that they committed the crime, it doesn't square with asking questions about the crime. If you're so sure, then why are you asking?

I saw an investigator go into an accusatory interrogation. After he accused the man, I saw the man sit back, looking like he had been caught red handed. Then the investigator stumbled over some words, which gave the suspect confidence. The suspect said he couldn't have done the crime because he was somewhere else at the time. The investigator stopped and asked questions about this supposed alibi. As soon as he did so, the suspect gained confidence and completely took over the conversation, which turned into more of an argument than anything else. The interrogation was finished with no new information found.

If the suspect had an alibi, the investigator should have given him an opportunity to voice that in the interview. Presuming he was provided the opportunity to give an alibi in the interview, the fact that the suspect suddenly remembered it during the accusatory phase is a clear indication of deception.

Next, please always remember that some suspects are innocent. Even if you choose to interrogate them because their guilt is reasonably certain, they still may be innocent. If your interrogation isn't going anywhere at all after you've presented your theories, consider stopping.

I think a lot about a video on interrogating innocent suspects made by a popular YouTube interrogation channel called Jim Can't Swim (JCS). In the video titled, "Guilty until proven innocent,"[4] the creators describe the case of Michael Dixon. Dixon was arrested for breaking into a jewelry store on August 15th, 2003 in Hamilton, Ontario. According to the JCS video, the 911 call described a small, white man, and somehow police arrested Dixon, a tall Black man.

When the investigator goes into the room, he launches into an accusatorial interrogation without asking any questions. According to JCS, the investigator read Dixon his rights and then said, "Ok, why we're here is because earlier tonight, you were arrested for breaking into a jewelry story in Jones Street South. Um...now...your innocence and guilt in this is...quite frankly isn't an issue." Dixon seems confused by the accusation, and he asks the investigator to ask him questions so that he can respond. The investigator refuses because, he claims, evidence of Dixon's guilt is conclusive, which is sort of crazy because...it isn't?

Always interview before you interrogate, especially on your cases where an arrest without a warrant has just been made. These types of cases are always going to be at a higher risk for error because arrests are often made in the heat of the moment. Mistakes can happen. If the detective in the Michael Dixon case had given Dixon a chance to respond before accusing him, he would probably have learned Dixon had nothing to do with the crime. Do not be this guy.

As mentioned above, it is possible and even likely you will end up accusing an innocent person of having committed a crime. Life is messy and complicated. There will be times when a person ends up in a situation where a good investigator might conclude based on good evidence that they probably did a thing when they actually did not. There are some steps you can take to reduce the chance of accusing an innocent person and, more importantly, to reduce the chance of extracting a false confession from an innocent person.

## Reducing the Likelihood of False Confessions

The cardinal rules of interrogation are the following: no threats or violence, no promises of leniency, and nothing that shocks the conscience. Any violation of these rules will not only make it likely your interrogation will be suppressed but also increase the likelihood of false confessions. Engaging in these practices, then, is neither moral nor practical.

An example of a threat is, "If you don't confess, you'll go to jail for the rest of your life." An example of a promise is, "If you confess, I'll make sure that you get probation." I think it's pretty evident how statements like these might lead to false confessions. Stay away from these. If you ever find yourself saying something that sounds like a threat or a promise, I recommend stopping and clarifying immediately. "What I just said may have sounded like a promise of leniency. It isn't. I do not have the authority to make promises like that."

Shocking the conscience is sort of a catch-all that is hard to define, like the famous Supreme Court definition of pornography, "I know it when I see it."[5] An example I would point to is in the Canadian interrogation of Michael Rafferty.[6] Rafferty was arrested for the rape and murder of an 8 year old girl named Torrey Stafford. During his interrogation, one of the detectives said, "So if you ask me why I'm sitting in this room, I'm sitting in this room for Torrey. Making you squirm. Putting you through some of the grief that you put her through. That's why I'm in here, Mike, and I'm having a good time." I understand why he said that, but I think it's shocking to hear a detective is interrogating a suspect in order to get back at him for what he did. Ultimately there is no bright line rule about what shocks the conscience, but a little common sense and decency goes a long way here.

Lying to a suspect about evidence is legal in the United States. As an officer, you can lie and tell the suspect you have, for example, their fingerprint at the scene. You cannot actually fabricate evidence by, for example, taking a random fingerprint card and writing the suspect's name on it. While it may be true it is legal to lie about evidence, I generally recommend against doing it for a couple of reasons: it increases the possibility of a false confession, you lose the moral high ground, and I think juries hate it. I've written more about lying in Chapter 12.

Saul Kassin Ph.D. wrote the book *Duped: Why Innocent People Confess - And Why We Believe Their Confessions*. In the book, he proposed a list of commandments in the interview room, "Along with, 'Thou shalt not physically harm or threaten a suspect or deprive a suspect of food, water, sleep, or contact with a loved one, for an extended period of time,' [he] would add 'Thou shalt not lie to a suspect about evidence.'"[7] He also advocates for a recording of the entire police interaction, but that is so commonplace now that I simply mention it.

Be careful about how long you interview and interrogate. In fact, my early training in interview and interrogation suggested once the accusations started, I should never leave the room until the suspect confessed or they invoked Miranda. I do not think this is right. As time goes on in the room, ask yourself, "Is anything changing? Are they adding to the story? Are there any nonverbal indicators of acceptance?" If nothing new is happening, it may be time to shut it down.

The Innocence Project writes that, "On average, people who falsely confessed were interrogated for up to 16 hours before admitting to a crime they did not commit (research shows that the reliability of confessions is greatly reduced after a prolonged interrogation)."[8] Although I've never seen the Innocence Project or writers like Saul Kassin, who wrote a book on false confessions, say so, I suspect most of these interrogations were happening before everything was video and audio recorded. I've never known a detective who engaged in a 16 plus hour long interview, so it's hard for me to imagine how 16 hours is the *average* length of an interrogation leading to a false confession.

Be careful with the very old, the very young and people with diminished mental capacity. I have yet to interrogate a person so old I suspected their mental capacities were diminished by virtue of their age, but I have interrogated a number of juveniles, and I have interrogated at least two definitely diminished mental capacity people. My recommendation to avoid problems in these areas is to avoid leading questions and keep your interviews significantly shorter than those with people aged between juvenile and the very old. It is particularly important with these groups to keep as many of the case facts to yourself as possible. This ensures you do not contaminate their memories.

## How to Think About the Interrogation

A good interrogation does not involve screaming, table pounding, or finger pointing. Rather, it is an accusation stated calmly and consistently, combined with a theory of why they did it other than, "Because you're a bad person." Humans want to save face as much as possible. We like people who are nice to us and willing to give us the benefit of the doubt. Yelling at, belittling, or in any other way making the subject feel small will cause them to resist telling you the truth. It all starts with believing. If you don't believe it, they won't believe that you believe it.

One reason investigators fail at interrogations is, I think, because they don't really, deep down, believe. They think, "I would never confess to a felony!" One of the reasons they think this way is because they haven't committed any felonies against others. Maybe they smoked some marijuana in college (a crime because we say it is), but they haven't raped anyone (a crime because it's universally repugnant). Maybe they drove drunk with a .16 BAC, but they haven't committed an armed robbery. I believe crimes against persons are weightier for the offender.

When I talk to co-workers about this, I tell them, "Imagine you've been cheating on your spouse." I believe the typical person can imagine cheating on a significant other whether or not they can imagine robbing somebody at gun point or raping a child. So we will use cheating as the example.

Imagine you've been cheating on your spouse. Really put yourself in that mental headspace. Try to feel what that feels like. You've been very careful about how you've done it. You've only met the other person at conferences. You've deleted your text messages. You named the other person a co-worker in your phone so your spouse doesn't get suspicious if a message comes through. Maybe you've accused your spouse of sneaking around in your phone so you've changed the passcode. Whatever you've done, you've been very careful. You know there is no way whatsoever you can have been found out. You probably feel awful, though. I'd guess there is a sense of foreboding that follows you throughout the day. Maybe you are thinking of having a talk with your spouse to let them know or break it off.

One day you come home from work (at the right time for once). You ask your spouse what's for dinner. Your spouse says,:

## Good Interrogation

*Spouse:* You've been cheating on me.

*You:* Wait, what? Me? I've been cheating?

*Spouse:* Stop. I'm not mad. I've been expecting this day to come for a long time. I've been really cold towards you. I know I drove you into their arms. I got distracted with work. I let the kid's activities run our schedules. I know I didn't leave much time or space for you. I'm glad you waited for so long. I appreciate you keeping it quiet so it didn't get back to our friends. Other people might not have been so kind. I really thank you for that.

*You:* But I would never do that!

*Spouse:* I know you wouldn't have when we first got married. I was a better spouse back then. I was 20 pounds lighter and a real party animal. These days I'm just trying to get by. It's because of all the good history we have that you've put up with me like this for so long. I've known about this for a while. You've been cheating on me, and I thought about when the best time to bring it up was. I've been avoiding it, but today is as good a day as any. I want you to know the time that has passed since I've known has let me go from being mad at first to just feeling resigned and guilty for not having done better when I had the chance. The one thing I really wanted to know is whether you did this because you hated me or if you did it because I wasn't fulfilling your needs. It's because I wasn't fulfilling your needs wasn't it?

If you were out there slipping around on your spouse and came home to this, you'd be in trouble. Better to just fess up now. He or she knows what's up. If you were able to put yourself in the headspace of a cheater, look through that exchange and ask yourself how that makes you feel. You weren't expecting this. You did such a good job of covering it all up. You know you cheated. That's the most important part of all of this. You KNOW you cheated. Here is somebody calmly telling you they know about that. While your mind is spinning trying to figure out how they could know, your verbals and non-verbals are putting off signs that will not be missed. You rally your defenses to object, but they smack it down and keep going. If you can really feel this monologue, you can feel what a suspect accused of a heinous felony against another person feels like.

Take this knowledge and really think through what that means for your interrogations. If you've decided to interrogate, you are reasonably certain the suspect committed the crime. It's possible to know in your head without really feeling it in your bones. No matter what happens with the rest of your interrogation, I want you to commit to the direct positive confrontation in a way that projects absolute certainty about the crime to the suspect.

I'm going to use the cheating scenario to show you what a typically terrible direct positive confrontation looks like a few paragraphs down. You'll want to read that, I promise. Before we get there, let's sift through a few elements of the confrontation above.

One thing about that direct positive confrontation, the speaker may or may not have really been there to talk about cheating. What if the speaker was being silly and accused their partner of cheating just to get a rise out of them? When they heard that first response – "Wait, what? Me? I've been cheating?" – they saw blood in the water. They remained calm and pressed forward.

I point this out for a reason. In a standard interview and interrogation, the interrogation is a planned event that happens at a distinct time and begins with an accusation. However, whether it's on street patrol or in your normal life, there may come a time when something you say by happenstance provokes an obviously deceptive response. If you are practiced, you might just be able to roll that into a monologue and a confession. Try to plan things, but don't miss the opportunity to let serendipity be your guide if that's the way it goes.

As the interrogation example progressed, we got to the alternative question. While you are building themes, you are always working towards the alternative question. You want to use this when the suspect has ceased to deny and object. This might be in a few minutes or a few hours. The alternative question above was: "The one thing I really wanted to know is whether you did this because you hated me or if you did it because I wasn't fulfilling your needs. It's because I wasn't fulfilling your needs wasn't it?" We all like using "Are you the awful guy or the not so awful guy" alternative. There are endless variations to this. No matter how you pose the alternative question, always remember to end it with a leading question that the suspect can answer with just a simple, "yes". The leading question here is, "It's because I wasn't fulfilling your needs wasn't it?"

If you are ever lost at sea during your interrogation, ask yourself if you've gotten to the alternative question yet. If you haven't, work your way over there. No matter how good you are, people rarely confess spontaneously. Your stories might be great, but at some point you need to get them to the alternative question (and by extension the leading question) to get them started. I write more about the alternative question further on in this chapter.

Now let's look at a bad suspect interrogation given the same scenario:

### Bad Interrogation

*Spouse:* I have no doubt in my mind that you've been cheating.
*You:* I haven't cheated.
*Spouse:* You're out late at night. You come back in different clothes. You never kiss me anymore. We haven't had sex in a year.
*You:* You're crazy. Those don't mean anything.
*Spouse:* Why are you out late at night then and why…
*You:* I'm out late because I have work. Don't you like the nice things I buy you?
*Spouse:* You never let me look at your phone.
*You:* Because I've been planning a surprise for you. There! I said it. I can't believe you've ruined that. It's so typical of you.
*Spouse:* What's the surprise then.
*You:* Forget it. You don't deserve it anyway. The surprise is off. I work my ass off to get you all the things you want. It's so typical of you to ruin it. You're lucky I haven't cheated on you. I've been faithful all this time and here you are…

Ouch. That one didn't go as planned. Believe it or not, the example above is most similar to the interrogations that go off the rails every day. In this scenario, our speaker's opening salvo didn't go the way they wanted. Panicked, they attempted to prove their case by listing the proofs they know. Instead of proving their case, it emboldens the suspect. The quick-thinking suspect understands now their partner only has suspicions and nothing concrete. Suspicions can be argued with. At first they were worried their partner had witnessed it or found messages they forgot to delete. It's not nearly that bad. Slowly, the suspect begins to take control of the conversation. We left them as the suspect was laying down a weighty guilt trip. My guess is this suspect is going to make it.

I see this style of attempting to prove the case during the interrogation all the time. This technique is disastrous. Put your cheating self in the place of the second cheater. Are you going to admit to anything under those circumstances? I doubt it. They are giving you specifics. Specifics are easy to fight against.

It's difficult to resist *unspecified* certainty. If you know you did it, and somebody says they know you did it, your mind will be reeling trying to figure out how they know. *If you know you did it and somebody tries to convince you that you did it, you will know on a gut level they don't really believe themselves when they accuse you.*

You must remember no matter how many times we tell suspects how certain we are of their guilt, the case doesn't sound all that good when you lay it out, even if it's a trial ready fact pattern. Do not lay the case out for the suspect. Every single fact or argument you lay out is something to argue with. If you give them something to argue with, they will. Is it possible that you could get a confession out of this approach? Yes. Is it probable? No.

The thing that made the first speaker so powerful was their absolute certainty. You should adopt this style when interrogating. This first speaker does not present specifics. They tell a story about how they failed their partner. Their partner, desperate to be anything but a cheat, hears this forgiving certainty and wants it so bad they feel forced to decide: Am I a cheat or somebody that was let down by their partner and led astray? There's nothing to argue with because there aren't any fact pattern specifics. What is the person with the guilty conscience going to say? You've been perfect and I cheated anyway? No.

Whatever crime you are investigating, if you decide to interrogate, go in with conviction. Look through these two examples and really understand what it's like to approach your suspect with conviction. A calm and steady gaze will combine with the inexorable certainty, and you will get the confessions you seek from the guilty.

## Process of the Interrogation

In an accusatory interrogation, accuse the person of committing (or having guilty knowledge of) the crime while providing them an explanation that allows them to save face.

The most common concerns I hear from new interrogators is they will run out of stuff to say or they don't understand theme building. I'll address both of these in the section that follows. Perhaps the most important thing to do during an interrogation is just to keep talking. Don't pass the mic. Don't use silence. Just keep talking. Ideally it would be related to the theory of why they did it (theme),[9] but any talking will do during the crucial period after the accusation. How can you do that?

My interrogations follow a basic process, which is as follows:

1 Accuse them
2 Present a theory or theme as to why they did it
3 Ignore denials
4 Storytelling
5 Accuse
6 Frameworks
7 Accuse
8 Alternative question

And so on until either their denials cause you to rethink your accusation or you start getting buy in from the suspect. The process is a bit like hammering a nail. Strike (accuse), Backswing (storytelling / frameworks), and Strike (accuse).

## The Accusation

The accusation should be stated as clearly and simply as possible. Avoid any words that modify your level of certainty. "You did it" is a good accusation. "I know you did it" is an okay accusation. "I think you did it" is a weak accusation.

When I make the accusation, my tone is quiet and my overall approach is calm sincerity. A person walking by the room who didn't know what was happening might think I was discussing the untimely death of an elderly relative. Calmness, sincerity, and perseverance are the keys here.

I think a suspect in a crime talks to police because:

1 They didn't do it and want to explain suspicion away from themselves
2 They didn't do it but want to understand better why they are being accused
3 They did it, but they want to know what you know
4 They did it, and they want to see if they can talk themselves out of it

When you accuse a person of committing a crime, you should expect a reaction. All four of the groups (listed above) that decided to talk to the police have their answer. They know they can't talk themselves out of it, and they know, broadly, what evidence you have against them. Now they have to decide what to do.

There are three common responses to an accusation. First, many suspects will nod and/or slump their shoulders when you accuse them. This is typically associated with a guilty person that is willing to confess to what they did. Second, some suspects will say, "Well, if you've decided I did it, then there's nothing more to talk about." Or perhaps, "If it's like that, then call my lawyer." These are obviously invocations of Miranda rights, and your interrogation is over. The third group of suspects will cross their arms, shake their head "no", and lean back. This group is resistant. You'll have some talking to do to find out how this interview is going to turn out.

Most accusations result in little change. They will nod acceptance, shake their head in refusal, or terminate the interview. Sometimes it goes sideways, though. I had one suspect who told me to shoot him in the head if he did what I was accusing him of. Then he called 911 and told an operator to send an officer to arrest him while sitting in the interrogation room. I've seen my partner accuse a man who stood up, flipped the table over, and threatened to assault him. Expect it to go well, but have a plan if it doesn't.

## Themes

> How must they [sex offenders] see the world so that their behavior seems rational and acceptable to them?
>
> Graham Hill[10]

When I teach, many questions I answer have to do with themes in interrogations. What are they? How do they work?

Essentially, a theme is an idea that is woven throughout the interrogation. This idea is used to minimize the importance of the crime. It provides an explanation for how the crime may have happened. Selecting the perfect theme is hard. But selecting a good enough theme is relatively easy. The theme does not have to explain how the actual crime happened but rather a way that it might have happened that morally excuses the suspect *without* legally excusing them.

For example, there is the YouTube video of the interrogation of James Rauch, a former professor caught for soliciting sex from a minor.[11] At one point in the interview, he said, "My own motivation is not to...to...to...um...just find somebody who's interested in me. Ok. Not young. Not old. Not fat. Not thin. Not...Someone who is interested in...in...who I am." You are lucky when you find somebody who spells it out for you like this. His theme is, *Everybody Deserves Love.*

Of course, Rauch is actually soliciting sex from underaged girls because he is sexually attracted to them. Maybe it's power and control issues. Maybe it's one of any number of unmet psychological needs. As working cops, it's not for us to understand what this man's sexual desires are. Rather, we have credible information he is soliciting sex from minors, and we need to test that information against his denials.

Using a theme like Everybody Deserves Love allows somebody like Rauch to save face because it offers him a moral excuse. I would be wrong to say anything that suggested excusing him criminally. For example, if I said, "Maybe you thought you were talking to an age-appropriate person. That would be ok. Wouldn't it?" That would be offering him a defense to prosecution. It's not soliciting sex from a minor if you thought the person was of legal age.

Having a person admit to a non-crime isn't exactly the truth you'd hope for from a guilty person. If we theorize to Rauch he did the crime because he was lonely and he agrees, his loneliness is not a defense to prosecution. That is a way of morally excusing him. If we theorize to Rauch he got confused and thought the person was of age, that is a defense to prosecution, which would criminally excuse him.

There are times when investigators might make a calculated decision to offer a suspect a theme that criminally excuses them in the hopes they can then use an admission to tie the person to the crime. I see this a lot in homicide cases. The investigator offers the suspect a self-defense claim, "Maybe you shot him because he was threatening you." If the suspect agrees to it, they are now committed to being the shooter, but they have a defense to prosecution that will have to be overcome.

If your case facts are strong enough, you may be able to overcome a defense to prosecution with evidence. In a case like this, having the suspect admit to committing the actions that caused the resulting criminal allegations may be worth the risk to the case. For example, I offered a self-defense claim to a suspect in a murder case once. In that case, I had good evidence that the gunshot didn't happen the way she said it did. I also had evidence she had taken steps to cover up her actions afterwards. I made the choice to offer that theme as a calculated risk.

If your case facts aren't strong enough, you'll have to progress the interrogation to the point the person then admits it wasn't actually self-defense or whatever other defense to prosecution they are claiming. My experience is that it is terribly difficult to get a person to move off of claims which criminally excuse them.

I recall one interrogation of a child abuse suspect where the detective got them to admit to doing the actions that caused the injury. In order to do it, they offered the theme that maybe it was all a horrible accident. When the detective came out, they were happy to have gotten the "confession." I asked them, "What are you going to charge them with, though?" In the interview room, the detective hadn't thought about how an accident didn't meet the culpable mental state required to charge a person with injury to a child.

If this detective believes the suspect purposefully committed the crime, they would need to build on the admission to move them past "accident." Now the actions are stipulated to, but the culpable mental state is not. The interrogation would then center around the culpable mental state rather than the actions themselves. "You said it was an accident, but we both know it wasn't. You may have lost control, but you knew what you were doing."

If you decide to offer them a criminal excuse as a tactic, do it knowingly as part of an overall strategy. Don't offer themes that criminally excuse the suspect unless you have a plan. That plan will be to lock them into an admission of committing the actions and *then* addressing the culpable mental state either through evidence or further interrogation to uncover the mentality.

## Selecting Themes

So how should you select your theme? Think through the crime, and ask yourself, "If they did it, how are they likely to have justified the crime?" Good themes arise from *likely* justifications. If your theme is based on a likely justification, it will seem infinitely more acceptable to the suspect than having done it because they are bad people. It doesn't really matter if the person justified the crime in a different way.

You'll find the theme follows on from the justification. Once you have selected a theme, the shape of your interrogation is formed. You'll use the theme to talk, provide examples, and give arguments for why you know they did the crime *and* why they should tell you about it. It helps to pull from life and work experience to fill out the things you will say. If you are at all worried about what to say in an interrogation, start with naming your theme.

Let's go through some examples for each of the major crime types. I provide a possible justification that a suspect having committed the crime might use. I then name a possible theme to address that justification. You'll see that the themes are not long or complex even though what you have to say about those words *will* be long.

***Robbery***: *A theft that is accomplished by threatening and/or assaulting the victim*

*Table 10.1* Examples of themes arising from justifications likely to be used by robbery suspects.

| *Justification* | *Theme(s)* |
|---|---|
| Peer pressure | With friends like these..., You would have done anything to fit in, If it weren't for Marshall... |
| Financial hardship | Times are hard |
| The other person made it so easy | Victim blaming |
| Getting even | They hurt you so you hurt them. Hurt people hurt people |
| Criminal history prevents them from normal work | Blame society, One wrong turn and a lifetime to pay |
| I didn't really hurt the person | You're a good guy, The other guy would have been worse |
| Things got out of hand | It was supposed to be easy |

This isn't an exhaustive list of justifications or themes. It doesn't have to be. Think about how the person may have justified the crime, and your theme flows from there. Choose a theme, and begin to work it. Let's keep going through some other crimes. Afterwards, we will look at how you might develop these themes in the interrogation.

***Burglary***: *a trespass and a theft*

*Table 10.2* Examples of themes arising from justifications likely to be used by burglary suspects.

| *Justification* | *Theme(s)* |
|---|---|
| Financial hardship | Times are hard, you wouldn't have done it when things were better |
| Just looking for a place to sleep | Things got out of hand, Victim blaming |
| I didn't hurt anybody | You're not out there *robbing* people |
| Insurance will cover it | Nobody actually got hurt |

Note: avoid any references to them having permission to take the items or permission to be in that location. Those would provide a possible legal defense to prosecution.

***Rape*** (adult victim): *non-consensual sex*

*Table 10.3* Examples of themes arising from justifications likely to be used by suspects in the rape of adults.

| *Justification* | *Theme(s)* |
|---|---|
| I was drunk | You wouldn't have done it if you were in your right mind, Bad input leads to bad output |
| She wanted it | You misread the situation, The male mind has trouble shutting down once sex is brought up |
| She's my wife / girlfriend | You thought you had a right to sex |
| I have unmet sexual desires | If you were getting what you needed at home..., You were lonely and looking for connection |
| I didn't *hurt* her | You're a good guy that did a bad thing |

Note: With adult rape crimes, **it is *never* appropriate to use the theme of Blame the Victim.** In these types of crimes, you would have to suggest the victim wanted sex with the suspect. If the victim *wanted* sex, then it is consensual sex and therefore not illegal. Blame the Victim can be very effective in child sex crimes where the victim is statutorily incapable of consent. While Blame the Victim is highly effective in child sex crime interrogations, I'd note victims are not to blame no matter what theme you may use to get their assailant to talk.

**Murder:** *intentionally causing the death of another without legal justification*

*Table 10.4* Examples of themes arising from justifications likely to be used by murder suspects.

| *Justification* | *Theme(s)* |
|---|---|
| Revenge | They started it |
| Bad upbringing | Other people made you who you are, If you had only had a chance |
| Drugs or alcohol | Sober you wouldn't have done that |
| Mental health problems | You've had a bad deal |
| Peer pressure | We've all acted differently around our peers before, If it weren't for bad friends... |
| The victim was a bad person | Blame the victim |
| The victim fought back and escalated it (during another crime) | If they would have just listened..., It was never part of the plan |

**Sexual Assault of a Child:** *either nonconsensual sex with a child and / or statutorily prohibited sex with a child.*

*Table 10.5* Examples of themes arising from justifications likely to be used by suspects in the rape of children.

| *Justification* | *Theme(s)* |
|---|---|
| Unmet sexual needs | If your wife had taken care of you..., When men don't get what we need... |
| I wasn't in my right mind | Curiosity and opportunity |
| Drugs / alcohol | Sober you wouldn't have done this, We've all made bad decisions when drunk |
| She wanted it | Blame the Victim |

Note: Again, no victim is to blame for their abuse. The use of this theme to get the truth is not an endorsement of any of the suspect's actions.

In whatever type of case you have in front of you, think about how the suspect may have justified the crime. Usually you won't know the suspect, so you'll have to do some thinking about their situation. It doesn't matter why *you* might have done the crime. Why did this three-time felon commit another robbery? Maybe he felt like he didn't have any other choice. Why did this school teacher touch his student? Maybe he thought the victim wanted it. Why did this stepfather rape his stepdaughter? Maybe he thought his sexual needs were unmet. The theme selection follows on from the justification.

The theme you select will be based on everything you know about the suspect. Ideally, you will have knowledge about them going into the interview. Then you will learn more about them during the interview. If you listen, most interviewees will tell you what's important to them. By the end of the interview, you will know a lot about the suspect. Now you take everything you know, and you think about how they may have justified the crime. Then you select your theme.

You don't need an official theme. It doesn't have to come from a list somewhere. Your goal here is to propose a theory for why the crime happened in a way that morally excuses the person without criminally excusing them. The theme you select is a way of addressing a likely justification for the crime.

I'll provide an example from each crime type listed above as to how the theme might be developed. A theme is not just a few words you say once and forget about. You can't just say, "I think you did it because of curiosity and opportunity. Tell me why you did it." You have to work on it. A lot of interrogation is talking with periodic accusations. A theme helps you stay on track when you run out of things to say.

**Robbery theme:** *Times are hard*

> I've been thinking about this case a lot, and it occurred to me crimes like this don't happen when times are good. You don't read stories about a guy making a living wage with a good home life out there sticking people up. No sir. They don't do it because their lives are easy. You haven't had an easy life. You've been living hard for a long time. You talked about a few jobs you've had along the way, but none of them have worked out. That shows you're trying! If you had just had a little more luck. If the inflation hadn't eaten up all that you earned. If those things were going well, you wouldn't have beat that man up for his money.
>
> I've worked cases where moms told me they were working three jobs to make ends meet. Even by working themselves to death they are barely making it. How's a guy like you with a felony conviction supposed to even get one job much less three? How's that supposed to happen? No, you beat that man up because you were frustrated. Everything's gone to hell, and you acted in a way you wouldn't have in a better world, a better economy. Once he was down, you saw his wallet, and you probably thought, "Here's a stroke of luck. Here's a chance to get ahead." You stole his wallet, and that's how we ended up here.

**Burglary theme:** *Nobody actually got hurt*

> You know, "burglary" sounds harsh. You went into that man's house, and you took a few electronics. Ok, you didn't have his permission for that. Ok, he's a little inconvenienced.

Who actually got hurt, though? Living in that fancy neighborhood you know he has insurance. He gets all new stuff. You get enough to eat and feed your drug habit. It almost sounds like everybody wins.

I remember when I was in high school, the school was broken into. The news reported it was this big thing. A burglary! I found out the next day they went in through an open door, and they took a few computers. What the news didn't report on, though, is that the computers were old, and they were going to be replaced anyway. I thought at the time, "How is this such a big deal if nobody even got hurt?" It's not right what you did. I'm not making you any promises about what's going to happen. If it's true, though, that you did what you did because you didn't think anybody would get hurt, then I think we need to talk about that. Let's tell your story and explain how this happened.

**Rape** (adult victim) theme: *You wouldn't have done it if you had been in your right mind*

Something that really confuses me about your case is how exactly a person like you could have done a thing like this. I lost sleep over it during the investigation. I finally realized it was probably because you were drunk. Sober Robert wouldn't do a thing like that. Sober Robert goes to work, plays with his kids, and turns his taxes in on time. Sober Robert is the kind of citizen we all want more of. He's the kind of friend we want to have.

Drunk Robert is different though. Drunk Robert does things that he shouldn't. When I was in college, I was friends with a guy named Duncan. Duncan was the nicest, friendliest person you could ever ask to meet. Drunk Duncan was a menace, though. Something twisted in his brain when he drank. He'd get in fights, collapse in his own vomit, and break anything in sight. The difference was night and day, and there was no doubt at all that it was the alcohol.

In your case, Robert, the drinking might not create such an extreme result, but it affects you nonetheless. Here you were on a date with a new girlfriend. You were probably feeling nervous, and you took to drinking. With all of the nerves, you drank way past your limit. When you two left the restaurant, it was Drunk Robert that took her up to her room.

Note: In Texas, the use of drugs and alcohol are not a defense to prosecution. Make sure this is the case where you work too or else you'd be criminally excusing them.

**Murder theme:** *Peer pressure*

Your actions led to his death. That much is true and we know it. Our investigation proves it. What our investigation doesn't show, though, is why you did it. Why would a guy out on the town with friends shoot a man to death? That's a question people are going to want to know, and I recommend that you tell them. Let me tell you what I think it was. I've been all over every aspect of this case. It dawned on me the other day you were probably pushed to do something you didn't want to because of peer pressure.

That man shoulder checked you, and your friends let you know only a wimp would let something like that pass. You may be a lot of things, but a wimp isn't one of them. You pulled out, and you let him have it. It never would have happened if those friends hadn't been there. You had a split second to choose what kind of guy you were. In that moment, you couldn't let yourself lose face.

We've all done stuff we wouldn't normally do with peer pressure. I remember being a kid. I had just gotten my license. Of course the first thing I did was pick up my friends. I got them all in the car, and we went out riding. We cruised the town until one of them started teasing me for driving like a grandma. Then they all took it up. Without thinking more about it, I gunned the car, and I raced through a series of red lights. That's when the police lights got behind me.

The thing is, every person that hears your story is going to understand what it means to experience peer pressure. They may not be able to understand killing another person over it, but they will all know what it feels like to be pressured by their friends. Most will know what it means to act in a way that isn't normal when they are around their friends. What you did isn't right, but if we can at least make it understandable, it humanizes you. It's harder for somebody to think you're a monster when they see the forces moving you are the same forces they've experienced before.

**Sexual Assault of a Child theme:** *Curiosity and opportunity*

You aren't the first person I've talked to about being involved in a situation like this. I've talked to dozens of other men that have been in your exact situation. What I've learned from those other men, is they aren't evil people. They are usually people who have thoughts they shouldn't have at the same time that they are presented with an opportunity they don't usually have. That's curiosity and opportunity.

We all have thoughts that we shouldn't. A presenter at a conference once told me "normal" people have sexual fantasies regularly. Of those "normal" people with sexual fantasies, the fantasies themselves are 90% normal, mainstream sexual fantasies. Stuff you might see on any mainstream porn site. What surprised me, though, was he said that even "normal" people have about 10% of their sexual fantasies that get weird, kinky, or deviant. This presenter said the reverse was true of people that suffer from deviant sexual thinking. Those people have 90% kink and 10% mainstream.

The point is even "normal" people have kinky thoughts that make them curious about stuff they probably shouldn't be doing. Fantasy is a type of curiosity. Usually it passes through your head, and there's nothing to be done about it, so it goes away.

On the other hand, any adult will have had sexual opportunities in their life that they didn't follow up on. Maybe they were in a committed relationship at the time. Or maybe they just weren't into the person. An opportunity without the curiosity or the willingness to follow up on it is nothing.

Now, where things go wrong, is when curiosity meets opportunity. That kinky thought comes to you at the exact time you have the chance to act on it. My experience talking to people who have been through what you're going through is that THOSE situations are where bad things happen. I think that's what happened in your case.

Once you get your theme going, you'll work it into the pattern of an interrogation.

1 Accuse them
2 Present a theory or theme as to why they did it
3 Ignore denials
4 Storytelling (Relate to theme when possible)
5 Accuse
6 Frameworks (Relate to theme when possible)
7 Accuse
8 Alternative question

Having a theme provides a way for the suspect to minimize their actions, but it also gives focus to what you are saying.

## Another Way to Think About Creating Interrogation Themes

An interrogation is like an academic paper. You come up with a thesis (theme) first. "Peer pressure is hard to resist for young people because fitting in is everything." Once you have the thesis, everything follows from that. You provide examples and supporting arguments. "I remember a time when I…" "I had a friend in school who…" "If you don't fit in with peers, you…" Then present conclusions. "When you did this, you had that same peer pressure pushing you." The grade for *this* paper is based on how well you stay on topic, not necessarily how good your arguments are. You shouldn't get lost because the topic is singular. Forgot what you're saying? "Peer pressure. Here's another example of peer pressure."

Fill in the blanks as though you were writing the outline for your paper on James Rauch, the music teacher soliciting sex from a minor, and his theme of "Everybody deserves love"? I'll list my answers on the next page, but do yourself the favor of filling these out or at least thinking of the answers before looking at mine.

What's an example?:____________________
What's a supporting argument?____________________
What's another example?____________________
What's your conclusion? ____________________

Do the same for a robbery suspect using the thesis (theme) of "One wrong turn and a lifetime to pay."

What's an example?:____________________
What's a supporting argument?____________________
What's another example?____________________
What's your conclusion? ____________________

Fill in the blanks as though you were writing the outline for your paper on James Rauch, the music teacher soliciting sex from a minor, and his theme of "Everybody deserves love"?

**What's an example?:** *I had a friend going through a divorce. His wife treated him terribly. She was always putting him down. They never had sex. It was a constant struggle, and he was miserable. He worried about being a failure, especially for his kids. Finally, I looked at him and I told him, "Failure sucks, but you deserve love too, man." It's true too! It's not my job to sort through who did what in their marriage. But if half of what he said was true, he was doing all of the work and receiving none of the love. Not getting love causes us to do things we wouldn't do otherwise.*

**What's a supporting argument?** *Love civilizes us. It gives us something to live for, and live right. If we don't have love, we act badly. You don't see well-adjusted people in loving relationships end up in situations like this. If you were in a loving relationship, you never would have gone into those chat rooms.*

**What's another example?** *I worked a case where a 35 year old man got into a relationship with his neighbor's underaged daughter. It wasn't right, and he knew it, but his wife had fallen out of love with him. She wasn't mean to him like my friend's wife. She just didn't do anything for him. It was always cold at home. Then he saw that his neighbor's daughter was being flirtatious with him. He started doing things that led to a full blown relationship with this young girl. None of it would have happened if he had gotten love at home.*

**What's your conclusion?** *You acted badly when you solicited sex from the girl in the chat room, but it came from a place of searching for connection. You deserve love too. You just went about looking for it in the wrong places.*

Do the same for a robbery suspect using the thesis (theme) of "One wrong turn and a lifetime to pay."

**What's an example?:** *I worked a case with a female robbery suspect. When I saw her mugshot from a previous arrest, I was surprised at how tattooed her face was. She had a whole list of mugshots. Curious, I followed them backwards until I found her first. She was 15 years old when she got that first mugshot. She was innocent looking, and maybe a little scared. She had been picked up for auto theft. Really, she was just in the car with the wrong person at the wrong time. The next mugshot was for robbery. She looked harder there, not as innocent. I noticed she had a tattoo on her neck. As time went on, each mugshot got a little harder with a lot more ink. She made one wrong turn and she has a whole lifetime to pay for it.*

**What's a supporting argument?** *Once you're in the system, nobody wants to help you out. Jobs won't hire you. All the charities don't want anything to do with you. Your family might not even let you come around, worried about the influence you have on others. In a way, it looks like you don't have any choices at all that aren't more crime.*

**What's another example?** *I talked to a crack addict once. It surprised me when I found out that she was addicted to crack. I asked her how it all started. What was the first time she smoked crack like? She told me it was so stupid. She was playing spades with a boyfriend of hers. He asked her if she wanted to try it. She said, "Sure." Everything was downhill from there. It wasn't long before she was stealing from family and turning tricks for money to buy crack. It was just the one wrong turn.*

**What's your conclusion?** *When you robbed that man, it wasn't an evil decision. Life has a way of sweeping you along whatever path you start down. One wrong turn and a lifetime to pay. What I want you to do today is to stop it. Instead of continuing on with denials until the next bad thing happens, stand up. Say you did it. Accept responsibility. That's how you stop the flow and open yourself up to the possibility of doing good again.*

Everything flows from the theme. A theme keeps you on track. It gives you focus. It provides the guilty suspect an opportunity to tell you the truth in a way that minimizes their moral guilt without excusing them criminally. Spend some time thinking about the right theme. It gets faster with experience. You should fear *not* having a theme far more than you worry about coming up with the perfect one.

### *Storytelling*

Storytelling is a relatively simple technique that allows you to talk more without having to think too hard about what to say. Essentially, you tell the suspect you worked a case just like theirs. In this other case, the suspect told the truth about what he did, and he felt better as a result. The trick of it is that the story you are telling them is just their story with a detail or two changed.

There are three main elements to Storytelling:

1 I worked a case just like yours (tell them *their* case with a few details changed)
2 That suspect admitted to what he did
3 He felt better after admitting to what he did

Note: It is vital you stick to "he felt better" instead of "that guy's out walking free." The former is just a state of emotional wellbeing for the suspect. The latter is a pretty clear promise of leniency, which could be grounds for suppression of your interview.

Say you are investigating a stabbing. The suspect is alleged to have stabbed a man in a bar for hitting on his girlfriend. After you accused the suspect of the stabbing, you introduced a theme of Drunk You Did Bad Things. After you talk about the theme for a while, you lose some steam. You can always launch into Storytelling.

> I worked a case just like this where a man beat his best friend with a baseball bat because his supposed best friend was texting his girl about going out. My investigation led me to that man. Time had passed. He wasn't mad anymore. He didn't have the baseball bat either! That man looked me right in the eye, and he admitted what he did. Afterwards, he told me that he felt much better for having admitted it.

In this Storytelling version, the knife became a bat and the bar patron became a best friend. In the story, the man tells the truth, and he feels better. That is not a major change from the initial story. That's something you should be able to come up with on the fly. It does not have to be an actual case you worked, but it's always best to stick as close to true things as possible, even in Storytelling.

As another example, you are investigating a father who is alleged to have performed oral sex on his son. After you accused him, you introduced the theme of Curiosity and

Opportunity. You may run out of things to say about your theme, and choose Storytelling. That might look like this:

> You know, Zach, one reason it's important to me that you tell me what happened is that my experience shows it will make you feel better. I worked a case just like this where a granddad put his mouth on his granddaughter's vagina. He had hidden it for years, but one day she told the family. I investigated. When I talked to that granddad, he sat in the same chair you are sitting in now, and he lied at first. Everybody does, and that's ok. At the end, though, he chose to tell the truth. He admitted what he did with her. When he walked out of the door, he thanked me for allowing him to tell the truth without any judgment.

Here is a similar situation. The suspect becomes a granddad. The victim becomes a granddaughter. The actions under investigation are essentially the same. The suspect resisted at first, but they chose to talk. Once they admitted their wrongdoing, they felt better.

This is a technique my partner and I present along with the next one, Frameworks, in our training on the Fundamentals of Interviewing and Interrogation. We have a long section on interrogation practicals. During those practicals, we ask the students to choose Storytelling or Frameworks, and they always choose frameworks. As you'll see in the next section, there's something punchy about that technique that people pick up on quickly.

Of course, I adapted to this resistance. Now, I have the first few students alternate. One will do a Framework. The other will do Storytelling. Then we do that again. By then, the others in the group have heard several examples of each. The others then get to choose which they want to practice. Once that happened, the usage rate went to about 50/50.

All that to say, if you are an interrogator, try the Storytelling technique out. It is very easy to use. It helps you talk without having to come up with totally new things to say. People like stories that reflect them and their situation. They especially like them when the person they see themselves in comes out better than expected.

### *Frameworks*

Frameworks are stories or examples you memorize in advance that provide shape and substance to your interrogation. They illustrate points, provide motivation to talk, and keep you from running out of things to say. These require a little bit of upfront effort, but I guarantee that the effort will be worth it as you continue on with your career interviewing and interrogating criminal suspects. I use frameworks in every single interrogation that lasts more than a few minutes.

An interrogation is like a building plan. Your preparation for the interrogation is like sketching out what you want your building to look like (you have themes, examples, and evidence). It looks good on paper. When you start to build it, though, the real world intrudes. Maybe the ground is bad or your measurements are off (unexpected things happen in the interrogation). Whatever the problem, your building starts to lean (your interrogation loses momentum). If you want to complete the project, you'll have to adapt by strengthening the weak areas. Just as you would shim up the weak areas in the structure, so too will you need to build out supports in your interrogation to keep it standing. This is where frameworks come in.

Let me provide an example up front so it is clear what a framework looks like. The framework I have used the most is **Three Things to Get Right**. It goes like this:

> You're struggling with this, and I can see it. The thing about that, though, is that you aren't doing the right thing by denying your involvement. There's three things that you gotta do to get right. You have to say what you did is wrong, you have to say you're sorry, and you have to say it won't happen again. That's a universal rule for everything.

The framework here is Three Things to Get Right. It always has the same three components, but the way I present it differs a little each time. I riff off of the content, allowing me to talk more. I have several variations of this framework I've used over the years. As an example:

> You're struggling with this, and I can see it. The thing is, though, you aren't doing the right thing by denying your involvement. There's three things that you gotta do to get right. You have to say what you did is wrong, you have to say you're sorry, and you have to say it won't happen again. That's a universal rule for everything.
>
> If you forgot to pick the kid up from daycare for example, you're wife's going to be mad at you. It's true you were wrong to miss the pickup time, but you had reasons! It doesn't feel like it's your fault. You might say, "It won't happen again," which is step three in this process. If you stop there, though, your wife isn't going to back off. That's because you haven't committed to getting right with your wife again.
>
> If you really wanna get right, you gotta say, "I screwed up. I got busy at work, and I forgot. I'm really sorry. It won't happen again." That's how that works! I've found the times in my life that I don't want to accept responsibility for my actions are the times I need it the most.
>
> Sometimes "sorry" is the hardest word to say. Let's leave that for a bit and start with step three. Can we agree that it's never going to happen again?

That's an example of a common riff I might do on the framework of Three Things to Get Right. In the above example, I'd try to get them to agree that the actions won't happen again. Then guide them to one of the other steps. This is a framework in action. It bolsters up your sagging interrogation, and it provides direction and opportunities to continue to project certainty in your monologue.

When my interrogation starts to falter, I reach for the framework. I may be working on the theme, adapting to the suspect, and, suddenly, I think to myself, "Where am I going to go from here? I'm just repeating myself." In other instances, I can see that the suspect has hardened himself to the theme or the monologue. He may cross his arms, shake his head "no," or in any other number of ways show that he isn't interested in what I am saying. When this happens, I reach for a framework. "Let me tell you, there are three things you gotta do to get right…"

Most of the frameworks I use came about during interrogations where I ran out of things to say. I had to think about ways to illustrate why telling the truth was so important, and my usual examples weren't getting through. In one such interview, I came up with Separate and Condemn Together, and it was exactly what I needed.

Here's how **Separate and Condemn Together** looks:

> You're lying about what happened with that boy. I've heard from you about your hard life. I agree with you that your life has been hard. When you get treated badly, you act badly. That's just a fact of life. The thing is, I'm not going to judge you on how you've been treated. It's not my job to judge you for the things you've done. But what I *am* going to judge you on is lying.
>
> Because as long as you're lying about what you did, you're holding onto that wrong thing. By doing that, when I'm looking at the wrong thing, I'm looking right at you. That's true of others too. What you need to do is tell the truth about what happened. When you tell the truth, you put the wrong thing down. Now when I'm looking at you, I'm just looking at a person that's been treated badly and acted badly as a result. That's a person I can understand.
>
> Now you and I can stand shoulder to shoulder together and look at the bad thing. I'll be right there with you. I will stand next to you, and I will look with you at the bad thing you did. Now you and I together will agree, "It's bad what you did." You can't control how people are going to think about you. Nobody can. But once you tell the truth about what you did, you can stand with your head up and know you've done what you can to fix it. However people judge you later, you will have taken back as much control of the situation as possible.

I taught a class in the middle of 2023 where I presented this framework. Days later, one of the students, a newly promoted violent crimes detective, sent me a link to an interview he had done using this particular framework. The suspect brought a gun into a bar in the downtown area, and he fired off two rounds, hitting multiple people with debris or shrapnel. I watched as this detective put the framework to work and got the man to confess to having the gun and firing off the rounds.[12] These things work!

The other framework I use the most is called **The Missing Puzzle Piece**. This is one I came up with as I was preparing for an interview with a window peeper. It goes like this:

> Have you ever done a jigsaw puzzle? These puzzles sometimes have a thousand pieces. If you've ever done a jigsaw puzzle, you know that every single time when you are about to finish one, you're missing a piece. Every time! When that happens, you have to go looking for the piece. You look under tables, under couch cushions, and anywhere else it might have gone. Nothing feels settled until you can find that piece. It's not possible to look at the 999 pieces of the puzzle without looking straight at the hole that missing piece creates.
>
> As long as you continue to lie about what happened, your story is that jigsaw puzzle with the missing piece. As long as you lie about it, nobody can stop thinking about that missing piece. Their eyes go right to it. It doesn't matter about the good things you've done in your life. Those good things make up the other 999 pieces. The times you cared for sick children, volunteered to work holidays at your job so your friends could be off, sent

> flowers to your mom on mother's day. All of those things big and small don't matter as long as this lie sits here like that missing puzzle piece.
>
> When you tell the truth about what you did, though, you put that final piece in the puzzle. Now nobody has to go crazy looking for it or wondering what that piece was. They can see it. Once that piece is back in the puzzle, it's still bad. It's bad what you did. But it isn't the first thing people look at. Their eyes see all of the other things that make up who you are and what you've done. That's what I want for you. I want you to see that denying having done this thing is the worst thing possible for your ability to get right with your family and community. Tell the truth. Let them stop worrying about it and start seeing you as the man you are.

Like the other frameworks, this one has elements that always show up. Everybody sees their lies. Their lies bring more attention to the crime not less. They are more than the crime. Once they tell the truth, it will still be bad what they did, but they can regain some of their standing in their family or community. Once I bring the framework out, I riff on it. It is never exactly the same.

I use a series of frameworks that I've come up with. These work for me. If my previous students are any indication, they can work for you too. Try this technique. Memorize some of these frameworks (not necessarily every word, but the substance of them), and use them when the interrogation starts to sag.

I am sure there are many more frameworks out there already in use or as yet to be discovered. Keep innovating on this front. Look for new frameworks, and share them with your partners when you have them.

Here are the main frameworks that I use.

## Three Things to Get Right

1 You have to say what you did is wrong
2 You have to say you're sorry
3 You have to say that it won't happen again

- Make it clear that you are not promising them legal forgiveness
- Focus their attention on the victim, the family, society
- Very effective changing sequence. Establish 2 then 3 then 1 OR 3 then 2 then 1.

## The Truth Sounds Like The Truth

"Right now, you aren't telling the truth. How do I know? Because the truth sounds like the truth, and you aren't there. It's not just about me, it's your family and friends too. It may seem like a good idea to avoid consequences by not telling the truth, but no matter what happens between us here today, your family is going to be thinking about what you said. They know you. They know her. They know how y'all interact, and this story here is going to leave them knowing that you weren't being honest. The truth sounds like the truth, and this isn't it. Let's be honest about what happened. When you are, it will be obvious. The truth sounds like the truth."

### Missing Puzzle Piece

"Have you ever done a jigsaw puzzle? I used to do them a lot. You have a 1,000 piece puzzle, but when you get to the end, there is usually a piece missing. It will drive you crazy. When you look at it, you can't look at the 999 things you got right. Instead, you stare at the missing piece. You keep looking around for it until you find it. As long as you continue to lie, that lie is like your missing puzzle piece. Everybody that knows you can't help but to focus on the lies. All of the good stuff that you do and have done is ignored because of this awful hole. When you tell the truth, it completes the puzzle."

### Separate and Condemn Together

"Right now, you and what you did are so tied together that you're inseparable from one another. When others see you, they see the bad thing that you've done. As long as you continue to lie about it, that will be the case. When you tell the truth about it, however, you separate yourself from your actions. When you do that, then you and I (or you and your society) can stand together side by side and condemn the action together."

### Everybody Knows

"Look, I know people lie because they see it as their last, best option to save face. I understand that, but I don't think it is saving face when everybody knows you are lying. It makes you look bad and remorseless. Right now, you have your head in the sand thinking people don't see you and your lies, but they do. When everybody knows you are lying, the best thing to do is to tell the truth."

#### *The Alternative Question*

In my experience, all difficult interrogations lead to the alternative question. This is where your first admission is likely to come. No matter how many times you review your theme or propose stories and frameworks, there will come a time when nothing is left to say. The suspect is nodding along with you. They are on board. But they haven't quite yet committed to jump. You've got to nudge them.

An alternative question is the nudge you need to get the first admission. It juxtaposes a scenario in which the suspect's actions are horrible and a scenario in which the suspect's actions are understandable. In one, they are a monster. In the other, they are just a guy who made a mistake. The alternative question is finished off by a leading question that links them to the more sympathetic scenario. It allows the suspect to admit their guilt with a one word answer: "Yes."

An alternative question has three parts. All three of the parts *must* be present for the question to be effective. 1. Bad scenario. 2. Less bad (but still criminal) scenario. 3. Leading question. The most commonly forgotten component is the leading question. *Do not forget the leading question.*

*The trick to the alternative question is that it does not make explicit the third option, which is, of course, that they didn't do it.*

Then there are patterns the alternative questions follow. The three main alternative question patterns that I use are:

1 Planned Vs. Unplanned
2 X number of times vs Y number of times
3 Monster or Just a Guy Who Made a Mistake

You might ask a murder suspect a Planned Vs. Unplanned alternative:

Is this something you planned out? Like some sort of cold blooded attack? Or is it just something that happened and you wish you could take back. You wish you could take it back right?

You might ask a child abuse suspect X number of times vs Y number of times alternative:

It's obvious that you had sex with her, but I've been bothered by one question since the beginning of this investigation: Is this something you did more than five times? Or was it just the one time? It was just the one time wasn't it?

You might ask a stabbing suspect the Monster or Just a Guy Who Made a Mistake alternative:

Are you some sort of monster that is just gonna stab people every time you get mad? Or are you a guy who just had a bad day and made a mistake? That's what it was, right? A mistake?

Note on this one: a mistake is still criminal. An *accident*, on the other hand, may not be depending on the culpable mental state required for the crime. Keep the word accident out of your alternative question. If possible, keep it out of anything to do with the interrogation.

A common mistake with alternative questions is one that isn't finished by a leading question. A perfect example comes from the interview with Ralph Shortey, an Oklahoma congressman arrested for soliciting sex from a minor.[13]

**Interviewer***:* Well, like I said, we don't think you're a bad guy. We think you made a bad decision. There's a big difference.

*(13 seconds of silence)*

**Shortey***:* I honestly don't know why he would do that.

Here, the interviewers failed to finish their alternative question with a leading question. Their results are similar to other incomplete alternative questions I've seen: nothing happens. There is no guarantee that Shortey would have said anything if they had used the leading question, but my experience says they would have been more likely to succeed. Never forget the leading question.

Timing is important. The alternative question is nearly useless if you ask it at the wrong moment. If you use it too early, the suspect isn't ready. If you use it too late, the suspect may have begun to suspect you aren't nearly as all-knowing as you are letting on.

An example of an alternative question delivered too early came up in one of our training sessions. We had the students role-play an interrogation. One had a child abuse scenario. My student chose the theme of Curiosity and Opportunity. The interrogation went like this:

> Look, I know you touched little Susie. I think maybe it was because of curiosity and opportunity. Are you some sort of monster that enjoys hurting little kids, or are you somebody that made a mistake? You made a mistake didn't you?

I've seen this style of interrogation plenty of times. It mistakes naming a theme for actually developing a theme. It delivers an alternative question way before the person is likely to have accepted the inevitability of their guilt. The bad news is this presentation is almost certain to be unsuccessful. The good news is all of the elements of a good interrogation are present, they just need fleshing out.

The alternative question that comes too late is just as ineffective. This one is harder to gauge than the too-early version. A mind switch of sorts can happen in the room where the person just gets fed up with what you're presenting. They start looking at their watch or checking their messages. They've left the world of the interrogation. They've lost interest. The real life version of this is pursuing a relationship where you never make that last move. You get stuck in the friend zone, and somebody else gets your love interest. Too fast is bad. Too slow is bad.

The *right* time to use an alternative question is when the suspect has stopped denying the allegations. Sometimes they will be very attentive as you describe their criminal actions. You may say, "Obviously you robbed the man" and look up to see them nodding. On the other hand, they may have slumped forward in a posture that reads as being ashamed. In both of these scenarios, the time has come to present the alternative question.

While the alternative question is likely to lead to your first admission, do not expect the suspect to be ready to confess everything immediately. I have seen this dozens of times in the interview room. The detective finishes with their leading question:

*Detective:* That's what happened isn't it?
*Suspect:* Yeah.
*Detective:* Tell me what happened.
*Suspect:* Nothing really.

Generally, open-ended questions are great, but this isn't the time for them. The suspect is just beginning to accept the fact that they are confessing. If you push too hard at this moment, they will shut down. You have to make this part easy for them.

When the suspect makes that first admission, stay calm. Let them know you knew what they just told you all along. You are glad they are telling the truth. Then ask another leading question. Then maybe one more. Now you have two or three admissions. The suspect is on the path towards a full confession. There is no hiding behind a claim they didn't know what they were saying.

At this point, you will be able to ask more and more open-ended questions. During this process, be on the lookout for statements that make it seem as though the suspect is trying to negate the admission that he just made. It may look like this:

*Detective:* Is this something you planned? Or is it just something that kind of happened? It just kind of happened right?

***Suspect:*** Yeah.
***Detective:*** That's what my investigation shows. I believe you. [*This statement locks the suspect in to what they just admitted to*] Did it happen more than five times or less than five times. It was less than five times right? [*Another alternative question instead of an open-ended question*]
***Suspect:*** For sure less than five times. **I hardly remember the one.** [*Another admission followed by an attempt to buy it back. This type of buyback statement is very common when the suspect begins the process of confessing. They seem to regret saying it happened, and they look to take it back. It is critical to lock them into the statement and address any buyback chances*]
***Detective:*** But for sure the once?
***Suspect:*** Yeah.
***Detective:*** Are you sorry for what you did?
***Suspect:*** Yes. Every day.

That's how you use alternative questions. If you find yourself lost at sea in your interrogation, look to see if you've asked the alternative question yet. If not, ask one.

As a final note on alternative questions. You can search YouTube for "alternative question interrogation" and find numerous videos about it being a psychologically manipulative tactic. The contention is innocent people may be tricked into admitting to something they didn't do because they weren't aware of the implicit third option which is, "None of those. I didn't do it."

I'm just a cop, which doesn't qualify me to dispute any of the psychology majors or PhD's that may make such a claim in their lane. Their lane is one of studies and research. I only know how to think about the question in my lane, which is infinitely more practical. Neither the crimes nor the criminals are hypothetical. The person being interviewed knows whether or not they did it.

On a practical level, read the following statements, and say out loud your initial, gut level response. This is not an exercise in being an imagined criminal. You are you. Don't overthink it. Just respond as the person you are, whoever that may be.

1 Look, Jim, did you put your finger in little Susie's vagina more than five times or less than five times? It was less than five times wasn't it?
2 Elise, I know you've been stealing from police equipment for years. Is this something that you planned out? Or is it just something that got out of hand? It just got out of hand didn't it?
3 Robert, there's no doubt you killed that man downtown. For a while, I worried that you were some kind of murderous monster that was going to go on a rampage. But after talking to you, I think you're just a normal guy that made a mistake. It was just a mistake wasn't it?
4 I know you've been cheating on me. Have you had sex with dozens of other people or just one? Please tell me it was just the one.

Is there any one of these scenarios in which you struggled to think of the unstated third option, "None of those. I didn't do it"? I doubt it. Add whatever pressure you want to that situation, you are going to know you didn't finger little Susie, you didn't steal from police equipment, you didn't kill the man downtown, and you didn't cheat on your partner.

Now do the reverse. Try to put yourself in the position of being Jim, Elise, Robert, and the accused cheater in scenarios where they did do these crimes. If you can really imagine those situations, you can imagine that it might indeed be hard to think of the unspoken third option in the moment. You desperately want to be the not so bad person in those scenarios.

That's my practical test for the technique. Is it so tricky that an average person would fall for it? I think not. I think an innocent person easily understands there is the third option of, "I didn't do it." I think the guilty person is left with few options except to save face if possible. That is a technique that I am willing to use.

Note: Any technique used in excess could result badly. Our typical interviews are 2-4 hours. The risk seems minimal in this time frame. The Innocence Project cites that the average length of an interrogation leading to a false confession is 16 hours.[14] I definitely believe a technique used repetitively for 16 hours could result in wearing down an innocent person's defenses. Be reasonable.

## Conclusion to Interrogation

That's how an interrogation goes.

Accuse
Ignore denials
Introduce your theme
Accuse
Storytelling or Frameworks
Accuse
Frameworks or Storytelling
Accuse
Alternative Question

If you're making progress, but they aren't quite ready when that first alternative question comes about, do it again. Progress looks like: subsequent admissions, head nodding, maintained rapport between you and the suspect. You might hear the suspect switch from denials to objections. A denial sounds like, "I didn't do it." An objection sounds like, "I couldn't have robbed him. I don't even own a gun!" Nothing is 100 percent when it comes to humans, but my experience has been a switch from denials to objections is progress.

It's hard to know when a guilty suspect will confess. I've watched interrogations that looked like they were lost when, out of seemingly nowhere, the suspect admits they did it. I've done interrogations where they confess immediately. The most common way for a guilty suspect to confess is a little at a time. A denial turns into, "I don't remember." I don't remember turns into, "Maybe if I was drunk." Maybe if I was drunk turns into, "It was just the once."

There isn't an exact time on how long all of this will take. My standard time for an interview and interrogation is between 3-4 hours. The interview takes about 2/3 as long as the interrogation. I've had interviews and interrogations go as long as 7 and 10 hours, but I am monitoring whether or not I am making progress.

Accusatory interrogations aren't pretty. You are accusing somebody of having committed a crime and you aren't listening to their denials. They are challenging to do well. Then, a few years later, you have the entirely separate pleasure of getting to defend them in court. If you are smart about how you do them, you'll be just fine. Just remember: no threats, promises of leniency, nothing that shocks the conscience.

If you aren't making progress in the interrogation, ask yourself if the suspect might be innocent! There are some indications I watch for that help me decide when it might be the right time to shut it down. Are their denials getting stronger? An example of denials getting stronger is when the interviewee starts out saying, "I didn't rape her" and they progress to saying, "I didn't rape her or anybody else! I've never raped anybody in my life!" Are they getting angry? Are they refusing to budge at all off of "I didn't do it"? If you are stuck after giving it a good try – say 30–45 minutes – consider shutting it down. Either they didn't do it, or they aren't going to come off of it.

Your worth as an interrogator *is not* based on confessions. Your worth as an interrogator is based off of the following criteria:

1 Did you try?
2 Did you conduct the interview and interrogation ethically?
3 Did you improve your case?
4 Did you give the suspect a chance to respond to the evidence against them?
5 Did you treat the suspect well?

The criteria I listed out are things you can achieve every single time. If you achieve those things every single time, you are a success regardless of whether or not the person confesses. Aiming for these criteria instead of only a confession will ensure the statements you do get are solid and defensible.

As with everything in life, you can read about it forever. Reading won't make you good, though. Practice will. Get out there. Get your reps in.

## Summary

This chapter outlines the accusatory nature of interrogations, which are used to challenge a suspect's claims of innocence and seek a court-admissible confession if appropriate. I emphasize the importance of conducting a thorough, non-judgmental interview before moving into interrogation. Key strategies include developing a theme that aligns with the suspect's likely justification for the crime and using techniques like Storytelling and Frameworks to maintain focus and momentum. The chapter also highlights the importance of ethical interrogation practices to prevent false confessions and ensure the integrity of the process.

## Notes

1 Roeloffs, Mary Whitfill. 2024. "Amanda Knox Convicted of Slander in Italy—Here's What We Know." Forbes. June 5, 2024. https://www.forbes.com/sites/maryroeloffs/2024/06/05/amanda-knox-convicted-of-slander-in-italy-what-we-know-about-the-man-she-wrongly-accused-of-murder/?sh=71c6103265db
2 These definitional word games are happening all the time. A presenter I know and like, Larry Braunstein, a lawyer out of New York, talks about how police insist on calling the victim "the victim", but he prefers to call the victim "the complainant." As he points out, complainant has the base word of "complain," which is a word with negative associations. Just as victim and complainant can be correct, so to can interview and interrogation.

3 Probably trademarked.
4 "Guilty until Proven Innocent." n.d. www.youtube.com. https://www.youtube.com/watch?v=BemHqUqcpI8.
5 Justice Potter Stewart in Jacobellis v. Ohio as referenced on Wikipedia Contributors. 2019. "I Know It When I See It." Wikipedia. Wikimedia Foundation. November 14, 2019. https://en.wikipedia.org/wiki/I_know_it_when_I_see_it.
6 Split across multiple videos but as viewed on Rd Circle Interrogation YouTube channel including this one Red Circle Interrogations and Confessions. 2020. "Michael Rafferty - Police Interrogation - Part 4 - the Murder of Tori Stafford." YouTube. June 25, 2020. https://www.youtube.com/watch?v=NA6VIrdKMNI
7 Kassin, Saul, *Duped: Why Innocent People Confess – and Why We Believe Their Confessions* (Blue Ridge Summit: Prometheus, 2022), 353.
8 The Innocence Project. 2024. "False Confessions." Innocence Project. 2024. https://innocenceproject.org/false-confessions/.
9 Discussed in detail later in this chapter.
10 As recorded in my notes from his presentation at the August 2023 Crimes Against Children Conference.
11 The Cappening Channel. 2016. "Music Professor Caught on to Catch a Predator James Rauch (Audio Boost!)." YouTube. August 14, 2016. https://www.youtube.com/watch?v=nuX6kgww1Is
12 James, A, Taylor Girtman, Jala Washington, and Mercedez Hernandez. 2023. "2 Arrested after Gun Goes off inside Man's Pocket in 6th Street Bar, Affidavit Says." KXAN Austin. July 24, 2023. https://www.kxan.com/news/local/austin/2-arrested-after-gun-goes-off-inside-austin-6th-street-bar/
13 KOCO 5 News, "Watch: Moore Police Interrogate Former State Sen. Ralph Shortey."
14 Innocence Project, "False Confessions."

## References

"Guilty until Proven Innocent." n.d. www.youtube.com. https://www.youtube.com/watch?v=BemHqUqcpI8

"I Know It When I See It." Wikipedia. Wikimedia Foundation. November 14, 2019. https://en.wikipedia.org/wiki/I_know_it_when_I_see_it

James, A, Taylor Girtman, Jala Washington, and Mercedez Hernandez. 2023. "2 Arrested after Gun Goes off inside Man's Pocket in 6th Street Bar, Affidavit Says." KXAN Austin. July 24, 2023. https://www.kxan.com/news/local/austin/2-arrested-after-gun-goes-off-inside-austin-6th-street-bar/

Kassin, Saul. 2022. *Duped: Why Innocent People Confess – and Why We Believe Their Confessions*. Blue Ridge Summit: Prometheus.

News, KOCO 5. 2018. "Watch: Moore Police Interrogate Former State Sen. Ralph Shortey after Being Found in Motel with Teen." YouTube Video. *YouTube*. https://www.youtube.com/watch?v=WJQ6_khlxnc

Red Circle Interrogations and Confessions. 2020. "Michael Rafferty - Police Interrogation - Part 4 - the Murder of Tori Stafford." YouTube. June 25, 2020. https://www.youtube.com/watch?v=NA6VIrdKMNI

Roeloffs, Mary Whitfill. 2024. "Amanda Knox Convicted of Slander in Italy—Here's What We Know." Forbes. June 5, 2024. https://www.forbes.com/sites/maryroeloffs/2024/06/05/amanda-knox-convicted-of-slander-in-italy-what-we-know-about-the-man-she-wrongly-accused-of-murder/?sh=71c6103265db

The Cappening Channel. 2016. "Music Professor Caught on to Catch a Predator James Rauch (Audio Boost!)." YouTube. August 14, 2016. https://www.youtube.com/watch?v=nuX6kgww1Is

The Innocence Project. 2024. "False Confessions." Innocence Project. 2024. https://innocenceproject.org/false-confessions/

Chapter 11

# Scenario-Based Case Studies

It's time to bring all of these concepts together. In these four scenarios, I walk you through exactly what I'm thinking as I process the information. I provide a step by step guide on how to come up with questions, think about evidence, interview, and interrogate. I hope these very specific examples provide insight into how you can work on your own cases.

## The Scenarios

The following scenarios will provide a chance to apply what we have discussed so far in the book.

### *Scenario 1: Robbery*

On Saturday, June 20th, the police received a call from Loretta Hawkins. Loretta reported she was walking by Moose's Tavern at 7 pm that night when two men robbed her. Loretta provided descriptions of the suspects. She described one of them as a white male (WM), approximately 5′11″ with a beard and a white t-shirt. The WM's t-shirt had a cartoon logo of some sort on it. The other male had a darker skin complexion, but she couldn't say what race he was. He had yellow shoes and mostly dark clothes.

Loretta said the WM pointed a gray handgun at her and demanded her purse. When she handed the WM the purse, he handed it to the other male. The WM then hit her across the head with his gun. Loretta stumbled to the ground. The two men ran away. Loretta reported that she had her phone and wallet in her purse. Her wallet contained various cards including a credit card.

While one officer spoke with Loretta, another canvassed the area for video. At Joe's Sandwich Shop, which is across the street from Moose's Tavern, the officer found a video camera pointed right where Loretta was robbed. On reviewing the camera feed, the officer was able to locate video of the robbery. The video showed two men get in front of Loretta. The WM yelled and pointed at Loretta and then took her purse. Due to the angle, no gun could be seen. The officer recorded the video for the detective.

The following day, police responded to a fraud call at the local mall. A man went into the shoe store to buy some new sneakers. The shoe store ran his card, and they got an alert saying the card was stolen. Police arrived, and they detained Javier Pozos, the man who provided the card to the cashier. On follow up, they found that Javier had provided Loretta Hawkins' credit card and Loretta had been the victim of a robbery the day before.

DOI: 10.4324/9781003663904-12

When officers contacted the detective, the detective asked what color shoes Javier was wearing. The officers reported that he was wearing yellow shoes. They then described Javier to the detective, and the detective found he matched the general (though vague) description of the second suspect in the robbery from the night before. The detective, suspecting that Javier was the second man who robbed Loretta the night before, authorized placing him under arrest for some warrants he had. The detective then asked the officers to bring Javier to the police station for questioning.

*Overview*

How many of you have decided that Javier robbed Loretta? He probably did, but I'd like to challenge you to approach scenarios like these with a more open mind. One of the things that leads to false confessions is the formation of conclusions which are never questioned. "Too often, however, police make a snap judgment based on an interview and a hunch."[1] Let's start our preparation for this interview by questioning what we "know."

Loretta told officers two men robbed her. This might be true, but sometimes victims are less than pure. Victims are on a sliding scale from pure victim to malicious liar. Police are often biased in favor of whichever person approaches them first. My experience has been most people complaining of victimization are telling the truth, but a little bit of caution goes a long way here because some lie. *Testing what you think you know makes your conclusions stronger not weaker.*

Officers found video of two men confronting her and taking a purse she had, but the officers didn't see either pointing a gun at her. Is it possible Loretta owes these guys money? Maybe *she* stole the purse from one of *their* friends and they were just getting it back. Javier was found using Loretta's credit card. Maybe Loretta found her wallet, didn't report it to police, and let her boyfriend Javier use it.

Some of these alternate scenarios stretch what we think is likely. That's ok. It's usually very easy to deal with them and dismiss them. Once you do that, you'll be left with the robbery just how Loretta described it. For example, in the last alternate theory, I pointed out maybe Javier had Loretta's permission to use her card.

*If*: Javier had Loretta's permission to use her credit card

*Then*: Javier knows Loretta somehow. Loretta gave him permission at some time. Loretta communicated this permission to him somehow.

*Therefore*: How do you know Loretta? When did she give you permission to use her card? How did she give you permission to use her card (witnesses / method)?

Or having to do with the possibility that Loretta stole their friend's purse and they were just getting it back:

*If*: They were just getting their friend's purse back.

*Then*: Their friend's purse was stolen. It was stolen somehow. It was stolen somewhere. It was stolen by someone. They noticed it at some time. They linked it's theft to Loretta.

*Therefore*: Who is your friend that had her purse stolen? When was your friend's purse stolen? How was it stolen? Where was she when it was stolen? When did she notice it was stolen? What made you think Loretta had your friend's purse? Did you report the theft?

There are a lot of benefits to testing your theories. I'll point out two. First, if Javier is innocent, this sort of exploration into the topic will provide him the space to proclaim his innocence and provide evidence. Second, if Javier is guilty (and he chooses to talk) he will probably claim something like one of these alternate theories. In that case, you'll have your questions ready.

What is Javier's situation when officers bring him to the detective for questioning? Is he under arrest? Yes. If he is being forced from the store to the police station, he is under arrest. It is a common misconception that police can "detain" a person suspected of a serious crime and transport them in handcuffs to the police station. This is not the case. Except for a safety situation (such as moving a suspected drunk driver from the side of the road to a safe parking lot for testing) your detention does not allow you to remove suspects from scenes no matter how serious the crime is under investigation. In this case, the detective has authorized Javier's arrest for a warrant.

Since Javier is in custody, you will read him his Miranda warning.

While officers are en route, think about designating a second detective to greet the officers and settle Javier in the room so that you can work.

Start thinking about evidence with the SUE technique.

*SUE Step One*: Analyze and rate your evidence. We have Javier using Loretta's cards listed as stolen and a video showing somebody generally consistent with Javier's description participating in confronting her and taking her purse. In terms of SUE, I'd recommend using the credit cards but avoiding the video. The video doesn't definitively show Javier but rather a person matching Javier's description. The video would be a good bait question, i.e. "Is there any reason you'd be on a video recording yesterday…"

*SUE Step One Continued*: Think of alternate explanations for the evidence. Maybe Loretta gave him permission (discussed above). Maybe he found the card.

*SUE Step Two*: Contact the suspect. This has been handled by patrol.

*SUE Step Three*: Give the suspect a chance to volunteer the information. This will happen during the interview after introductions, custodial issues, and rapport building. The questioning should go from very open to very specific, focusing on the robbery the day before.

You might start with: "In as much detail as possible, tell me about your activities from midday yesterday until you were arrested by police at the mall today." Listen to his account. Ask follow up questions. Look for ways to either corroborate or disprove his statement. The robbery happened at 7pm. Focus on that time of day. Have him list everywhere he was and everybody he was with. Finally, if he has neglected to mention that he was at Moose's Tavern and in contact with Loretta Hawkins, ask him directly, "Were you at Moose's Tavern?" "Did you have any arguments or conflicts with other people?" "Were you involved in taking anything from another person?" Of course, you'll ask questions about his association with Loretta and any sort of found property he may have come across. "Do you know Loretta Hawkins?" "Have you found anything that doesn't belong to you recently?"

*SUE Step Four*: Here is where you will lay out the evidence. SUE step four happens in three moves going from vague to specific.

*Step Four, Move One*: "I have some evidence you were involved in the robbery yesterday. Please tell me about that." Whatever he says, follow up on it. There is no rush to move to the more specific move two. This step is where you start learning information you didn't know going into it. It introduces a mind virus of sorts in the guilty person's mind. Did the other guy turn on him? Is there video evidence? Did the woman pick him out of the lineup? Maybe he tells you about a new alibi or adds information about his whereabouts. Ask questions.

*Step Four, Move Two*: "In fact, I have evidence you were in possession of Loretta's stolen property after the robbery. Please explain that." Here, you may find he suddenly remembers finding the credit card on the ground or a friend giving him the card. Whatever he brings up, ask questions about it.

*Step Four, Move Three*: "The thing is, you were using Loretta's stolen credit card at the mall the day after she was robbed. Please explain this." Now you've shown your cards. They may relent and tell you all about it, or they may stay stuck on the lie. My experience with using SUE has been that moves one and two on step four yield the most new information. If they make it to move three without giving it up, they are probably going to stay stuck on "I don't know."

By now, Javier is probably seated in the interview room. You've planned out your SUE technique questions. Now go ahead and type out your questions. My document might look like this:

Case: 23-XXXXXXX
Incident: Robbery
Victim: Loretta Hawkins
Suspcct: Javicr Pozos
Date / Time / Location: (Date), 7pm, in front of Moose's Tavern

## BIO Data / General Questions

- Name
- Identification type
- Physical address
- Phone number
- Email Address
- Work
- Vehicle
- Who do you live with?
- Who do you most often associate with?
- Are you in a relationship with anyone?
- How do you know Loretta Hawkins?
- What types of stressors do you have now? Money issues?
- Describe your usage of drugs and alcohol.
- What health conditions do you have?

## Case Data

- In as much detail as possible, tell me about your activities from midday yesterday until you were arrested by police at the mall today.
- Who have you spent time with?
- Were you with another guy yesterday?

- Tell me about him.
- Did anything unusual happen?
- Any problems with other people?
- Any misunderstandings?
- Let's focus in on the hours of 5 pm–9 pm yesterday. Please tell me all about that time period.
- Did anybody give you anything?
- Were you at Moose's Tavern?
- How did you get around yesterday? Car? Other people? Uber? Etc.
- Tell me about today.
- Tell me about getting arrested. What was happening just before?

## SUE

1. I have some evidence you were involved in the robbery yesterday. Please tell me about that.
2. In fact, I have evidence you were in possession of the victim's stolen property after the robbery. Please explain that.
3. The thing is, you were using Loretta's stolen credit card at the mall the day after she was robbed. Please explain this.

This is a pretty good question list. The list is not intended to be a rigid dictation of exactly what to say and in what order. Rather, the question list helps you get back on track if you get lost in the interview. Interviews can go so many different directions. You'll want to follow the natural flow of conversation. Use continuers – "Go on" "And then?" – reflections and summations to keep the suspect's response to open-ended questions going. Remember that open-ended questions keep the suspect talking. Closed / direct questions force you to do more talking and limit what you learn.

You'll also want to think about possible themes should you choose to do an accusatory interrogation. Your best themes come from the suspect themselves. If they did it, they've justified it somehow so it seems rational and acceptable to them. You're likely to hear hints of what that justification is when you interview the guilty suspect. However, it's good to think of a theme in the event that you miss the justification. This theme operates as a sort of theory. It is not set in stone so be willing to trash it.[2]

The first one that comes to mind on this one is, The Other Guy Took it Too Far. If you get to the end of the interview with Javier, and you decide that his guilt is reasonably certain, then put the unidentified suspect in the driver's seat. You didn't plan this Javier. You didn't go downtown trying to rob somebody. You were with your homeboy, he decided to hit a lick, and you didn't stop him. You were wrong to take her purse, and you were wrong to use her card, but it never would have happened except the other guy took it too far.

With this done, you'd be ready to step into the interview room and get started. Once you do this a few times, this whole process could take as little as 15 minutes or so. If you investigate serious criminal offenses, that is time well spent.

My approach to Javier would go something like this:

*Greeting / Pre-Miranda Monologue*

*DL:* (enters room) Hello. Javier? I'm Darrel Lambert, a senior detective here. (Shake hands) Here's a bottle of water for you (hand water). I'm glad we are going to have a chance to talk today. I'm sure you have some questions about what's going on. That's a good thing. I have some questions too. This isn't how I would have chosen to have the conversation, but here we are. Those patrol officers put you under arrest for some warrants. I can't undo those warrants. It is true that whatever we talk about here today, you'll have to go to jail after. That's out of my control.

The reason I had those officers bring you in, though, is because your name came up in an investigation having to do with a woman who had her purse taken from her yesterday evening. That's an investigation I do have some control over. I'll be straight with you, I have some evidence that links you to the case. I want to show you that evidence. If you choose to talk to me today, we'll go over all of it. I want you to tell me if I'm looking at it wrong or if there is some other explanation. If you had something to do with that incident, I want to understand why. On the other hand, if you didn't have anything to do with that incident, I'm hoping you can help point me to some evidence you weren't involved.

My job is to find the truth. Although your name came up in the investigation, if you didn't have anything to do with it, my job, then, is to prove that. If there is evidence or there are witnesses I need to talk to, just point me in the direction, and I'll go look for them.

While we talk today, if you need water or coffee, I'll get those things for you. If you need to use the bathroom, I'll show you where those things are. I promise to listen to you and to treat you with respect.

Before we talk, I want to make sure you understand your rights. (Read Miranda warning).

Assuming Javier agrees to talk with you, there will be a period of gathering basic information and building rapport. I'll usually transition out of the Miranda warnings by gathering some obvious details. Confirm the spelling of your name. Confirm your address. What's the best telephone number for you?

Then I'll say something like this, "I've heard quite a bit about you from reports and other sources, but I don't know you. I find it's easier to be fair to people we know. With that in mind, before we get started, tell me about yourself so I can get to know you better."

A common complaint from robbery and aggravated assault detectives is, "That kind of stuff doesn't work with our guys. They're hardened crooks!" I disagree. I've used these kinds of rapport prompts on murderers, shooters, rapists, and everybody in between. Almost everybody will share information about themselves. I don't care what their rap sheet looks like or how many face tattoos they have. Do not skip rapport building. We talk to people we like. We resist people we do not like. *The quality of your connection with the suspect will largely determine how good your interview is.*

I want to focus in on gathering the suspect's story because the questioning process is often misunderstood. Once you gather biographical data and establish good rapport with your suspect, you will transition into the questioning. In Javier's case, you have an initial prompt planned out. Let's look at how that might unfold.

***Detective:*** In as much detail as possible, tell me about your activities from midday yesterday until you were arrested by police at the mall today. [*Question*]

***Javier:*** What do you want to know?
***Detective:*** Everything that happened.
***Javier:*** Ok, well yesterday. Let's see. I woke up around 10 am. I've been separated from my wife for a while. I've been sleeping in cheap hotels. The night before last I was at the Motel 6. I goofed around in the hotel room. I skipped lunch to save money. At one point, I met up with some friends to hang out. Drank some beer. Had an argument with one friend, and I left. I came back to the hotel. Then today? I woke up, and I came to the mall. That's about it.
***Detective:*** What else? [*Encourager*]
***Javier:*** Not much else to say. I spent some time between yesterday and today trying to figure out other places to live. I'm tired of cheap motels.
***Detective:*** Other places to live? [*Reflection*]
***Javier:*** Yeah. Like I said, my wife and I are separated. It's so expensive to live these days. I'm thinking about saving money by camping outside until I can get settled.
***Detective:*** So I heard you say that yesterday you woke up at 10 am. You skipped lunch. You met up with some friends. You drank some beer, had an argument, and left. Today you woke up and went to the mall. You've spent some time looking for a new place to live. Did I get that right? [*Summarize*]
***Javier:*** Yeah.
***Detective:*** Ok, I'd like to redirect your attention to yesterday. You said you met up with some friends, tell me more about that. [*Redirect / Focus*]
***Javier:*** We usually meet up downtown. Its a small group of guys. Usually Jeff, Bill, and Damian. We hang out. Shoot pool. Stuff like that.
***Detective:*** Uh huh. [*Encourager*]
***Javier:*** Bill and Damian skipped out yesterday so it was just Jeff and another guy that I hadn't met before.
***Detective:*** Another guy? [*Reflection*]
***Javier:*** Yeah he was Jeff's friend. Like I said, I don't know him.
***Detective:*** Could you describe him?
***Javier:*** (description)
***Detective:*** You said you usually meet up downtown. What did you do yesterday?
***Javier:*** We met up at Moose's around 5 pm.
***Detective:*** Tell me about being at Moose's. [*Open-ended question*]
***Javier:*** It was normal. Me, Jeff, and the other guy watched football and drank beer. We shot some pool. There wasn't any problems.
***Detective:*** You said earlier you had an argument with a friend but you also said that there wasn't any problems, help me understand. [*Nonjudgmental confrontation*]
***Javier:*** Me and Jeff didn't have any problems but that other guy, yeah. He wanted to hit a lick, and I didn't want any trouble. We argued, and I left.
***Detective:*** Hit a lick? [*Reflection*]

This would be a good interview pattern. It allows Javier plenty of space to talk and answer questions. A good interview division is 80% him talking and 20% you. Using open-ended questions, encouragers, and reflections helps to accomplish that. You'll notice there aren't any closed questions. A closed question is one that can be answered in one or two words. For example, "Were you with Jeff?" Or "What time did you get there?" Most interviewers default to closed questions. Closed questions should be the very last resort after you have provided lots of open question opportunities to answer.

As you reach the end of your interview, you will have given Javier lots of opportunities to bring up his excuses for why he had Loretta's credit card. If he hasn't taken those opportunities to explain himself, it will be time to present your evidence. The SUE presentation should take place toward the end of your interview and before any sort of accusatory interrogation (should you choose to use that method). Present the evidence using the steps you've already planned.

If you finish the interview and still think it is more likely than not Javier was part of the robbery, you may choose to confront Javier in an accusatory interrogation. My readers in Europe and Canada won't be able to go along with this part. Those areas have moved away from accusatory interviews entirely. They will have plenty to gain from the other portions of preparation for this interview, but this next part is for investigators that still work in places using accusatory interrogations.

*Initial Confrontation*: Javier, I'm glad we had the chance to talk today. I have quite a bit of evidence in this case. I wanted to make sure you had the opportunity to respond to that evidence. At the end of the day, it's clear to me you were in fact involved in the robbery in front of Moose's Tavern yesterday. I expect this case to get stronger as more evidence comes in. I want you to know that I'm not judging you for that at all. What you did was wrong, but I don't think it ever would have happened except for the fact The Other Guy Took it Too Far.

That friend of Jeff's wanted to hit a lick, and he did. What you didn't count on was him including you in his plan. The evidence shows that he was the leader. He was the one who had the gun, but afterwards, he handed you the purse. Instead of reporting him, you figured you were in too deep. You decided to get something for yourself out of it too. That's where you went wrong.

*Storytelling*: I've been in situations like yours where things have gone too far. I remember being a kid and setting off fireworks in my backyard. It was supposed to be just a couple of bottle rockets. My friend wanted to go bigger. He started setting off black cats and roman candles and mortar shells. It turned into a real show. Next thing I knew, I was dropping a mortar shell into the tube as the cop's flashlight lit up my face. My friend must have heard the cop coming because he was nowhere to be found. He left me holding the bag.

*Accuse*: That's what's happened to you here, too. Jeff's friend has literally left you holding the bag. You took that purse and you used her credit cards. Where is Jeff's friend? The guy that had the plan? He's not here, and I bet he'll point the finger at you when I do talk to him.

*Framework*: The truth sounds like the truth Javier, and what you've told me today doesn't sound like the truth. I'm just one person, but I've worked with my bosses long enough to know when I tell them your story, they aren't going to believe you either. I think as we spend time in this room together, it becomes you and me. Sometimes the people I talk to in here think I'm the guy they are up against. They think they need to convince me and that's it. That isn't the case. I work in a team. My bosses look at what I do. My coworkers look at it. The courts look at it. I've worked with those people long enough. I know not a single one of them is going to hear this and think, "He's telling the truth."

*Accuse*: When you took her purse from Jeff's friend, it was wrong. When you used the lady's credit card, it was wrong again. All those things are true, but there's more to talk about.

*Framework*: When you do something wrong and you lie about it, it's like you're holding that thing close. When I'm looking at the bad thing, I'm looking right at you. When you tell the truth about it, though, it's like you set it down on the ground. When you do that, then you and I can stand shoulder to shoulder and look at the bad thing. We can both agree that the thing is bad. Now when I'm looking at you, I'm looking at a person. A person flawed like anybody else, but a person trying to make it right. That's what I want to see. And that's what I want others to see too.

*Alternative Question*: When you took that purse from Jeff's friend, I don't think it was something you had planned. I think it was something that just happened. It just happened didn't it?

### *Scenario 2: Aggravated Assault*

At about 3 am on February 12th, the Main Street Hospital called to report that they had a stabbing victim in their emergency room. He was preparing to go into surgery. When officers arrived, they found Marshall Boynton on a stretcher. He had deep gash wounds to his abdomen and chest. Marshall told officers he had been at Pearl's Dance Hall until about 1 am, when he left. Outside, in the parking lot, he was approached by a woman in a red dress. He didn't remember how it started, but they were kissing and then, next thing he knew, the woman was cutting him. He fought her off, landing a hard punch to her eye. He saw the woman get into a silver sedan with the first three of the license plate being DXB. Then Marshall got in his car, and he drove himself to the hospital. The officers didn't have time to ask more before Marshall was wheeled into surgery. They noticed a strong odor of alcohol coming from him as he spoke.

Officers knew Pearl's drew a rough crowd. Their plain clothes team regularly made prostitution arrests there. A search of police records showed plain clothes officers arrested an Angelique Kelly in a silver Mazda with the license plate DXB5093 just two weeks prior at Pearl's Dance Hall.

When they drove to the scene, the manager of Pearl's refused to release any video without a subpoena or a warrant. He did admit, however, he saw Angelique Kelly in the bar the night of February 12th. He saw her wearing a red dress. He remembered her because she used to work for him as a bartender.

Police present Marshall with a photo lineup once he is out of surgery. He picks Angelique Kelly out of the lineup with an 80% certainty.

Police drove to Angelique's last known address, but she no longer lived there. The detective put out a BOLO on Angelique and her vehicle. About a month later, she was stopped by patrol officers. Angelique agreed to come in for an interview with the detective.

#### *Overview*

In this scenario, we have a date and an approximate time of occurrence. Although a month has passed between the stabbing and the potential suspect coming in for questioning, there is good reason to believe she would remember where she was on a day a month before.

We have a drinking establishment with a rough crowd. Marshall may not be the most sympathetic character. We know he was drinking. We know he was getting on well enough with the woman in the parking lot that they were kissing one another. Something changed that led to him getting stabbed. A little bit of experience investigating matters like these will suggest two likely scenarios: either he became aggressive with her in a sexual sense or she was setting him up for a robbery. There are other possibilities, but these are the most likely.

If Marshall became aggressive with Angelique, she would have a plausible claim of self defense. This might be true, and we will want to know more about that. If, however, Angelique is the criminal in this scenario, you could expect her to claim self defense. The problem for her, though, is to claim self defense, she has to admit to being on scene and in contact with the victim. If she denies being on scene and in contact with the suspect during her initial statement, it will be impossible to go back and claim self defense later.

#### *Custodial Issues*

In this scenario, Angelique is not under arrest. She has been invited in to make a statement. This is a non-custodial interview. You do not have to read her Miranda warnings, but you will need to advise her that she is free to go. You need to let her know that you will meet her biological needs (water, bathroom breaks etc).

#### *SUE*

*SUE Step One: Analyze and rate your evidence.* The manager of the bar has refused to release video, which probably would have been your best evidence. Marshall said he didn't know the woman who stabbed him, but he picked her out of a lineup. Although he picked her out of a lineup, he was only 80% certain. Your second piece of evidence is the bar manager's statement. Despite not being helpful with the video, he admitted Angelique Kelly was at the scene on the night in question wearing a red dress. As far as rating the evidence, both are pretty good but with different strengths. The photo lineup is pretty good evidence for Angelique being the suspect (strengthened by the license plate return), and the other is very good evidence for Angelique being at Pearl's.

*SUE Step One, continued: Think of alternate explanations for the evidence.* Here we are focused on the bar manager identifying Angelique and saying that she was there that night. It's possible the manager is lying. If he is lying, why? Is there some sort of bad blood / negative interaction? Maybe he is covering up for somebody else. If so, who? Maybe he just agreed to whatever name the police said to get them out of the bar. Maybe he was mistaken and it wasn't actually Angelique. Maybe Angelique was there, but she left before Marshall left or never had any interaction with him at all. February 12th is just a few days before Valentine's Day. There may have been a lot of women in red dresses that night.

As to the photo lineup, the main alternate explanation is Marshall is mistaken.

For all of these alternate theories, make questions to address them. Put these questions on your question sheet. You'll see that I did so below.

*SUE Step Two*: This is where you contact the suspect. This has been handled by patrol.

*SUE Step Three*: Give the suspect a chance to volunteer the information. This will happen during the interview after introductions, custodial issues, and rapport building. The questioning should go from very open to very specific, focusing on Angelique's association with the bar, the bar manager, and her whereabouts on February 12th.

During the interview, you'll probably want to give Angelique the opportunity to bring up working at Pearl's Dance Hall. Ask her about where she works. Ask her about where she has worked in the past. This might come up during rapport building and background.

Move the conversation towards where Angelique hangs out. If she isn't volunteering a discussion of Pearl's Dance Hall, you may have to ask her directly, "Do you ever go to Pearl's?" You always want to give the interviewee the chance to volunteer information before asking them directly. You might want to ask, "In the past two months, have you gone to Pearl's?"

Explore other topics that will give Angelique an opportunity to volunteer being at Pearl's and in a disturbance. Remember, if she is going to claim self-defense, she is going to have to put herself on scene and in contact with Marshall. "In the past few months, have you been involved in any fights?" "In the past few months have you physically hurt another person?" "Have you been threatened or intimidated at all recently?" You can be creative in how you ask the question, but you are looking to see if she will bring up the disturbance at Pearl's. Ultimately, you'll ask her if she used a knife against anybody on the night of February 12th.

If Angelique doesn't volunteer her association with Pearl's, you'll gather her statement as to her activities on February 12th. "Angelique, I'd like to direct your attention back to February 12th. That would be two days before Valentine's day. What can you tell me about that day?" If you need to let her check her phone or do something else to refresh her memory, do it. Once she is talking about February 12th, prompt her, "In as much detail as possible, without leaving anything out, tell me about that day."

If Angelique admits to being at Pearl's but denies hurting anyone or being hurt herself, gather a detailed description of her activities that night. You won't need to go to step four (evidence presentation) with the bar manager's statement about her, but you will go to step four with the evidence she was involved in an altercation.

*SUE Step Four*: Here is where you will lay out the evidence. SUE step four happens in three moves going from vague to specific.

*Step Four, Move One (bar manager)*: "Angelique, I have some evidence you were at Pearl's on February 12th. Can you please tell me about why that might be." Whatever she says, follow the conversation.

*Step Four, Move Two (bar manager)*: In fact, I have an eyewitness who puts you on scene and in the bar on the night of February 12th. This eyewitness is a person who knows you. Can you tell me why that is?

*Step Four, Move Three (bar manager)*: In fact the bar manager, your former employer told us you were at Pearl's that night and he is sure of it. Can you explain that?

*Step Four, Move One (photo lineup)*: I have evidence you were involved in attacking a man that night. Please explain that.

*Step Four, Move Two (photo lineup)*: I have an eyewitness who has made a sworn statement saying you stabbed a person that night. Tell me about that.

*Step Four, Move Three (photo lineup)*: The stabbing victim identified you as the person who stabbed them. Why?

*Preparation*

Now is the time to make your question list for Angelique. My document would look something like this:

Case: 24-XXXXXXX
Incident: Stabbing at Pearl's
Victim: Marshall Boynton
Alleged Perpetrator (AP): Angelique Kelly
Date / Time / Location:

**Bio data**

- Name
- Identification type
- Physical address
- Phone number
- Email address

**General questions / anticipatory questions**

- Work
- Prior work experience
  - Ever work for any bars or dance halls
- What sources of income?
- Previous bosses
  - Any problems with previous bosses?
- Relationships
- Vehicle
  - Anybody else ever use your vehicle?
  - If so, who and when?
- Hangouts
  - Ever go to bars? If so, which ones? Any others?
- Alcohol and drug use. Any addictions?
- Recent injuries
  - How received? How treated? Did any of them create police reports?
- Recent altercations
  - Who with? Why? How did they resolve? Did anybody get hurt?

**Case data**

- Please tell me about your connection with Pearl's Dance Hall.
- Last visit there?

- (If she says she hasn't been) Would anybody say you've been to Pearl's in the last few months?
- In as much detail as possible, tell me about your activities on February 12th from beginning to end without leaving anything out." What helps you remember?
- (If denies being at Pearl's) Alibi Witnesses. How to prove?
- Please tell me about anybody you had more than casual contact with.
- On February 12th, did you kiss anybody at Pearl's? Hook up?
- Did anybody try to kiss or hook up with you?
- Did you do anything to injure anyone that night?
- Did you cut or stab a man in the parking lot?

## SUE

(If she denies being at Pearl's)

### Bar manager

1. Angelique, I have some evidence that you were at Pearl's on February 12th. Can you please tell me about why that might be.
2. In fact, I have an eyewitness who put you on scene and in the bar on the night of February 12th. This eyewitness is a person who knows you. Can you tell me why that is?
3. In fact the bar manager, your former employer told us you were at Pearl's that night and he is sure of it. Can you explain that?

(If she denies being in an altercation at Pearl's)

### Photo lineup

1. I have evidence you were involved in stabbing a man that night. Please explain that.
2. I have an eyewitness who has made a sworn statement saying you stabbed a person that night. Tell me about that.
3. The stabbing victim identified you as the person that stabbed them. Why?

This is a pretty good question list. The list is not intended to be a rigid dictation of exactly what to say and in what order. Rather, the question list helps you get back on track if you get lost in the interview. Interviews can go so many different directions. You'll want to follow the natural flow of conversation. Use continuers – "Go on" "And then?" – reflections and summations to keep the suspect's response to open-ended questions going. Remember open-ended questions keep the suspect talking. Closed / direct questions force you to do more talking and limit what you learn.

You'll also want to think about possible themes should you choose to do an accusatory interrogation. Your best themes come from the suspect themselves. If they did it, they've justified it somehow so it seems rational and acceptable to them. You're likely to hear hints of what that justification is when you interview the guilty suspect. However, it's good to think of a theme in the event that you miss the justification. This theme operates as a sort of theory. It is not set in stone so be willing to trash it.

In all cases, and particularly in a case like this, you have to be careful to choose a theme that morally excuses them without criminally excusing them. For example, if you said, "Angelique, I think he was trying to attack you and you defended yourself." You would have criminally excused them by giving them a self-defense argument. In my experience, once a suspect finds safe ground like an excuse that will be a solid legal defense, it is nearly impossible to advance the conversation further.

> I want to stress that Angelique might be innocent! When I write about interrogating her, I'm assuming you have interviewed her first. When we give the interviewee chances to bring up situations, it isn't just some elaborate ruse to catch her lying. It may catch her lying, but, importantly, it may give her the chance to tell the truth in a way we hadn't thought of before. For example, it was February 12th, days before Valentine's Day. Most of the women in the bar were probably wearing red. What if Marshall was stabbed by a different woman in red then saw Angelique (not the suspect) get into her car and assumed it was her? With the fact pattern we have, Angelique probably did it, but it is certainly not an open and shut case. We need to be open to the real possibility she didn't do it.

What are some ways we might be able to minimize the seriousness of the crime? Assuming it was robbery, some possible themes are: blaming a drug addiction,[3] blaming the victim, or blaming poverty. Remember, with themes, we just need a better explanation for why something happened; it doesn't have to be the truth. If Angelique robbed Marshall, she probably did it because she was greedy. Being greedy isn't easy to admit to, though.

In fact, most people will have rationalized their wrongdoing in some way already. Your goal is to guess what that rationalization might be and build a theme around that. You'll enter into the interview with a hypothesis and then test that in the room. If for example, you guessed drug addiction would be the best explanation, you would ask questions during the interview related to drug usage. If the person admits to having a problem with drugs, this may be a good theme. If, on the other hand, they deny ever having used drugs, you'll need to come up with another theme (obviously). During the interview, listen for what the person says in order to modify your theme. Since we don't have the input as to what Angelique thinks is important in this hypothetical, we'll select drug addiction as the theme.

With this done, you'd be ready to step into the interview room and get started. Once you do this a few times, this whole process could take as little as 15 minutes or so. If you investigate serious criminal offenses, that is time well spent.

My approach to Angelique would go something like this:

*DL:* (enters room) Hello. Angelique? I'm Darrel Lambert, a senior detective here. (Shake hands) Here's a bottle of water for you (hand her water). I'm glad we have the chance to talk today. [*Custodial Issues*] Thanks for coming in today. I want to make sure you understand that you are not under arrest. At any time you want to leave, the door is open. You can open the door, walk out to your left and head into the lobby. We are here because your name came up in a criminal investigation as possibly being involved, but I have not made any final decisions in the case. At any time you want to use the restroom, just say so, and I'll show you where it is. If you want water or coffee, let me know, and I'll bring them to you. If you are done talking at any point, you don't need my permission to leave. Just head on out and do what you need to do. Does all of that make sense to you? Do you have any questions?

*Angelique:* I understand all that, but what's this about?

*DL:* It's about a fella who got hurt at a bar last month. I want to get into that, but before we do can I say a few more things?

*Angelique:* Ok.

*DL:* Thanks! I want to tell you a little bit about myself. I've been an officer for over 18 years. I've investigated everything ranging from simple assaults up to and including murder. One thing I've learned is to listen without judgment. If we talk about any subject that is embarrassing for you, just know that I won't judge you for it. It's important we talk about true things, even if we find them embarrassing.

I've heard quite a bit about you from reports and other sources, but I don't know you. I find it's easier to be fair to people we know. With that in mind, before we get started, tell me about yourself so I can get to know you better [*Rapport*].

*DL:* Thank you for helping me get to know you. I know you're anxious to hear more about why we are here today. I want to share as much as I can with you. Sometimes I keep things back because it helps me make sure the things we talk about are true. If I tell you everything I know, and you just tell me those things back, how can I know if it's true or not? In fact, there are some questions I'll ask you that I already know the answer to. The reason I ask those questions is to make sure you are telling the truth. Do you promise to tell me the truth today? [*Your first behavior provoking question. Watch and listen carefully.*]

*Angelique:* Yes.

*DL:* I told you before we were here because of a man who was hurt at a bar about a month ago. What can you tell me about that? [*The first real question of the interview.*]

*Angelique:* I don't know anything about a man getting hurt at a bar. Why would I?

*DL:* Ok. I hear that you don't know anything about a man getting hurt at a bar. Let's talk a little about your situation.

[*A period of questions from the list about work, relationships, drug usage, familiarity with Pearl's etc.*]

*DL:* Directing your attention back to February 12th of this year. Please tell me all about your activities that day from beginning to end without leaving anything out.

*Angelique:* Well, that's near Valentine's Day. I broke up with my boyfriend on February 7th. I remember because of how close it was to Valentine's day. I know I didn't do anything on Valentine's Day. I don't remember what I did a few days before.

*DL:* Really? [*Encourager*]

*Angelique:* Is that so hard to believe?

*DL:* (silence)

*Angelique:* Ok. I see it's important. Let me think. I probably went out that night? Was it a Saturday? (Looks at phone) Yeah it was. I usually go out on Saturday.

*DL:* Go out on Saturday? [*Reflection*]

*Angelique:* Yeah I have my usual spots. G&S Lounge, Whiskey Bottoms, I used to go to Pearl's, but I don't go there much anymore.

*DL:* You mentioned Pearl's. Tell me more about that.

*Angelique:* Pearl's Dance Hall. I used to work there, but I quit last December. I've only been there a few times since.

*DL:* Go on please. [Encourager]

*Angelique:* Is this about that thing that happened at Pearl's? I did hear that a guy got shot or stabbed or something. My old boss told me.

*DL:* Maybe that's the same. Can you tell me all you know about that?

*Angelique:* (checks phone) Ok. Yeah. That was the 12th. I see a message with my old boss about it. He said something crazy went down and a guy got stabbed. Said ambulances were there and everything.

*DL:* Ok. Now that we are talking about the same day. Can you please tell me all about that day?

*Angelique:* I remember now. I went on a date with Brandon. We just met on the apps. We went to dinner at a tex-mex spot. He got too drunk on margaritas. I made my excuses, and I left.

*DL:* And then? [*Encourager*]

*Angelique:* And then I probably went home. I don't know.

*DL:* Did you go anywhere else that night?

*Angelique:* Not that I can remember.

*DL:* Ok. So just to summarize. You used to work at Pearl's Dance Hall, but you quit last December. You still have communication with your old boss. On February 7th, you and your boyfriend broke up. On February 12th, you went out on a date with Brandon. Brandon got drunk, and you left. At some point in the night, your old boss from Pearl's texted you to say that a man was stabbed at Pearl's. You think you went home after that, but you don't know. You don't remember going anywhere else. Is that right? [*Summarize*]

Once you reach the end of the interview, begin your presentation of evidence. I've listed out the exact SUE questions I would ask in the question sheet. Use them if she has left out either or both of the issues they address (being at the bar and stabbing Marshall).

If you get to the end of the interview and SUE, and you are reasonably certain that Angelique is the person that stabbed Marshall, it's time to get ready for the interrogation. We still think that drug addiction is the best theme for Angelique. Some techniques recommend leaving the room for a few minutes then re-entering to start the interrogation. Sometimes I do this, but generally I start when I see an opening.

Note: there is a common misconception you have to read the suspect Miranda before accusing them or after they start admitting to the crime. This isn't true. The same three pronged rule exists for when Miranda is needed: In custody, by police, and being questioned. If their custodial status hasn't changed, Miranda doesn't apply. Some jurisdictions may have more restrictive policies. This book isn't legal advice. Follow your policies and procedures.

*DL:* I really appreciate you spending the time to talk about February 12th. At the end of the day, though, it's clear to me you are the person who cut the man with a knife in the parking lot of Pearl's Dance Hall. [*First Accusation*]

*Angelique:* No I…

*DL:* Now, hold on. I've let you talk and now it's my turn to talk. [*Shut down denials*] I'd like you to hear what I have to say first. I've spent a lot of time thinking about this case. It didn't make sense to me until I realized that it was probably the drugs that led you to make these decisions. [*Introducing the drug addiction theme*] I've known and loved addicts in my own life. It took me a lot of work to learn about how addiction is a disease. It's a disease that affects our choices. Now, addicts are still responsible for their actions. There's no doubt about that, but there's some understanding that can go with that too.

When you cut that man in the parking lot, [*Accusation*] I'd bet your head was filled with a need for more dope. You weren't thinking of Marshall as a person – that's his name, Marshall – you were just thinking of him as a wallet you could take, a car you could steal, and some odds and ends you could pawn. That's it! He had those things. You needed those things. If you could just get one more fix, maybe you'd go to rehab after that.

You see, though, there's three steps you have to take to get right when you're wrong. [*Three Things Framework*] You have to say what you did was wrong. You have to say you're sorry. You have to say it won't happen again. That's it! It won't change the past, but it will make it so you did what you could.

When you cut that man, [*Accusation*] it was wrong what you did, but that doesn't make you a bad person. Good people do bad things. Let me tell you a story. [*Storytelling*] When I was a kid, my mom had a friend who stole from her. This was her best friend. They spent every single day together. When my mom found out about the theft, she was wrecked. The theft wasn't the worst part, though. When my mom confronted the woman, the woman denied it. She yelled and screamed and made my mom the bad person. My mom was willing to forgive the theft, but she couldn't stand the lack of accountability. I think about that woman a lot. I think she must have been scared. She never thought she would be caught. When she did get caught, her instinctual response was aggression. "I'll lie and make her back down." Once she started down that path, though, there was no going back.

When you cut Marshall, [*Accusation*] you weren't thinking about fixing it. You were hardly thinking at all if we're being honest. If you were thinking, it was about dope. Getting your fix. [*Theme*] But now it's all out. The question isn't whether you did it or not, the question is what are you going to do about it now? You're probably scared right now, but I want you to think about your next steps carefully. I want to be able to go to my bosses and say, "Angelique messed up when she stabbed Marshall, but she admitted what she did was wrong, she said she was sorry, and she said it would never happen again." That's some accountability that can set things right for you. Don't be like my mom's friend. There's no fixing that. I'm not making you any promises as to the outcome, I don't have any authority to do that. What I *can* promise you, though, is I will present everything you say and give as complete a picture I can as to what happened and why.

When you cut Marshall, is that something you planned to do, or is it something that just happened? It just happened didn't it? [*Alternative Question*]

*Usually your first admissions will come after the alternative question.* Once you get the first admission, work towards another small admission. It's a mistake to get the first admission and then say, "Tell me everything that happened." They aren't ready for that yet. Maybe ask, "This was was the first time something like this has happened, wasn't it?" Aim for questions that are one word answers here.

After a few of these admissions, look to expand what you know. A confession is not complete until you learn new details about the crime that you didn't know before. Some topics you might have her expand on could be:

1 What she did with the knife
2 What she did with Marshall's property
3 How she treated her injuries
4 Who she told
5 What sorts of internet searches she made about the crime (looking for news stories)

At the end of all of your suspect interviews – both custodial and non-custodial – ask them, "How do you feel like I've treated you today?" I've had numerous people who just confessed to serious felonies tell me about how well I treated them. I can't think of anybody that's ever claimed I treated them badly. Some have asked to come back and talk to me another time. This question is important because it addresses future allegations their defense might make about the coercive nature of the interview.

### *Scenario 3: Burglary*

On April 22nd, 2024, Melissa Chen arrived home to find her house had been burglarized. Melissa lives in the 1300 block of E St John's Ave in Austin, Travis County, Texas. She was alerted to the burglary by the front door being wide open. As she got closer, she saw the door jamb was completely shattered. Melissa called the police.

Melissa, who works from home, reported she left her house at 12:30 pm and returned at 1:30 pm. The door had been closed and locked when she left. She noticed a suspicious looking woman loitering nearby when she left. The woman was wearing a black Metallica tank top, torn jean shorts, and red basketball sneakers.

During the on scene investigation, officers discovered a footprint on the front door, suggesting that the front door had been kicked in. There were also fingerprints discovered on the medicine cabinet in the main bedroom.

Melissa did a walkthrough with the officers. Melissa indicated the following items had been stolen:

- Her 16″ Macbook Pro laptop
- A bottle of Hydrocodone prescribed to her for back pain
- $200 in cash

Melissa agreed to submit the serial number for her laptop.

On April 23rd, 2023, Detective Buck received a notification that Melissa's laptop had been pawned at the First Best Pawn Shop located at the intersection of Reagan Hill and

Cameron Rd. The person pawning the laptop is identified as Darlene Byrd, a known drug addict in the area. Generally speaking, Darlene matches the description of the suspicious woman Melissa saw outside of her house the day of the burglary. Detective Buck writes an arrest warrant for Darlene for burglary. She is arrested a few days later.

*Custodial Issues*: In this scenario, Darlene is under arrest. You'll want to do a solid greeting followed by a pre-Miranda monologue. You'll use the pre-Miranda monologue to let her know she is under arrest, but you want to show her the evidence used to make that decision (inspire curiosity). Also, you want to know if she has any evidence that can show she didn't do it (inspire hope). Let her know she will be treated fairly and respectfully (reduce fear).

#### *Overview*

We want to approach this interview with a little bit of humility. Darlene probably committed the burglary, but it's possible she's innocent. A drug addict pawning a $2,000 laptop the day after it was stolen in a burglary that also involved the theft of drugs? I'd write a probable cause affidavit on that. Are there other explanations that don't involve her being the burglar? Yes. *Even though it is probable, your interview is conducted in order to test the truth of that belief.* Having the humility to know you might be wrong is an essential mindset to have in the interview.

As investigators, it is easy to forget complainants lie too. What if Melissa didn't get burglarized at all? Maybe she staged a burglary to commit insurance fraud, threw away her computer to make it seem believable, and poor Darlene went peeking in that dumpster? Is it likely? No. Is it possible? Yes.

It's useful to think of likely motivations for the crime, and explore those with the suspect. For example, a person burglarizing others is usually not doing well financially. Explore their finances. How do they make money? Do they have any savings? Are they stressed about money? Darlene is a known drug addict, and we know drug addicts will do desperate things to fund their habit. Ask her about her drug use.

Another thing to keep in mind, a common deceptive tactic is to deny involvement *and* pretend like they don't remember the day in question. Since one of the most effective questioning techniques for a denied event is a careful timeline examination, this is a problem. How are you going to do a timeline examination on a day they claim not to remember? It's a good tactic because, of course, innocent people forget things too.

If the day of the incident is within a week or two, this is relatively easy to address. You can walk them back through the week(s) day by day until you get to the day in question. Otherwise, you could pick out significant events and work around the edges of those until you arrive at the day. For example, I worked a case where the suspect was the boss of his co-conspirator. In order to understand more about that relationship, I had to focus him on the events he acknowledged remembering: the days he paid the co-conspirator. I had a calendar printed out. I circled the pay days moving backwards until we got to the time of the crime. With agreed upon anchor points, I was able to get him to acknowledge remembering more about the date of the crime. Once you arrive at the date in question, establish a timeline.

If too much time has passed, or your suspect refuses to agree they remember anything about the day in question, you have to adjust your tactics. In these cases, you can focus on generalities related to the crime. Darlene here is suspected of burglarizing a home. You might ask, "At any time in the past month, have you been in somebody's house without permission?" "In the past year, have you sold anything that doesn't belong to you?" "Have you come into possession of any valuable property recently?" Questions like this will allow you to talk around the crime without having an agreed upon date.

*Evidence:*

1 Darlene pawned Melissa's laptop, which she reported stolen.
2 Darlene frequents the area where the burglary happened.
3 Darlene matches the description of the woman Melissa saw lurking around the area the day of the burglary.
4 Darlene is a drug addict.
5 Drugs were stolen.

*SUE Step One: Analyze and rate your evidence.* In this case, the best piece of evidence is obviously Darlene pawning Melissa's laptop. We could work with a woman matching Darlene's description in the area at the time of the crime as well. Realistically, though, I would probably use a bait question for this one because I don't *really* have the goods here. SUE is for when you have the goods. Bait questions are for when you don't have them yet or at all (example: waiting on a DNA return or waiting on a video canvas). An example of a bait question: "Is there any reason why a witness would say you were there the day of the burglary?"

*SUE Step One, continued: Think of alternate explanations for the evidence.* What are some other reasons Darlene might have Melissa's laptop? Here are some possibilities: Melissa gave it to her. Darlene found it. Somebody else gave it to Darlene. Darlene bought it secondhand. For each of these possibilities (and any others you think of), come up with some questions. If she is innocent, she should readily give you one of these answers either straight away or in response to your questions.

The first situation – Melissa giving the laptop to Darlene – necessitates Melissa and Darlene know one another fairly well. "Do you know Melissa Chen?" "How would you describe your relationship?"

For the others, you might come up with questions like: "Have you recently found anything valuable?" "Has anybody given you anything valuable in the past few weeks?" "What valuable electronics have you sold recently?" "Have you bought any electronics recently?"

*SUE Step Two*: This is where you contact the suspect. This has been handled by patrol.

*SUE Step Three*: Give the suspect a chance to volunteer the information. Never struggle for anything you can get easily. Here we give Darlene a chance to admit being in the area, knowing Melissa, or committing the burglary. Your first step when you get to these case specific questions is to guide the suspect's attention to the day in question. As I discussed in the overview section, this may be easy or hard depending on the age of the crime and how cooperative the suspect is.

Once you get to the day of the crime, ask for information in big, open-ended questions that encourage long, narrative responses. Encourage them to give you more and more with continuers. "Go on" "What else?" And so on. Then summarize what they have said, clarifying any details. If the suspect has not admitted to being involved in the things under investigation, ask more and more specific questions until you finally ask, "Did you go into the house without permission?" "Did you steal a laptop?" "Did you pawn a laptop that didn't belong to you?"

Note: the way I use SUE, step three is part of my overall interview process. I'm asking other questions as well as these. Finally, there will come a point when the suspect has had all of the opportunities to volunteer an explanation for the evidence that has implicated them in the crime *including a direct question asking if they did or didn't do the crime*. At that point, it's time to move on to the evidence presentation, or step four.

*SUE Step Four*: Here is where you will lay out the evidence. SUE step four happens in three moves going from vague to specific.

*Step Four, Move One (pawning computer)*: Darlene, I have some evidence that you did, in fact, steal things from that house on St. Johns. Let's talk about that.

*Step Four, Move Two (pawning computer)*: In fact, the evidence I have that you stole things from that house is strong, and we need to address it. Please tell me about that.

*Step Four, Move Three (pawning computer)*: Darlene look at these (show video footage or receipts or whatever you have). I've got you pawning that stolen computer the day after it happened. Nobody is going to doubt this evidence. Let's talk about what happened.

Let's use our If, Then, Therefore process to think of some more questions for Darlene.

*If*: If Darlene entered into Melissa's house without permission between 12:30 and 1:30 pm and stole items to include a laptop and drugs...

*Then*:
Darlene would have to have been in the area at that time
Darlene may be familiar with Melissa and her schedule
Darlene didn't have permission to enter Melissa's house that day
She broke into the house in some way
Darlene would have to be physically capable of breaking into the house in that way
She did something while she was inside
She transported the items in some way
She got away from the house in some way
She did something with the computer between the entry and the pawning
She did something with the drugs

*Therefore*:
Where were you on the day of April 22nd?
Were you ever in the area of the 1300 block of E St Johns on the day of April 22nd?
Do you know Melissa Chen?
Have you ever been in Melissa Chen's house with her permission?
How would you describe your physical health?
Do you have any problems with your neck, back, knees, or legs?
Do you have any physical limitations?
What did you do inside the house?
Describe any bags you carry with you.
Where were you on the afternoon of April 22nd?
Can anybody vouch for you?
Have you had any drugs that don't belong to you in the past few week?

I like this process for getting started on thinking through the problem. I'll select the questions that fit, and I'll type them into my question list. I may or may not get through with asking all of them.

Question list:

My question list would look something like this:

24-XXXXXX
Burglary
Location: 1300 E St Johns
Victim: Melissa Chen
Alleged Perpetrator: Darlene Byrd
Date: April 22nd, 2024
Time: Between 12:30 and 1:30 pm

### Bio data

Name and DOB
Address. If recent change, previous address
Phone number
Email address

### General questions / anticipatory questions

- How would you describe your drug use?
- How are your finances?
- Do you know Melissa Chen?
- If so, how would you describe your relationship?
- Have you ever been in Melissa Chen's house with her permission?
- Do you have any physical limitations?
- Have you
- Have you recently found anything valuable?
- Has anybody given you anything valuable in the past few weeks?
- What valuable electronics have you sold recently?
- Have you bought any electronics recently?

### Case data

- In as much detail as possible, tell me all about your activities on April 22nd.
- Where were you on April 22nd?
- Where were you on the *afternoon* of April 22nd?
- Were you ever in the area of the 1300 block of E St Johns on the day of April 22nd?
- Did you go into a house without permission that day?
- What did you do inside the house?
- Describe any bags you carry with you.
- Can anybody vouch for you?
- Have you had any drugs that don't belong to you in the past few week?

### SUE

1 Darlene, I have some evidence you did, in fact, steal things from that house on St. Johns. Let's talk about that.

2 In fact, the evidence I have that you stole things from that house is strong, and we need to address it. Please tell me about that.
3 Darlene look at these (show video footage or receipts or whatever you have). I've got you pawning that stolen computer the day after it happened. Nobody is going to doubt this evidence. Let's talk about what happened.

This is a good question list. The list is not intended to be a rigid dictation of exactly what to say and in what order. Rather, the question list helps you get back on track if you get lost in the interview. Interviews can go so many different directions. You'll want to follow the natural flow of conversation. Use continuers – "Go on" "And then?" – reflections and summations to keep the suspect's response to open-ended questions going. Remember that open-ended questions keep the suspect talking. Closed / direct questions force you to do more talking and limit what you learn.

You'll also want to think about possible themes should you choose to do an accusatory interrogation. Your best themes come from the suspect themselves. If they did it, they've justified it somehow so it seems rational and acceptable to them. You're likely to hear hints of what that justification is when you interview the guilty suspect. However, it's good to think of a theme in the event you miss the justification. This theme operates as a sort of theory. It is not set in stone so be willing to trash it.

In all cases, and particularly in a case like this, you have to be careful to choose a theme that morally excuses them without criminally excusing them. For example, if you said, "Darlene, I think Melissa gave you that laptop to sell." You would have criminally excused her. It's not stealing when you have permission. In my experience, once a suspect finds safe ground like an excuse that will be a solid legal defense, it is nearly impossible to advance the conversation further.

My approach to Darlene would go like this:

***DL:*** (enters room). Hello. Darlene? I'm Darrel Lambert, a senior detective here with the department. (Shake hands). Here's a bottle of water for you (hand her water). I'm glad we have the chance to talk today.

*Pre-Miranda Monologue* I have a lot of questions for you, and I'm sure you have some questions for me. Those officers arrested you today on a warrant. I can't do anything about that right now. I want you to know, though, a warrant is based on probable cause, not absolute certainty. Sometimes those are put out when there is still a real possibility the person didn't do the crime. Like I said, probable isn't certain. When we talk today, I want to show you the evidence that led to you being looped into this. There's a very real chance you may look at that evidence and help me see it in a way I hadn't understood it before. If we got it wrong, help me see it right. Also, if you have any evidence at all that you weren't involved in the crime, I want you to point me to that. Tell me who I can talk to or where the evidence is and I'll go get it. No matter what we talk about here today, I promise to treat you with respect, and I hope you'll do the same for me. If you need water or coffee, I'll bring them to you. If you need a bathroom break, I'll take you to where those are.

*Custodial Issues* Read Miranda within your policy and using whatever card or warnings you use.

*DL:* I want to tell you a little bit about myself. I've been an officer for over 18 years. I've investigated everything ranging from simple assaults up to and including murder. One thing I've learned is to listen without judgment. If we talk about any subject that is embarrassing for you, just know that I won't judge you for it. It's important that we talk about true things, even if we find them embarrassing.

I've heard quite a bit about you from reports and other sources, but I don't know you. I find that it's easier to be fair to people we know. With that in mind, before we get started, tell me about yourself so that I can get to know you better [*Rapport*].

*Darlene:* What do you want to know?

*DL:* Anything you'd like to share!

*DL:* Thank you for helping me get to know you. I know you're anxious to hear more about why we are here today. I want to share as much as I can with you. Sometimes I keep things back because it helps me make sure the things we talk about are true. If I tell you everything I know, and you just tell me those things back, how can I know if it's true or not? In fact, there are some questions I'll ask you that I already know the answer to. The reason I ask those questions is to make sure that you are telling the truth. Do you promise to tell me the truth today? [*Your first behavior provoking question. Watch and listen carefully.*]

*Darlene:* Yes.

*DL:* What's your understanding of why you're here today?

*Darlene:* I have no idea!

*DL:* Ok. Well, we definitely need to be talking about the same thing! We are here because items were stolen from a house in the St. Johns area a few days ago, and your name came up as possibly being involved. What can you tell me about that?

*Darlene:* Nothing at all.

*DL:* Fair enough. Let me ask you some questions that can help me verify that.

[*A period of questions from the list about daily activities, census data, drug usage, familiarity with the St. Johns area etc.*]

*DL:* Today is May 1st. April 22nd happened on a Monday, which would be two Mondays ago. What can you tell me about your activities that day?

*Darlene:* I have no idea. My life is pretty chaotic. I don't know what I did yesterday.

*DL:* Chaotic? [*Don't be so focused on getting to the day in question that you miss an opportunity to follow up on a detail like this. This is a reflection to prompt more.*]

*Darlene:* I'm on the streets. I get a hotel room when I can, but it's mostly living in tents. I've had a drug problem in the past.

*DL:* You've struggled with addiction.

*Darlene:* Yeah.

*DL:* How are you doing with that now?

*Darlene:* I haven't wanted to use in days. [*She hasn't denied using, though.*]

*DL:* I hear you, if we talked about major life events or news events would that help you remember?

*Darlene:* Probably not.

*DL:* Ok. Darlene, tell me this: how often are you on St Johns?

*Darlene:* Not often.

*DL:* Really? [*Encourager*]
*Darlene:* Maybe once a week. I'm usually in the Rundberg area north of that.
*DL:* Usually? [*Reflection*]
*Darlene:* Like I said, I move around a lot. My campsite is on Rundberg. I have some friends down on St. Johns.
*DL:* Who are your friends?
*Darlene:* Ray J, DB, Perro, Emily. I don't hang out with many people.
*DL:* What about Melissa?
*Darlene:* I don't know anybody named Melissa.
*DL:* You're sure?
*Darlene:* Yeah.
*DL:* Have you been in anybody's house without their permission in the past couple of months?
*Darlene:* Not that I know of.
*DL:* What do you mean?
*Darlene:* I've stayed in bandos[4] sometimes. I don't really think of them as belonging to anybody because nobody lives there. I haven't done that recently, though.
*DL:* Besides bandos, have you been in anybody else's house without their permission?
*Darlene:* No. That wouldn't be right.
*DL:* So to make sure I have this right, you usually camp in the Rundberg area. Your life is chaotic because of homelessness and drug addiction. You sometimes go down to the St. Johns area because you have friends down there including Ray J, DB, Perro, and Emily. You don't know anybody named Melissa. Other than abandoned houses, you haven't been in anybody's house without their permission. Did I get that right? [*Review the story.*]
*Darlene:* Yeah.
*DL:* I thought of something while I was talking. Were any of the abandoned houses you stayed in near St. Johns? [*When you review the story, you usually find something you forgot to ask about.*]
*Darlene:* No. Those are other places.

Continue on with the interview. Give her all the opportunities possible to volunteer the information you are seeking. Ask her about the laptop. Ask her if she pawned it. Ask all of those things. If you get to the interview, and Darlene still hasn't told you about pawning the laptop, it's time to use the SUE presentation of evidence.

*DL:* Darlene, I have some evidence you did, in fact, steal things from that house on St. Johns. Let's talk about that. [*SUE step four, move one.*]
*Darlene:* If it's about that Makita drill, I found that. That was mine. [*Here, Darlene brings up stuff you aren't looking for. It's tempting to pass it up and focus on the computer, but you should spend some time talking about these suddenly remembered things. See if they relate.*]
*DL:* Tell me about that.
*Darlene:* Nothing much to say. I found it near a bus stop. Nobody was around. I took it. I pawned it. [*An admission to pawning other items.*]
*DL:* Tell me about pawning it.
*Darlene:* I walked right into the pawn shop at Rundberg and Lamar, and I sold it.
*DL:* Anything else?

*Darlene:* That's it!

*DL:* In fact, the evidence I have that you stole things from that house is strong, and we need to address it. Please tell me about that. [*SUE step four, move two.*]

*Darlene:* There's nothing else! [*Darlene has not added anything new to follow up on. Go to the next move.*]

*DL:* Darlene look at these (show video footage or receipts or whatever you have). I've got you pawning that stolen computer the day after it happened. Nobody is going to doubt this evidence. Let's talk about what happened. [*SUE step four, move three.*]

*Darlene:* Oh that! Yeah. Some lady gave me that. I pawned it for money. It was mine so what's the big deal?

*DL:* Tell me all about the lady giving you that laptop.

*Darlene:* (continues with her story, but not in a way that convinces you)

If Darlene gets to the end of the interview without convincing you she didn't have anything to do with the crime, you'll probably move into an interrogation. At this point, you have good evidence, but you don't have any good explanations. It's more likely than not Darlene burglarized Melissa's home.

What themes might we use for Darlene? Drug addiction. Jealousy (she has so much and you have so little). Impulsiveness at an easy opportunity. Victim blaming (she made it so easy). For this example, I'll use Impulsiveness as the theme.

*DL:* Darlene, let's get real. You went into that house and stole the laptop. The evidence is overwhelming and more is coming in. Let's talk about this so you can move on and I can move on.

*Darlene:* But I…

*DL:* No. I let you talk. Now it's my turn to talk. [*Shutting down denials.*] What I want for you here is to help me understand the reason why you did it. [*Give them a reason to talk.*] I've been thinking about this case. What makes the most sense to me is this was a spur of the moment decision. You acted on impulse. I think you were in that area when you saw the homeowner leave. The homeowner has all that nice stuff just sitting in plain view. You thought, "Why not?" Here's a quick lick you could hit. You get money to get by, the rich lady won't hardly notice. Who loses? You said yourself that your life is chaotic. Chaotic people don't have a plan! [*Introducing a theme of impulsiveness with some elements of victim blaming.*]

What's good about your case is it comes across a lot different when people go around planning and organizing crimes. Anybody that hears your story will have at least one example of when they themselves acted impulsively. Not a lot of people on the other hand can wrap their heads around pre-planning a crime like this. Now, Darlene, you broke into that house, but you didn't plan it. I worked a case just like this recently. [*Storytelling describing a similar case where the person admitted to wrongdoing and felt better because of it.*] A guy who was living in his car, one step above living on the streets, saw a shop owner leave for the day without locking the door behind them. He ran in, grabbed an armload of their stuff, and he took off. He told me that he wouldn't have done what he did, but the opportunity was right there. He just couldn't resist it. Once he told me about what he did, he felt a lot better about it.

When you went into that house, I think it was the same thing. [*Accuse again*] If she had left 5 minutes later or earlier, you wouldn't have been there at the exact

> time it had to happen. You gotta know that denying it doesn't make any sense at all. Have you ever done a jigsaw puzzle? [*Introduce framework*] If you've ever done any of the big ones, you'll have the experience of finishing everything except that last piece. There will be a hole you can't look away from. That missing piece here is you accepting responsibility for what you did. Once you do that, the puzzle is complete. That piece that had been missing? The one about you having taken that lady's stuff? It's bad. I'm not going to lie to you about that. But now it's just one piece in hundreds. It starts to blend in to the rest so it isn't always the first thing you look at.
>
> When you went into that lady's house and took her laptop, I don't think it's something you planned. I think it's something that just kind of happened. It just kind of happened didn't it? [*Alternative question*]

*Usually your first admissions will come after the alternative question.* Once you get the first admission, work towards another small admission. It's a mistake to get the first admission and then say, "Tell me everything that happened." They aren't ready for that yet. Maybe ask, "This was was the first time something like this has happened, wasn't it?" Aim for questions that are one word answers here.

After a few of these admissions, look to expand what you know. A confession is not complete until you learn new details about the crime you didn't know before. Some topics you might have her expand on could be:

1 What she did with the money from the laptop sale
2 What she did with the drugs
3 What steps she took to cover up the crime
4 Who she told
5 What sorts of internet searches she made about the crime (looking for news stories)

At the end of all of your suspect interviews – both custodial and non-custodial – ask them, "How do you feel like I've treated you today?"

#### *Scenario 4: Child Abuse*

On August 12th, 2023, Melissa called the police department to report her daughter Terry had been molested by a friend of the family. Melissa reported to officers that she goes to car club meet ups in the park. A man named Raymond usually parks next to her in his pickup truck. Today, when she got back home, her 10 year old daughter – Terry – told her Mr. Ray had touched her private part. Melissa called the police.

Melissa reported she remembered seeing Terry look scared next to Mr. Ray earlier that day. Melissa had been chatting with a friend when she didn't see Terry. Melissa went looking for Terry, and she saw Terry next to Mr. Ray in his truck bed. Terry's eyes looked scared. Melissa went and grabbed Terry. She asked Terry what happened, but Terry just said she wanted to go home.

Responding officers saw Terry in the apartment crying and looking anxious. Due to her age, they didn't ask her any questions at that time. They did, however, schedule a sexual assault exam for Terry. Terry went through with the exam. Swabs and samples were taken from her body, and her clothing was collected.

The lead detective went out to the scene to look for video. There were, in fact, video cameras around the lot where Melissa and Raymond hang out. However, when the investigator went to request the footage, the apartment complex manager informed him that the cameras don't work and hadn't worked in years.

About two weeks later, the lead detective had Terry forensically interviewed. During the interview, Terry said Mr. Ray has known her mother for about a year. He parks next to them when they go to the car club meet ups. On the day her mom called the police, she had been playing in the parking lot where her mom was parked. Mr. Ray called her over to where he was sitting in the bed of his truck. He started singing and looking around as he put his hand down her pants, under her underwear, and rubbed on her vagina with his fingers. Terry felt frozen. When her mother came over, Mr. Ray told her not to say anything or he would hurt her.

The detective went by Raymond's house and asked him to come in for an interview. Raymond agreed. The detective and Raymond met later that day.

*Custodial issues*: Raymond has agreed to come in for an interview. He is not under arrest, and he is free to go. Therefore, this is a non-custodial statement. You'll want to thank him for coming in, offer him water at a minimum, offer him bathroom breaks, and make sure he knows he can leave at any time.

#### *Overview*

Unlike many child abuse cases, this case has quite a lot to work with. We have a known person accused of the crime. Melissa saw her daughter with Raymond looking scared and it was later that day her daughter outcried to Raymond touching her. Terry had a sexual assault exam done. Terry also went through with a forensic interview, in which she outcried to Mr. Ray rubbing her vagina.

In Texas, the crime to be investigated is Indecency with a Child by Contact, a 2nd Degree Felony. To charge indecency, the investigator has to show the purpose of the subject was to achieve sexual gratification. In this instance, Terry was able to articulate that Mr. Ray was rubbing her vagina in isolation (the truck bed) and secrecy (no explanation to the mother).

Other than sexual gratification, the primary reasons for a person to touch a child's vagina are for hygiene, helping them use the bathroom, and medical purposes. Raymond isn't a part of Terry's household, and he isn't mother's boyfriend. It is unlikely that he will have any credible excuses of these sorts to bring up, but we still want to explore them. We want to ask questions like, "Have you ever helped Terry use the bathroom?" "Have you ever given Terry medicine or any other medical attention?" "At any time, did you help clean Terry's body?"

With any allegation against a specific person, there are three main possibilities: It's true, it's false, or there is a misunderstanding. If Raymond admits it's true, we will have a relatively easy interview. If he says it's false, then there has to be some reason. For what reason would Terry accuse him of rubbing her vagina except that it happened? Those reasons might be money, revenge, or mental illness, for example.

In a case of a serious false allegation, the receiver of that false allegation could usually be expected to know why the other person wants to see them in trouble. Even in cases where the child is accusing a person, the accused often tries to shift focus to the child's parent and claim they have it out for them. The investigator will want to find out if there are any alternate motivations for Terry or her mom to accuse him of touching her. Has Raymond done anything to upset Terry? Does Melissa owe Raymond money? Is Melissa trying to extort money from Raymond? Have any threats been made?

A misunderstanding is the other possibility. If this is the case, Raymond should readily offer that information up, because he could be expected to remember. For example, Raymond might say, "I know what she's talking about. She was sitting next to me in the truck. I was serving a customer. While I talked to the customer, I reached over without looking to grab their item. I accidentally touched Terry, and she started acting strangely." If it's true, Raymond should be expected to say so right away. If it's false, he has exposed himself to a certain amount of danger by admitting the contact happened but it wasn't what the child thought.

What are some potential motivations for Raymond to touch Terry? We would include possible justifications that aren't based in reality. For example, he may say Terry came onto him. This is not likely to be true, but it is common for child sexual abuse offenders to say so. He may be a sex addict, engage in excessive masturbation, have fantasies about children, or be sexually repressed and / or unsatisfied. For these reasons, we would want to ask Raymond about his sex life. Is he satisfied? Does he suffer from intrusive sexual thoughts? Has he fantasized about Terry? For those that don't regularly investigate this topic, just realize sexual deviance is broad and deep. As revolting as it may be, you must approach the interview with a non-judgmental attitude. If a sexual deviant feels you are judging them, they will not talk to you.

Finally, consider using Dr. Darrel Turner's Analysis of Patterns of Denial (APOD) questions to prepare. I've written more extensively on that in chapter 12. As a quick introduction, though: adult male sex offenders use a common group of tactics to lie about involvement in sex crimes. These include: denigrating the victim, excessive detail, and claims of asexuality. There are 12 of these tactics. For interviews like this, I often include the list of 12 tactics on my question sheet. If I observe them, I put check marks next to them. The APOD is helpful in building your confidence in the guilt or innocence of your interviewee.

*Evidence*: Perhaps your best evidence isn't in hand yet. Terry had a sexual assault exam done, but the results won't be back for months. For that piece of evidence, you'll need to use a bait question instead of SUE. "When those results come back, is there any reason your DNA will be on Terry's vagina?" The same could be said for video footage. There are in fact cameras, but there isn't footage due to the cameras not working. This would also be a situation for a bait question. "If I check those cameras, will they show you touching Terry?" Some might choose to bluff (lie) about actually having the evidence. That is legal in the United States, but I prefer to avoid it. What if Raymond knows the cameras don't work?

What you actually have in hand and ready to go: Terry has made a clear outcry of Mr. Ray rubbing her vagina. That is evidence. Melissa witnessed Terry with Raymond in the truck on the day of the outcry; Terry was looking scared. That definitely corroborates Terry's statement.

*SUE Step One: Analyze and rate your evidence.* I would regard Terry's forensic interview as the strongest piece of evidence that is eligible for the SUE technique. Melissa's observations would be second best. Melissa's observations have quite a few alternate explanations whereas Terry's accusations have fewer alternate explanations.

A question I've been asked while instructing on the technique is which order the investigator should present the evidence in: weakest to strongest or vice versa? I don't know of Dr. Hartwig having said one way or another about this aspect of her technique. For me, I usually choose to start with the strongest. I have found that some interviewees will shut down or leave as the pressure mounts with the presentation of evidence. I like having their reaction to the best evidence in hand in case they cut the interview short.

*SUE Step One, continued: Think of alternate explanations for the evidence.* What are some reasons why Terry might accuse Raymond of rubbing her vagina? I addressed some of these in the overview section. She might be mistaken. She might have it in for Raymond for any number of reasons. Maybe he made fun of her or refused to give her money. The possibilities for why a child might seek revenge are too numerous to list, but Raymond could be expected to know of the situation if it existed. Maybe her mother put her up to it. If so, Raymond could be expected to know of what Melissa was so mad about that she would direct her child to accuse him of sexual abuse.

Some questions we could ask to address these different situations: "Describe your relationship with Terry / Melissa." "What kind of person is Terry / Melissa?" "Is there any reason Terry / Melissa would want to see you get in trouble?" "Would either of them gain if you were arrested?" "Was there any contact between you and Terry that the child might have misinterpreted as being sexual?" "Have either of them ever threatened you?"

*SUE Step Two*: This is where you contact the suspect. In this instance, the investigator chose to go in person, make contact, and set up a non-custodial interview.

*SUE Step Three*: Give the suspect a chance to volunteer the information. You'll list the questions you came up with to address alternate or innocent explanations for the evidence. Remember you always want to question from broad to specific. The most reliable corroboration comes from a suspect who has volunteered the information before being asked specifically about it. For example, if you said, "Tell me about Melissa." This is about as broad as can be. If Raymond says, "She's always had it in for me. She started threatening me the minute I set up my little shop." This is a statement – whether true or false – that has more value than one coming from a specific question like, "Has Melissa threatened you?"

At some point, you'll want to know if Melissa has threatened him, because that is one alternate explanation for the evidence against Raymond. If the interviewee doesn't volunteer threats with the open-ended questions, you'll *eventually* ask them specifically if Melissa has threatened him or not. A statement is always more powerful when it comes from the other person without a specific prompt. In order to give the interviewee the fairest chance, though, we will need to ask them *specifically* if they don't bring it up *generally*.

Note the way I use SUE, step three is part of my overall interview process. I'm asking other questions as well as these. Finally, there will come a point when the suspect has had all of the opportunities to volunteer an explanation for the evidence that has implicated them in the crime *including a direct question asking if they did or didn't do the crime*. At that point, it's time to move on to the evidence presentation, or step four.

*SUE Step Four*: Here is where you will lay out the evidence. SUE step four happens in three moves going from vague to specific.

*Step Four, Move One (Terry's accusation)*: Raymond, I've heard you say you haven't touched Terry's, but I have evidence you did touch her vagina. Can we talk about that?

*Step Four, Move Two (Terry's accusation)*: The evidence I have indicating you touched Terry's vagina is strong. I need you to be very clear and help me understand why there would be evidence like that.

*Step Four, Move Three (Terry's accusation)*: In fact, Raymond, Terry has made a sworn statement to independent experts that you rubbed her vagina. We need to talk about that.

Note: Although I haven't seen anything from Dr. Hartwig and her team on this topic, I sometimes will not use step four move three with witness testimony as the evidence. I'll get through move two, hear what they say, and move on from there. My reasoning is that it's easy for somebody to say, "Well, they're a liar" once you identify their accuser. On the other hand, if you stop at having strong evidence, you leave the guilty person with a mind virus of sorts. "What do they have? How do they know that? Did I overlook something?" The innocent person doesn't suffer from these same thoughts. The mind virus causes the guilty to experience increased cognitive load, which is good for the interviewer.

Question list:
My question list would look something like this:

23-XXXXXXX
Indecency
Location: 500 block S Pleasant Valley Rd
Victim: Terry
Victim's Mom: Melissa
Alleged Perpetrator: Raymond
Date: August 12th, 2023

### Bio data

Name and DOB
A photograph of Raymond
Address.
Phone number
Email address
Primary relationships
Other household members

### General questions / anticipatory questions

- How are you employed?
- Where do you hang out?
- Are you familiar with Melissa?
- Tell me about her.
- Have you two ever been in a relationship?
- What about her daughter? Tell me about her.
- How would you describe the daughter?
- Describe any physical contact you have had with the daughter.
- Anything else?
- The last time you saw the daughter, describe any and all physical contact you had with her?
- Was there any physical contact that the child may have misinterpreted as being sexual?
- Was the daughter ever in your truck bed?

- What about the last time you saw her?
- Does Melissa have any reason to want to see you in trouble?
- What about the daughter?
- Have either of them ever threatened you?

### Questions about sex

- How would you describe your sex life?
- What is a normal sex life?
- Do you have any intrusive sexual thoughts that bother you?
- How often do you masturbate?
- Have you had any sexual fantasies about children under 14 years of age?
- Do you think Melissa's daughter has had any sort of sexual thoughts about you?
- Has Melissa's daughter touched you in a way that made you feel uncomfortable?
- When her daughter's sexual assault exam results come back, is there any reason your DNA will be on her vagina?

## SUE

1. Raymond, I've heard you say that you haven't touched Terry's vagina, but I have evidence you did touch her vagina. Can we talk about that?
2. The evidence I have indicating you touched Terry's vagina is strong. I need you to be very clear and help me understand why there would be evidence like that.
3. In fact, Raymond, Terry has made a sworn statement to independent experts you rubbed her vagina. We need to talk about that.

This is a good question list. The list is not intended to be a rigid dictation of exactly what to say and in what order. Rather, the question list helps you get back on track if you get lost in the interview. Interviews can go so many different directions. You'll want to follow the natural flow of conversation. Use continuers – "Go on" "And then?" – reflections and summations to keep the suspect's response to open-ended questions going. Remember that open-ended questions keep the suspect talking. Closed / direct questions force you to do more talking and limit what you learn.

You'll also want to think about possible themes should you choose to do an accusatory interrogation. Your best themes come from the suspect themselves. If they did it, they've justified it somehow so it seems rational and acceptable to them. You're likely to hear hints of what that justification is when you interview the guilty suspect. However, it's good to think of a theme in the event that you miss the justification. This theme operates as a sort of theory. It is not set in stone so be willing to trash it.

In all cases, and particularly in a case like this, you have to be careful to choose a theme that morally excuses them without criminally excusing them. For Raymond, you might choose Blame the Victim. This is very effective for child abuse suspects. It doesn't criminally excuse them because – in Texas at least – a child under 14 cannot consent to sexual contact. Consent is not an issue like it would be for adult sex crimes. Other possible themes could be Loneliness and Curiosity and Opportunity.

My approach to Raymond would go like this:

*DL:* (enters room). Hello. Raymond? I'm Darrel Lambert, a senior detective here with the department. (Shake hands). Here's a bottle of water for you (hand him water). I'm glad we have the chance to talk today.

*Custodial Issues* I want you to know you are not under arrest. You knew that right? I haven't made any final decisions in this investigation. You are free to go at any time. That door is open, and you know where the lobby is. If at any point you are done talking, just get up and walk out. You don't need my permission to leave when you are ready to go. Do you have any questions about that?

*Rapport*

*DL:* With all of that out of the way. I'd like to know you better. What can you tell me about yourself. *Continue on with rapport for long enough to establish a baseline and set the interviewee at ease. For me, this is typically about 20 minutes.*

*Transition*

*DL:* Thank you for helping me get to know you. I know you're anxious to hear more about why we are here today. I want to share as much as I can with you. Sometimes I keep things back because it helps me make sure the things we talk about are true. If I tell you everything I know, and you just tell me those things back, how can I know if it's true or not? In fact, there are some questions I'll ask you that I already know the answer to. The reason I ask those questions is to make sure you are telling the truth. Do you promise to tell me the truth today? [*Your first behavior provoking question. Watch and listen carefully.*]
*Raymond:* Yes.
*DL:* What's your understanding of why you're here today?
*Raymond:* Is it about Melissa?
*DL:* Why do you ask?
*Raymond:* She hasn't been at the car club meet ups and she hasn't answered my calls. She was acting strangely last time I saw her.
*DL:* Strangely? [*Reflection*]
*Raymond:* Yeah. She wouldn't look at me.
*DL:* What might that be about?
*Raymond:* I have no idea.
*DL:* Melissa's daughter has made some allegations about you touching her inappropriately. What can you tell me about that? [*Identify the issue at hand.*]
*Raymond:* I don't know what she's talking about.
*DL:* Well, let's look at the situation together.

[*At this point, I would go back into historical issues between Raymond and Melissa. Find out about their relationship, any problems, any changes and so on. Your question list will help you here. Once I had as much information as possible about those issues, I would ask him to recount the last time he saw Melissa and her daughter.*]

*DL:* That has helped me understand a lot about what's going on. I'd like to direct your attention to the last time you saw Melissa and her daughter. If you could please, tell me all about that last time from beginning to end without leaving anything out. No detail is too small!

*Raymond:* The last time I saw her? It would have been at the parking lot where we hang out. I think it was last Friday. I usually get there about 10 am. Melissa usually gets there about noon. She had her daughter with her. I thought it was strange that her daughter wasn't in school. I think Melissa isn't a very good mom. I've heard CPS was looking into her. Things were fine though. We chatted about small things. Her kid was mostly inside of Melissa's car playing on her phone. At some point Melissa seemed upset. She grabbed all of her stuff and left in a hurry. I haven't talked to her since.

*DL:* What else? [*Encourager*]

*Raymond:* We usually chat throughout the week. It's weird she hasn't called me.

*DL:* And that's unusual. [*A prompt to elaborate more.*]

*Raymond:* Yeah. Very unusual.

*Me:* You said Melissa's kid was mostly in Melissa's car. Where else was she?

*Raymond:* Oh, she'd walk around some. At one point she sat in my truck bed with me. I look after her when I can. Her mom doesn't pay much attention to her. [*Here, you may be tempted to jump into the part where Melissa's child is in the truck bed with Raymond. If possible, let that be for a minute and come back to it.*]

*DL:* It sounds like you don't think highly about Melissa as a mom. Tell me about that.

*Raymond:* (talks about Melissa being a bad mom)

*DL:* Interesting, you mentioned that Melissa's kid was in your truck bed with you. Describe what happened there.

*Raymond:* There's nothing to describe. She sat next to me looking at her phone. At one point, Melissa charged up and grabbed her kid, and that was the last I saw of her.

*DL:* Was there any reason she would have had to be upset?

*Raymond:* No. I wasn't doing anything when she came up to us.

*DL:* Describe any and all physical contact you had with Melissa's kid that last time you saw her.

*Raymond:* I may have patted her head. I don't think I touched her anywhere else.

*DL:* Is it possible you touched her in another way?

*Raymond:* It's possible, but I don't remember.

*DL:* If you did remember...

*Raymond:* I don't.

*DL:* Did you ever touch her vagina?

*Raymond:* Why would I do a thing like that?

*DL:* Did you?

*Raymond:* No.

[*Continue on with the interview like this. Give him a chance to talk about the evidence. Ask him the questions that you prepared. Remember to use reflections, continuers, and summations. Ultimately, Raymond has not explained away the evidence against him. When all the rest of the interview is done, it's time to use the SUE method for evidence.*]

*DL:* Raymond, I've heard you say you haven't touched Melissa's kid's vagina, but I have evidence you did touch her vagina. Can we talk about that? [*Step four, move one.*]

*Raymond:* No way. That definitely didn't happen. Uh uh. [*Nothing to follow up on, move on.*]

*DL:* The evidence I have indicating you touched Terry's vagina is strong. I need you to be very clear and help me understand why there would be evidence like that. [*Step four, move two.*]

*Raymond:* It's probably her mom putting her up to it. She's been trying to get back at me ever since she found out I overcharged her for some car parts.

*DL:* Interesting. Tell me about that situation. [*New information is brought up. The interviewer follows up. In this situation, where the accuser is known to the suspect, I rarely move on to step four, move three. Once Raymond responded fully to move two, I'd move on to the next piece of evidence.*]

If your interview with Raymond doesn't explain the evidence against him, and you are reasonably certain of his guilt, you'll move into an interrogation. An interrogation is accusatory. It's purpose is to get the truth. In order to get the truth, it is sometimes necessary to accuse the person. That accusation will test a truthful denial in a way that should help you gain confidence in the person's innocence. On the other hand, the accusation will test a guilty person's denial in a way that will hopefully lead you to the truth, which may be a confession.

I've found one of the strongest themes for an interview with a child abuse suspect is curiosity and opportunity. The idea of the theme is sometimes you have the opportunity but you aren't curious so nothing happens. Sometimes you are curious but don't have the opportunity so nothing happens. When curiosity and opportunity meet, though, things happen that wouldn't have otherwise. Let's look at how that might go.

*DL:* Raymond. I came into this with an open mind. At the end of everything, though, there's simply no doubt you rubbed Melissa's daughter's vagina. It's obvious and we need to talk about it because I want to know why that happened.

*Raymond:* It didn't happen!

*DL:* [*Ignore and keeps talking.*] The evidence in this case is overwhelming. We've been through some of the evidence. There is more, though, and more coming. I've spent a lot of time thinking about this case. It occurred to me this probably happened because of curiosity and opportunity. I've investigated so many of these cases, and this is something I hear a lot. A man comes in and he tells me he's suffered from some intrusive sexual thoughts. They come into his head without him wanting them there, and they rattle around giving him fantasies he didn't want. This is curiosity. Sexual fantasies like that are hard to control and hard to direct. A lot of guys tell me the fantasies started about their wife, then they became about her friend, then about her mom, and finally about her kid. The fantasies are there, but they usually happen when the person isn't around. That means there is curiosity (the fantasy), but there isn't opportunity (access to the person). This happens a lot.

My experience has been that problems happen when curiosity meets opportunity. For example, I talked to a guy last month who told me he was in the bathroom masturbating. He was thinking about some of the fantasies he had. When his stepdaughter walked in, he told me that it was the perfect storm. The opportunity was there at the same time the fantasy was there. He admitted to touching his stepdaughter. Afterwards, he told me he felt a lot better at being able to tell another person about it. It's a big burden to carry those experiences around without talking. [*Storytelling and theme building.*]

When you touched Melissa's kid, I think it was something similar. It was curiosity and opportunity. [*Accuse again.*] I think your mind wandered while you were out there without a lot of others around. You started edging into fantasy. Just then, Melissa's kid jumped in the truck bed with you. That's when that mixture of curiosity and opportunity happened. If she hadn't been there, you wouldn't have touched her. You never sought her out. It never happened before. It was the perfect storm.

You touched Melissa's kid. There's no doubt at all about that. [*Accuse again.*] There's three things my bosses are gonna ask when I present this case to them. They are going to ask: "Did he cooperate? Did he tell the truth? Is he sorry for what he did?" [*Framework*] Those are serious questions! I want to be able to go to my bosses and tell them yes to all of those.

Raymond, is this something that you planned out, or is it something that just kind of happened? It just kind of happened didn't it? [*Alternative question*]

—

Usually your first admissions will come after the alternative question. Once you get the first admission, work towards another small admission. It's a mistake to get the first admission and then say, "Tell me everything that happened." They aren't ready for that yet. Maybe ask, "This was was the first time something like this has happened, wasn't it?" Aim for questions that are one word answers here.

After a few of these admissions, look to expand what you know. A confession is not complete until you learn new details about the crime that you didn't know before. Some topics you might have him expand on could be:

1 How many other times has he done this?
2 What did he do to cover up the crime?
3 Was he worried about being found out? If so, what did he do about it?
4 Did he tell anybody else about what he did?
5 What sorts of internet searches he made about the crime. For example: searches about punishments for touching children, DNA, or similar things.

**At the end of all of your suspect interviews – both custodial and non-custodial – ask them, "How do you feel like I've treated you today?"** This question is important because it addresses future allegations their defense might make about the coercive nature of the interview.

## Notes

1 Kassin, *Duped*, 56.
2 Example: I had a case where a man raped an autistic 14 year old. I had a theory that he had sexualized the victim in a way that projected a sort of sexuality onto him. When I floated this idea in the interview, he vehemently rejected the thought. It was clear to me that this would not be a good theme to present.
3 Only use drug addiction as a theme if she admits to having a problem with drugs. Even if it's obvious to you and everybody else, an addict that hasn't accepted their addiction will fight the label.
4 Street slang for "abandoned house."

Chapter 12

# Short Essays on Interview Related Topics

## APOD, Statement Analysis, and Other Techniques

### *APOD*

APOD stands for Analysis of Patterns of Denial. It was developed by Darrel Turner, PhD. He calls this technique an "instrument." According to him, there are certain ways in which people deny involvement in sexual abuse cases. Dr. Turner has identified 12 themes that people use to deny involvement. These include: Victim Denigration (blaming the victim), Hero, Legal Technicalities, Excessive Detail, and Hedge Phrases. The average guilty person uses more than 4 of these themes. It is common to see guilty people using 6,7, or 8 of them. The average innocent person uses two or fewer. There are no innocent people who used five or more. Essentially, if you find a person using five or more of these techniques, you have strong evidence that they are lying. He has written a peer-reviewed paper that has lent credibility to his findings.

Some disclaimers up front: his instrument is calibrated for adult male sex abuse offenders. There is some interpretation used in identifying which statements fit the identified themes that will lead to variation in counting the themes. You should attend his training if you find what is being discussed here interesting.

I was introduced to Dr. Turner's work around 2019 while I attended the Dallas Crimes Against Children Conference (CACC). Since that time we've become friends. I did an interview with him that is available on my YouTube channel in which he discusses his APOD instrument. When I was first introduced to his work, I immediately recognized the themes he discussed as techniques I have seen interviewees use in the room, and I began looking for them in my interviews. Once you are looking for them, you will see them all of the time. Several of us in Child Abuse regularly use this technique to analyze interviews while we are watching our partners in the room. When our partner will come out we will say things like, "I heard Victim Denigration, Excessive Detail, and Hero, what did you hear?"

As an example, let's look at Excessive Detail and Hedge Phrases. Let's say you asked a person, "When she says that you squeezed her breasts is she lying?" And the person responds, "Yeah. She does that. One time we were on a trip in Tennessee. We flew into the Nashville airport. The flight was delayed and we had the hardest time getting our bags. Matter of fact, one of my bags is still missing! Then we got to our AirBnB and found it was broken into. We told the management and went downtown to get some drinks while we waited for the house to get repaired." You would count this as excessive detail. It isn't about her lying. It is sort of related because the victim was there, but it is a lot of detail about nothing. If, on the other hand, it was a detailed story about a specific lie the victim

DOI: 10.4324/9781003663904-13

told, then it wouldn't be counted because it is responding to the matter at hand. Listen for excessive detail where people avoid talking about the issue and tell you long stories about their work or families or anything like that.

As to Hedge Phrases, these are going to be counted when the person responds with qualifiers and squishy phrases to questions that should be simple and clear. If you asked, "Why is she saying you pointed a gun at her?" And your interviewee responds, "That pretty much never happened" or "I mostly avoid guns." These are hedge phrases. If you asked, "What time were you downtown yesterday?" And they respond, "I hardly go downtown" or "I usually go downtown around 5 pm." I would count those as hedge phrases. Make sure you have established a baseline before you score this. Turner uses a funny example in his training where he interviewed a guy that hedged everything. He asked, "Hey, what's your name?" And the guy responded, "Basically, Jimmy." Some people just talk in hedge phrases as a way of life.

Dr. Turner believes the APOD will ultimately be applicable to other crimes as well, but, as of now, he has made clear his research only supports its use in cases of adult male suspects of sex abuse. Any other usage would need separate studies. He is a scientist so he has to say that. I am not a scientist, and I can say I think these themes will pop up in interviews pertaining to other crimes as well. Others think so, too. For example, I was teaching a class in 2023 to a group of investigators. An arson investigator told me he had observed a number of these themes in interviews he has done with arson suspects. Hopefully, we'll see more research from others in this branch of deception detection.

The way I use the APOD is to bolster my confidence in the suspect's guilt or innocence as one more aid in determining whether or not to interrogate. Remember, we only want to interrogate when the guilt of the suspect is reasonably certain. When I hear four or five of these themes pop up in sexual abuse investigations, I am much more likely to interrogate.

If I did an interview where my case facts were good against the suspect, and his responses were unsatisfactory, I would move to an interrogation with or without the APOD being in my favor. My take on the APOD at this moment is it's one more tool. It isn't everything. That might change in the future as I continue to apply the technique.

During a video interview I did with Dr. Turner, I asked him if he would be willing to declare a person innocent if he listened to an interview where the suspect used zero APOD themes. He responded, "No! Of course not. Absolutely not." He went on to say APOD is just evidence. He mentioned that fingerprints, eyewitnesses, etc., "Everything's just evidence...Nobody is allowed to get on the stand and say, 'He's guilty because [of a specific piece of evidence].'" Here Dr. Turner has identified something very important in the field of lie detection. Evidence of a thing is not proof of a thing. I think this gets lost in some of the academic literature on lie detection. It seems to me that a writer like Aldert Vrij, for example, will point to a study on nonverbals, for example, say it led to mixed results, and imply that therefore nonverbals aren't useful. When you think of anything from APOD results to nonverbals, if you think of it as just evidence and not a definitive proof of guilt, then you're on to something.

I think the instrument Dr. Turner has created is one of the most compelling and useful that is out there. It is also relatively easy to understand and put to use right away. If you are serious about it, you'll want to go to one of his trainings and get certified. Dr. Turner has a website where you can check out his work.[1]

### *Statement Analysis*

Statement Analysis (SA) is a careful evaluation of what exactly the person writes. The practitioner then goes word by word to look for deception. The system was designed around written or transcribed statements, but I believe there are some elements that can be used live. For most of us, it's what we can do live that will get the most use.

> What most people do not realize is they will always word their statement based on all their knowledge. Therefore, their statement may include information they did not want to reveal. Even though they may feel they are sharing very little information, people will provide you with more information than they realize.[2]

While studying this topic, I read *Don't Be Deceived and I Know You Are Lying* by Mark McClish and *Wise As A Serpent; Gentle As A Dove* by Peter Hyatt. *Don't Be Deceived* has the ambitious subtitle "The definitive book on detecting deception." I want to distill some of what I have taken from those books that I think you can put to work right away. I encourage readers to look into training in these areas if they find the concepts of interest.

Some interesting concepts in SA:

*Reliable Denial*: In his book *Wise as a Serpent, Gentle as a Dove*, Peter Hyatt makes the bold statement that when a person says "I didn't [kill / rape / assault etc ... accusation]" without a bunch of extra words, then you should believe them. He claims that this is a 90% true rule. I struggle with the definitiveness of his statements to these effects, but this is something that comes up a lot. For one of my cases, I reviewed a statement by the suspect on a previous allegation. The allegation is he went into his patient's room and groped the boy's penis. Look at this exchange:

***Detective:*** Have you ever been in J***'s room with him alone?
***Suspect:*** No. Never. I ... to be honest with you, I haven't been there in so long, I don't know what room is his. So that even makes me feel more comfortable with his story because yeah I have no idea.

This looks like a strong denial, but it doesn't meet the criteria. On this case, you'd want to hear, "I didn't go into his room alone." Or "I didn't grope his penis." SA says that simple statements are the best. All words that are added to those necessary to answer the question are suspect.

Let's look at Suspect's response again, but this time I'll bold the word(s) necessary to answer the question and italicize everything extra.

***Detective:*** Have you ever been in J***'s room with him alone?
***Suspect:*** No. *Never. I ... to be honest with you, I haven't been there in so long, I don't know what room is his. So that even makes me feel more comfortable with his story because yeah I have no idea.*

That's a lot of italics. Basically, it's kinda sus. As the author writes, "The deceptive often go beyond the boundary as they feel the need to persuade."

*Normalcy*: Anytime a suspect describes themselves or an action as "normal" they are almost certainly abnormal. Hyatt talks about how we are trained from a young age to expect when somebody starts a story with, "It was a normal day…" that things are about to get weird. For a suspect's description of himself as normal, there is likely to be a history of people calling him or her other than normal.

*Changing nouns or pronouns:* When a person, place, or thing is introduced into a story, that person, place, or thing, will be referred to in the same way unless there is some change in reality OR there is deception. Example: "My wife and I have kids. My wife and I live in Middletown. Pam owns some miniature donkeys. My wife is a good cook." If "my wife" and "Pam" are the same, why did I refer to her differently? Something happened around the subject of miniature donkeys. The answer is that I find them a pain. They are very much her animals.

In one case, I had the mom write a statement about her son David (name changed for privacy purposes) getting injured. She referred to him as David at every point in the story except towards the end when she began referring to him as Davey. She then referred to him as Davey for the rest of the document. So, we look back at where David became Davey (Note: original punctuation kept). "…while I was holding David. then he came back from dropping her off. we started to get all the kids ready. [sic] when my husband noticed our son Davey wasn't really moving his arm."

What happened? At the moment the injury happened or was observed, reality changed, and, as a result, the way the writer referred to her child changed. In this case, the change isn't necessarily deceptive because it coincides with a change in reality. But what if the boy's name changed without having stated the change that led to it? That's something we can pick up on and direct questions towards.

Hyatt writes, "Principle: Change of language should represent a change in reality. If there is no apparent change of reality within the statement, it may indicate deception on part of the subject."

*The Disappearing "I"*: This is one I see a lot when I ask people to tell me all about their day but lie about everything. It's a tough exercise that forces people to lie on the spot. Here is part of a student's response in late 2023.

> My wife…uh…had to get up early yesterday so she woke me up early…um…She was really horny. She wanted to have sex before she went to work. So…um…did that. It was pretty quick. And then we…She went to work. Um. I got my son. We went to … uh… Took him to school. Came back. Ate some breakfast…Let the dogs out (one of the dogs has been sick). Put the dogs away.

Here, you'll notice sentences you would expect to have an "I" in front do not. "Came back" would usually be, "I came back." "Ate some breakfast" would usually be, "I ate breakfast." Statement Analysis says that the Disappearing "I" shows a lack of conviction. If you pick up on this technique being used during your interview, consider asking more questions in the areas where the "I" disappeared.

> The lack of the pronoun 'I' in a statement is an indication the person is not committed to his story. If we are to believe a person did something, the person has to tell us he did

it by using the pronoun I. If the pronoun I is missing, then we cannot believe the subject performed the action unless there is a justifiable reason why the I is missing.[3]

*When a question is avoided, the question, itself, is sensitive*: We've seen this concept before in Don Rabon's writing. He says an interview format should be Question/Answer, Question/Answer. It's often a problem if you get Question/Question or Question/Statement.

Here's a recent example from my personal life. My wife was watching a zombie show. I had never seen any of the episodes. A guy who looked like a main character died. The following exchange happened:

*Me:* Did you like that character?
*Wife:* He's been in the show since the beginning.
*Me:* You didn't answer the question.
*Wife:* I didn't like him.

I correctly identified that she avoided the question. I followed up. I got the real answer.

As an important aside: Anybody who learns about Statement Analysis really wants it to be definitive and incontrovertible. I believe it is one more tool in the toolbox. Please don't decide somebody is guilty because they avoided a single question or didn't give a Reliable Denial. It's a tool that you can learn and deploy to identify the areas that need more exploration in your interviews.

To use the tool live, learn the markers and place more questions in the areas where you notice them. If you hear when I stop saying "my wife" and start saying "Pam," ask me more about that topic. "You said Pam has miniature donkeys?" If you hear the guy with the disappearing "I" in his statement. "You said, 'ate some breakfast.' Tell me more." Ask yourself if the suspect provided a Reliable Denial.

## Juvenile Suspects

Many investigators have questions about how to interview juvenile suspects. While juveniles are one of the three classes of people that require extra care in the interview room (elderly, juveniles, and IDD), they are also responsible for crimes ranging from petty theft to murder. You can't exactly ignore them. There is a balance required to treat them ethically and to get the truth. The matter is not helped by the fact that laws about their treatment are buried in case law, policy, and miscellaneous government codes.[4]

There are three main ways an investigator can talk to a juvenile suspect: while they are under arrest, in a non-custodial setting, or while they are at school. While a typical interview with an adult suspect in custody simply requires the investigator to read them their Miranda warning, where I work, a juvenile suspect has to be magistrated before being questioned in a custodial setting. That means to say they will be taken before a judge and, out of the presence of any officers, a judge will inform them of their Miranda rights.[5] In my experience, most juveniles elect not to talk after being read their rights by a judge.

The most common way to interview a juvenile suspect will be in a non-custodial setting. In this scenario, the investigator calls the parent, and asks them to bring their child in for an interview. Here is where I tread perhaps more cautiously than is technically necessary.

I'll tell you what I do and why I do it. If you or your senior investigators have a different approach, do what works for you as long as it's legal and within policy.

When I call a parent of a juvenile suspect, I let them know what the allegations are against their child. I recommend they talk to their child and decide together if they should come in. I don't use trickery or deceit as to what the consequences could be. A typical call goes like this:

> Good afternoon. My name is Darrel Lambert, I'm a detective for the Police Department. Your kid's name came up in an investigation having to do with the sexual assault of a child. Have you heard anything about the allegations? Well, look, I'm at the part of my investigation where I'd like to interview your child about the allegations. You should know the allegations are serious. What I recommend is to talk to your child about this. Have a real talk with them about what they did or didn't do. If they didn't have anything to do with this, it might help them to come in and talk to me. On the other hand, if they did have something to do with this, and they tell me that, it could be used against them. I'll check back with you in a few days.

I freely admit this is overboard. It would absolutely be legal and within policy to tell the parents that you just have a little matter to talk over with their kid and would they be so kind as to bring them in to clear that up? I take my route for several reasons. First and foremost, I'm a parent, and I wouldn't want cops tricking me into bringing my child in for an interview. Second, this approach builds trust with parents because it's a sort of anti-sales tactic. Whatever happens afterwards, they will remember I was fair. You should know many parents still bring their child in. Either their child convinces them they didn't do it, or the parent wants their own child to be held to account.

> Apart from the legal issues surrounding the handling of juveniles, I believe there is a moral component each investigator will need to sort out for themselves. How pushy should you be with parents? In Texas, the age of criminal responsibility is 10 years old. I worked with a detective who investigated an aggravated assault where a 10- or 11-year-old chased his family member with a large knife. The case resulted in a warrant against the child. I was at the main police station when the child was brought in by his mother. He was maybe four and a half feet tall. He looked like the small child he was. I investigated another case where a 6′ tall 12 year old boy raped his stepmother and committed acts of bestiality against his pet. Does one make you want to approach the family notification differently?

The third way an investigator can interview a child is while they are at school. In Texas, the school is acting "in loco parentis" to the child while the child is in attendance. That means, legally, the school staff can make legal and medical decisions related to the child while they are in their care. If you go to the school, and the school staff agrees to present the child for an interview, you can interview them right there. Should you, though?

For example, if you asked a parent to interview their child, and the parent said, "no," you could legally attempt an interview with the child while they are at school.[6] In this scenario, you may be legally right but, in my opinion, morally wrong. In a different scenario, what if you are investigating a serious crime, but the parents won't answer calls, texts, or any other good-faith attempts to contact them? In this scenario, you owe it to your investigation to attempt an interview with the child at school. In general, I think the school interview with a juvenile suspect should only be attempted when either the busy parent asks you to take that route or all reasonable attempts to get in touch with the parents have failed.

In a 2022 case, Chicago area teen Martell Williams was suspected of shooting a store clerk. Police went to his school, and they interrogated him for several hours, resulting in a confession. Williams stated he was coerced into confessing by promises of going home and getting McDonald's. Charges were dropped later when his sister found video of Martell playing in a basketball game miles away from the crime scene and at the time the crime occurred![7] I don't have inside knowledge of this case, but it looks like this is a situation where the police purposefully went to school to avoid going through the parents. As I wrote before, this may be legal (depending on your jurisdiction), but it might not be right.

Those are the main ways a juvenile suspect interview will happen. There are many variations of scenarios that can occur, and my experience is answers are hard to come by. What if a 20-year-old adult is picked up on a juvenile warrant? Can you interview him? What if a juvenile is a suspect of aggravated assault but also a victim of sexual assault? Should you do the forensic interview only? In general, if neither department policy nor legal advice gets you a firm answer, err on the side of actions that have the least impact on the juvenile.

When it comes to juvenile suspects, I prefer to tread cautiously, well away from the line of what I technically can do. No matter how heinous the crime you are investigating, the interview is just one piece of evidence in that case. If your case is so weak you have to have a confession to file it, you may not be able to file charges on that case. I've had to have tough conversations with victims to tell them, "I'm not saying it didn't happen, I'm just saying I can't prove it." *Remember, a strong case with a confession is airtight. A weak case with a confession is strong. A weak case without a confession is weak anyway, so don't worry about it.*

As to the actual conduct of interviews with juveniles, we know that juveniles figure prominently in the list of false confessions. Here is an excerpt from Ariel Spierer's New York University Law Review article, "The Right to Remain a Child":

> Studies have found that juveniles are two to three times more likely to falsely confess than are adults. Additionally, Professors Steven Drizin and Richard Leo found that juveniles accounted for approximately one-third of all 125 known false confessions. In another study that analyzed 340 exonerations, forty-two percent of children were found to have given false confessions while only thirteen percent of adults did the same. Under a variety of circumstances, results from other studies have mirrored these troubling findings.[8]

With juveniles figuring so prominently in false confessions, investigators should scrupulously avoid threats, promises of leniency, and anything that shocks the conscience. These are to be avoided in all suspect interviews, but even more so with juveniles. In the Martell Williams case referred to earlier, news articles say he was promised that he could go home after confessing. That would definitely violate the restrictions on promises, so the restrictions needed to prevent Martell's false confession already exist.

Another step to safeguard the juvenile suspect and your investigation is to avoid lying to the juvenile suspect. Although the ability of police to lie to suspects was enshrined into law in Frazier V. Cupp, it is a tactic that also figures prominently in false confessions. This is another situation where you technically can, but maybe you shouldn't. In Illinois, Governor Pritzker signed measures into law banning law enforcement from lying or offering leniency to juveniles during interrogations. Other states are following suit.[9] It's probably only a matter of time before laws like these are on the books everywhere.

Finally, you should avoid excessively long interviews.[10] For me, I have in my head 2 hours or less as my time frame when I go into an interview with a juvenile. This is *not* a hard and fast rule. If the juvenile suspect and I have a lot to talk about, it may take longer. What that number is, for me, is a reminder that I am on a compressed time schedule with a juvenile suspect. I want to gather their account and clarify discrepancies. I do not want to wear them down.

If I move into an accusatory interrogation, the goal is to shut it down sooner rather than later, even if I might have continued on if the suspect had been an adult.

Besides these extra guardrails, the same processes discussed throughout this book apply to interviews with juvenile suspects. Prepare in advance. Strategize about evidence. Build rapport. Be non-judgmental. Even if you think their guilt is certain going in, interview them first. Everybody should have a chance to account for themselves.

## Interacting with Defense Lawyers

*"Did you ask my client about his version of events?"*

"I called him, and I asked him to make a statement. He told me to call his lawyer."

*"And what did you do?"*

"I issued a warrant for his arrest."

*"I'm his lawyer, why didn't you ask me?"*

- An exchange between defense counsel and myself during a trial for an aggravated assault case.

I learned early on in my detective career an interviewee asking for a defense lawyer is not necessarily the end of the road for gathering the suspect's statement. In fact, I would estimate anywhere from one-third to one-half of defense lawyers agree to bring their client in for a statement. Once they are in the interview room, it's anybody's guess what you'll gather from the interview.

If the suspect says, "I want a lawyer" in a non-custodial context, I never argue or try to persuade them otherwise. I'm thankful to live in a country where such protections exist. There are a couple of other questions I ask at that point, though. I'll ask, "Do you have a lawyer now?" If they do, I ask for their names, and I direct all future inquiries through them. If they don't, I tell them:

> Here is my business card with my cellphone number written on the back. Once you find a lawyer, please have them contact me. I have to make some decisions on this case, and I'll need to know if they will be bringing you in for a statement. Sometimes they do! If I

> don't hear from you in a week or so, I'll send you a text message to ask about their information. As soon as I know who is representing you, I'll direct all other questions to them.

When I prepare for an interview where the suspect will have a defense attorney, I make a few adjustments. First, I expect to shorten the dedicated section on rapport. Second, I focus on factual questions. Third, I make arrangements for them to have a place where they can consult away from recordings.

Why shorten the rapport portion of the interview? While rapport is very beneficial to the successful conduct of an interview, the purpose of "chatting" may not be obvious to a paid-by-the-quarter-hour representative. Of course, it might be obvious to them what the purpose is (increasing the likelihood of information yield), and they might prefer you don't obtain that benefit.

As we know, rapport helps in two primary ways: it establishes a baseline for how the interviewee responds to questions and it reduces anxiety for the interviewee. Without a dedicated rapport-building conversation, you are unlikely to have a reliable baseline for how the suspect responds. That's just the way it is. You can work to reduce anxiety, though, with a monologue and consistent friendly demeanor. I'll say something like:

> I'm glad you two were able to come in today. A little bit about the room. You and your attorney are, of course, free to go at any time. No charges have been filed in this case. If you want water or coffee, I'll get them for you. If either of you needs the restroom, I'll show you where that is. This room is recorded. That's required for my interactions with you all, but it isn't what you might want for consultation with your attorney. If you two need to consult away from a recorded room, there are two options. I've set up a room next door that is not recorded. You can use that. You'll see cameras in those rooms, but they are *not* recording. Some people have felt more comfortable conferring in the lobby or outside. That is totally fine. I'll just need to scan you back in when you are ready.
>
> A little bit about me. I've been a police officer for 18 years. I've done all sorts of jobs in this department from patrol to gangs to robbery and now in homicide. I investigated child abuse cases for years because I found the work rewarding. Children are vulnerable in a way that others aren't. On the other side, people *suspected* of child abuse are often misunderstood. Investigators sometimes jump to conclusions. That's not me. I'm a fact finder. Some of my questions may be hard, but I'm not asking them from a place of judgment. I know that sometimes people do things they shouldn't. I also know that innocent people are sometimes accused of things they didn't do. When we talk today, I'm approaching this situation with an open mind. I haven't made any final decisions about the case.

Here, I've addressed the biological needs of both suspect and attorney. I've also acknowledged they may want to consult with one another in a room that isn't recorded. By anticipating and facilitating this consultation, I've laid the groundwork for rapport. I demonstrate I am attuned to their needs. I also demonstrate I am not trying to trick them by, say, leaving them to consult in a recorded room.

Another adjustment I make while interviewing suspects along with their defense counsel is to focus on factual questions. I had the experience of asking a suspect, "What do you think should happen to somebody that abuses children?" His attorney appeared exasperated as she let me know that he would not be answering hypothetical questions. This led me to think more deeply on what exactly the expectations are in an interview with an attorney. I decided they might object to hypothetical questions, but they couldn't really object to factual, case-based questions (although they might refuse to answer).

When an attorney brings their client in to make a statement to a police detective, there is a reasonable expectation they are there to cooperate with the investigation. How cooperative can you actually be if you refuse to answer factual questions? If a suspect is in on, say, suspicion of robbery, there isn't much to object to when it comes to questions about his alibi, handling of weapons, and enemies he may have. If a suspect is alleged to have used their social media account to set up the crime, it's reasonable to have them verify which social media accounts belong to them.

In a way, having an attorney present might actually facilitate the gathering of factual information. If their client said something they knew to be false, it would probably be in their client's best interest to have them correct that statement. Sometimes the details about a phone number, a social media account, or what kind of car they drive could make all the difference to solving a case. *When you go into an interview like this, redouble your focus on provable, factual information.*

From my observations, the traditional expectation is that not much will come from a suspect interview that includes a lawyer, but that hasn't been my experience. I had one defense attorney go so far as to help me interrogate their client! With typical expectations being negative – an assumption the lawyer will interfere with everything – I recommend you elevate your expectations to neutral. Maybe you'll have a successful interview. Maybe not. The negative assumption going into an interview like this will prevent you from preparing like you should.

One attorney brought their client in, made some early statements about ground rules and representation and then sat back and texted on their phone while I asked their client all of the questions I had to ask. On the other end of the spectrum, I've had attorneys object to questions, rush the process, take consultation breaks and other similar actions. There's no telling what is going to happen in the room with or without an attorney.

I remember one interviewee who was in on suspicion of having a minor perform oral sex on him. At one point he denied having had a relationship with the girl. His attorney turned to him and said, "Now John,[11] that's not what you told me. Tell the detective the truth now!" That attorney was a bit unorthodox by assisting in the interrogation of his client. If it weren't for having had it happen in other interviews of my own and those of my teammates, I would have assumed it was a one-off.

I have had the experience of an attorney who said they will bring their client in, but then won't answer my calls or consistently puts off the meeting to some later, unspecified date. You need to provide the attorney a reasonable chance to meet with their client and review the case, but that doesn't give them an unlimited time horizon. If I speak to an attorney and they say they need to meet with their client. I ask them when I can expect to hear from them. Sometimes, I have to set that timeline myself. "I have to make some decisions in this case. Can you get me an answer by next Thursday?" If they ask for reasonable accommodations, I, of course, make them.

Some attorneys have asked me to submit my questions in writing. I have done this on three or four occasions. I've never received a response back from these written questions. I assume the attorneys are taking the chance to get insight into the case without giving up anything. At least I've demonstrated my commitment to giving the suspect a chance to respond to the allegations.

When you talk to a defense attorney on the phone, be prepared to share some information, but be aware they may try to extract more from you than you should give them. A suspect's counsel can't reasonably make decisions about whether or not to bring their client in if they don't know what their client is being investigated for. You should tell them the crime being investigated, approximately when the crime is alleged to have happened, and who is involved if safe and appropriate to do so.

I have found being friendly and conversational (without revealing more than would be proper) has resulted in increased cooperation from attorneys. They may have called me expecting a fight or a surly attitude, but instead they got professionalism and cooperation. I find that there is a sort of reciprocity that exists in these conversations where the more I share with them the more they share with me. Of course, balance has to be struck between too much sharing and too little.

A good conversation of this type might look like this:

*Lawyer:* I'm calling because I represent Luis Forte, and my understanding is you are assigned to the case.

*Detective:* I'm glad you called! I've been looking into this case for a while now, and I thought I might be hearing from you. I'd like to talk to your client. When would be a good time to set that up? I'm available Tuesday or Thursday of next week. [*Friendly approach. Make your ask.*]

*L:* What are the allegations against my client?

*D:* There are allegations of sexual abuse of a child against your client. He is accused of rubbing a child's genitals. [*The detective tries to be as broad as possible.*]

*L:* So is that like Indecency or Aggravated Sexual Assault of a Child? Is penetration being alleged? [*The lawyer asks for more specific information.*]

*D:* No. Not at all. No penetration is being alleged. This investigation is an Indecency case.

*L:* Who is he alleged to have touched? When? [*The lawyer asks for more.*]

*D:* The allegations are coming from a niece of his. They are from the 2018-2019 time frame. [*The detective gives a little more.*]

*L:* What evidence do you have? [*The lawyer makes a big ask.*]

*D:* There is some evidence, but I'd like to discuss that with y'all in person. [*The detective denies the big ask and reiterates a desire to meet.*]

I've had conversations substantially similar to the one above at least a dozen times. I include this section on what to expect here because I have seen a lot of confusion from other detectives as to their interactions with the defense in these situations. The overall tendency is to avoid providing any information at all. You may have a different approach, and that's ok! Above is what my conversations look like, below I discuss why I do what I do. Take what works for you, and leave what doesn't. As always, have a reason for doing what you do.

Obviously, the lawyer needs to know what their client is being investigated for if they are going to advise them on whether or not to make a statement. In addition they need to know who has been hurt, approximately when it happened, and what it is you are asking of them. In the above conversation, the detective provides enough information for the attorney to effectively consult with his client, but he refuses to disclose evidence or specifics that might compromise the case.

The attorney usually asks for more than you want to give them. Think through your case, and be purposeful about what you provide them and what you refuse to provide them. You would not want to say, "Melinda says your client rubbed her vagina in her mom's room on New Year's Eve, 2019 while she was wearing cartoon pajamas and watching movies. She has provided a forensic interview and been seen for a non-acute sexual assault exam." That would be too much information.

When interacting with defense attorneys, be respectful but do not be fearful. Avoid assuming that they will refuse all requests for cooperation. Prepare for these interviews with an increased focus on provable, factual information. You may be surprised at how helpful the attorney will actually be to your case. Finally, be reasonably accommodating without being a pushover. You may need to set concrete deadlines.

## Lying

As a police officer in the United States, can you lie to the suspect in the interview room? Yes.[12]

Should you lie to the suspect? That's a harder question. For me, the answer is "it depends." If you lie, you'll have to work with the Assistant District Attorney to explain that you lied to a jury. That's a weird place to be. You'll risk losing rapport if the suspect knows you're lying. That makes your interview harder. There are also ethical concerns that need to be weighed. That's your conscience on the line.

Let's start with the background on what makes it legal for police officers to lie to a suspect about evidence: Frazier v. Cupp 394 US 731 (1969). Frazier was convicted of murder in 1965. He confessed to murder after being lied to by police that his co-conspirator had implicated him. After his conviction, his counsel appealed to the US Supreme Court. One of the arguments was that Frazier's confession should be suppressed because the police lied to Frazier in order to obtain it.

As to the lying, the court held, "The questioning was of short duration, and petitioner was a mature individual of normal intelligence. The fact that the police misrepresented the statements that Rawls had made is, while relevant, insufficient, in our view, to make this otherwise voluntary confession inadmissible. These cases must be decided by viewing the 'totality of the circumstances...'"[13] This case has featured prominently in subsequent legal decisions on police deception in interrogation rooms.

One ethical concern is lying to the suspect about evidence is correlated with false confessions. In his book on false confessions, Dr. Kassin writes about this topic, "There is no dispute as to the danger of this tactic. False evidence has singlehandedly precipitated countless proven false confessions, resulting in thousands of years of wrongful incarceration."[14] So if you choose to lie about evidence, you'll have to weigh the benefit against a weighty negative.

It's easy to imagine how lying about evidence can impact the way the jury sees you. You are sworn in on the stand as a law enforcement officer. You are sworn to honesty. Your integrity is a vital foundation for the trustworthiness of what you say on the stand. Then you have to admit you lied to the suspect. It creates dissonance. This can be explained as a tactic which is legal and permissible, but it is a point that is given to the defense.

Can you lie to the suspect? Yes. It shouldn't be done recklessly, though. You should balance how vital the sought after piece of information is against the drawbacks. You may destroy all rapport. You increase the risk of false confession. You undermine yourself for later courtroom testimony.

While it is legal to lie to a suspect[15], it ***is not*** legal to manufacture fake evidence. You can *say* you have DNA evidence linking them to the scene, but you can't cut and paste the suspect's name onto a document and present that to them as proof. You can't create a fake witness statement, doctor a lineup, or any other thing that creates or alters evidence that isn't real. If you do those things, *you* will be the criminal. [16]

## Serial Offenders

Serial offenders create unique challenges. They thrive on the investigator's inability to focus on a single crime. Besides the normal best-practice approach of rapport-based, nonjudgmental interviewing, there are two other techniques I'd recommend using. Focus on one crime or victim at a time; start with your strongest case, and then proceed to your weaker cases. Elicit statements from them showing them to be the type of person that would do the crime.

The serial suspect will thrive on your inability to focus.

I recommend you stay laser-focused on one crime at a time during the interview and later during the interrogation. If you had 3 crimes, you would *interview* on crime 1, 2, and then 3, then you would *interrogate* on crimes 1, 2, and then 3. This is hard to do because it creates such a daunting task. If one crime might require a 4-hour interview, what could it mean for a series of three or more crimes? This seemingly impossible task causes the interviewer to rush and take shortcuts that they shouldn't. Remember how you eat an elephant? One bite at a time. Choose your best case and get started.

The first time I realized I needed to focus on one victim at a time was on a man who had sexually abused several family members. There was a female victim and a male victim. The female was about 11 years old when he abused her, and the male was about 15 when he was abused.

During the interview, the suspect made multiple comments that suggested he had (or wanted to portray) a negative view on gay men. When I got to the end of the interview, I formed the conclusion the suspect's guilt was reasonably certain, and I decided to interrogate him.

I intuitively knew it would be messy to talk about both victims at once. I decided to interrogate the suspect about one victim and then the next, but which victim should I start with? His crimes against the female constituted the more serious offense due to her being under 14, so it would seem reasonable to start with the male and then proceed to the female. However, I recalled the suspect seemed to want to portray a bias against gay men. I interrogated him about the female victim first even though it was the more serious charge because it didn't require him to express a sexual interest in males.

The strategy was successful. He first confessed to his crimes against the female, and then, when he was entirely done with that, I shifted the topic to the male. He confessed to his crimes against the male too. It took patience to go all the way through with the process for one and then do the same thing for the other. At the conclusion, though, I had solid confessions about both.

The next time I thought about the process of focusing on one victim at a time was when I helped another unit interview a serial masturbator. I felt a lot of pressure to get this interview right. There had been a community uproar about this man. He had escalated from masturbating and leaving the scene to masturbating and chasing the victims. I sorted through the cases, and I saw there were three in particular with good evidence and a fourth that was a maybe.

In the best evidenced case, the victim took a picture of him with his penis in his hand. You couldn't quite see the penis, but it was clear from his hand, body position, and general expression what was happening. The victim got a description of his car as well. This was for sure the one to start with. The next best case had a suspect and vehicle description. This was a scary one because he chased the woman, and she fell and hurt herself badly. The third case had a suspect description and a license plate. The fourth was an out-of-county case with a not-very-good photo that generally matched his build and hair color.

Once again, I went one at a time, in depth. Something like, "There was an incident where a woman took a picture of you. Can you tell me all about that from beginning to end?" Then we go over the story. He admits to being there and having his penis in his hand, but he claims to have been peeing. I go through the story, testing it asking tough questions like, "Have you ever masturbated in public?" After a full interview (alibi, means, opportunity, motive, etc.), I move to the next best case, and I do another full interview. Then on to the next one.

Ultimately, the man confessed to having masturbated something like 9 times in public. He said he got a thrill out of the possibility he might be seen, but he claimed he did not want to actually be seen. I think this case would have been quickly derailed if I asked one or two questions about each case before moving on to the next one. It's tempting to see a case like this as having such overwhelming evidence that an extended, non-accusatory interview seems pointless. This interview took me over 4 hours, but I got the truth one case at a time.

The next tactic I'd recommend for dealing with serial offenders is to elicit statements from them showing they are the type of person who would commit the crime. This, in my opinion, would be particularly good when you have a series of crimes without any one crime having really good evidence pointing directly at the suspect (video, DNA, reliable eyewitnesses). Without great evidence, it is difficult to make a strong assertion of confidence in their guilt. This is common in child abuse cases where physical evidence on delayed outcries is scarce.

For example, a coworker of mine had a case with a school teacher who had multiple students over the years indicating that he had had sexual contact with them. For a variety of reasons, the statements from these children had problems. They didn't know exactly when it happened. They had outcried then recanted. The school seemed to have meddled over the years. Essentially, there was a lot of smoke but not a lot of fire. What to do?

Without focusing on one specific crime, you can search for means, motive, and opportunity. Means is the physical ability to perform the act, so this is not particularly difficult. Motive is richer ground to develop. Search for both his motives and the motives of the accusers. Does he have a sexual interest in children? Has he been questioned by police or his employers about sexual contact with children? What is it about him that would lead children to lie about him? These are all general questions without being specific to one case, but they can point you to people or situations you need to know more about.

Without great evidence, it is hard to say for sure what happened, but there are responses suspects will give you that will increase your confidence you have the right guy. For example, here is an exchange I had in a recent interview with a father accused of sexual contact with his daughter:

*Me:* "Has your penis ever had contact with her face?"
*Him:* (Confused look on his face) "Not that I know of?"

You won't be shocked to hear this response gave me great confidence that I had the right guy. In the more general cases you might ask, "Have you ever been alone with a naked child that wasn't your own?" "Have you ever thought about robbing somebody?" "Is there any reason why your name would have come up in a burglary investigation before?" If a man responds to *that* question with, "Not that I know of?" You're probably onto something.

Then you explore opportunity. Continuing with the example of the accused teacher, you might ask, "Were kids ever over at your house?" "Did you have private meetings with the children?" With issues like this you are listening for their responses and looking at what they do when they respond. Many times it will be apparent which questions the suspect has problems with.

I am NOT saying we should hope to charge people on mere suspicion. You still need good evidence. You should always be testing your theories with counterarguments like, "What if they are innocent?" "Is there another explanation for this fact pattern?" I AM saying this suspect came on your radar somehow. You owe it to the victim to seek information as diligently and skillfully as you can. In my experience, guilty offenders that are questioned in this way end up making graduated (ever expanding) admissions (before I told you he never saw my penis but come to think of it ...) or telling stories which are so ridiculous they are suspicious (I've lived with my stepdaughter for 12 years, but I never hugged her).

If you decided to move into an accusatory interrogation, you might consider starting nonspecific and then gradually becoming more specific. "There's no doubt you've had sexual contact with children" instead of "There's no doubt you [specific actions with specific child]." In a robbery series, you'd want to start with something like, "You've definitely been involved in taking people's things" instead of "You definitely robbed the woman at 7th and Cedar last night." Then, once they have admitted to general acts, you can become more and more specific.

In summary: for serial offenders, focus on one crime at a time when you have well-evidenced cases. Otherwise, explore the general motive and opportunity issues while looking for issues to narrow in on.

## Definitional Ignorance and How to Combat It

When I hear people use the phrase, "fight or flight" I always mentally correct them by thinking "fight flight or freeze." This matters in the interview room because there are three main options for responding to questions. To fight is to tell the truth. Flight is to lie. Never forget the third option, freeze, which is to hide from the question in some way. One of the ways to hide from a question is to plead "definitional ignorance."

Definitional ignorance is a strategy employed by deceptive interviewees in order to claim that they told you the truth based on how they define the words. To prevent definitional ignorance, we must throw out assumptions and clearly define the terms we are using in our interviews. Every time an interviewee denies anything, they are doing so based on the definitions which they choose to use at that moment. Typically, they will choose to use the definition which is most convenient for them whether or not that is how you meant it. I encourage every interviewer to be crystal clear as to the definitions they are using regarding any term that is crucial to the case.

If you were not clear in your definition of terms, then you can't know if the interviewee is lying or telling the truth with different definitions. Sometimes interviewees will redefine a term. This redefinition can happen explicitly – said out loud – or implicitly – thought about but not said. If you were clear in your definition, then the interviewee who redefines the term without including you in the redefinition is almost certainly lying to you.

Example of an interviewee redefining a term but not including the interviewer:

*Q: Have you ever robbed a store?*

A: (Implicit redefinition / internal monologue: Robbing means pointing a gun or a weapon and stealing stuff. I stole stuff, and punched the guard, but I didn't use any weapons.) "No."

Example of an interviewee redefining a term but including the interviewer (therefore not deceptive):

*Q: Have you ever robbed a store?*

A: What do you mean?

*Q: I mean taking the store's stuff and assaulting or threatening somebody in the store in order to get away with it.*

A: Does breaking and entering when nobody is there count?

*Q: No.*

A: Then, no, I haven't.

I saw a fascinating interview clip with suspected murderer Michael Peterson in which he vocalized a thought process usually left unsaid. Here is a transcript of the clip (it's a minute and seven seconds):

> Hmm ok...yes...well...if you say, 'relationships,' that would mean...that would imply more than...you know, sex for instance. And that never happened. I mean I'm very...I'm not that multi-faceted, you know, that I could have more than one relationship. I'm a monogamous person in the sense that I don't...there was Kathleen. And she took up my whole life. Could I have sex? Yes. That could exist. But not a relationship. I could not... go to dinner or you know have a ... no it would be inconceivable that...that...because she fulfilled all of that and actually fulfilled...certainly sexual. Uh, but there was this other aspect of me that just existed, and I...uh...yes did have sex.[17]

Out here in the real world, having sex with somebody other than your wife when you are supposed to be in a monogamous relationship is cheating. That is probably your definition too, but, if you had asked Michael Peterson, "did you ever cheat on your wife?", he might have denied that he had ever done so without lying by his definition, which means he could rely on definitional ignorance. Cheating to him is … I don't know … companionship? Sex isn't cheating.

When somebody is motivated to lie, we cannot assume even relatively obvious things like a definitional understanding that having sex outside of your marriage is cheating. **In order to combat definitional ignorance, establish everything. Assume nothing.**

The Michael Peterson clip is instructive because this same type of reasoning – which is a form of mental distortion – is occurring all of the time inside the heads of interviewees without them saying it out loud. The "bad" questions allow for the Michael Peterson-esque mental distortions to assist the interviewee in lying. The "better" questions are asked in a way that remove loaded terms and make it harder to lie. The interviewee can still lie to the better questions, but they have to do so without the defense of, "I didn't understand the question because that's not how I define that word."

Bad

*Q: "Did you rape Vanetta?"*

A: (Internal redefinition / monologue: Rape means penis in vagina. I put my penis in her mouth. Therefore, I didn't rape her.) "No."

Better

*Q: Has your penis ever gone into Vanetta's body without her consent?*

Bad

*Q: "Did you stab Vanetta?"*

A: (Internal redefinition / monologue: she grabbed the knife and it sliced across her palm. Slicing isn't stabbing.) "No."

Better

*Q: Have you ever injured Vanetta with a knife?*

If they can justify their response, they will not necessarily see it as deceptive. If they don't see it as deceptive, they will not display the signs of deception we are trained to look for. Definitional ignorance is a specific mental strategy used by deceptive people. They know what you mean, but they intentionally twist definitions in order to lie while maintaining an out. It should not be confused with an honest person redefining a term. Let me provide some examples of what I mean by discussing murder and dating.

Murder has a very simple definition in our penal code. "A person commits an offense if he intentionally or knowingly causes the death of an individual." I know several police officers who have been involved in fatal shootings in the line of duty. I believe if they were being interviewed and were asked, "Have you ever murdered somebody?" they would probably say, "no" without any sign of deception because their internal redefinition of murder has to do with committing a crime. It doesn't matter the interviewer might mean the literal sense of the word if they don't say so. Since their shootings were legally justified, the officers probably don't define their actions as murder.

If the questioner were to rephrase this and ask, "Have you ever caused the death of another person?" The officers in question – if they chose to answer a very rude question –

would say, "yes." This does not necessarily mean they were being deceptive to the first question. It means the interviewer and the interviewee did not share the same definition of the term. Since the redefinition happens internally, you won't necessarily know it happened.

To be clear about the difference, here is what an explicit redefinition of the question "Have you ever murdered somebody?" would look like: "Murder? Like in a criminal sense? No, I've never murdered anybody." In this response, your interviewee redefines the term while including the interviewer, and then gives their answer.

Explicit redefinitions are used by truth tellers to make sure they understand the question; they are used by liars to alter the question and thereby give themselves permission to deceive. If Michael Peterson had used this tactic it might have sounded like, "If by relationships with other women you mean going to dinner with them and having an emotional connection, then, no, I haven't had other relationships with other women." When liars do it, you are in luck because their technique is easy to spot.

What does it mean to date another person? For my part, I would define it as having regular romantic contact with another person you aren't married to, but if I'm interviewing somebody about who they date, they will respond to a question about this topic based on how they define dating unless I define it for them. If you've been paying attention these past twenty years or so, you may have noticed definitions of dating vary wildly from person to person and generation to generation.

Imagine Marty. He lives by himself. He gets on apps daily looking for hookups. For the last six months, he has met up with Chris twice a week to watch movies and have sex, but he hasn't stopped using the apps to look for other hookups. Let's say I know about Chris before I start interviewing Marty. If I asked, "Are you dating anybody right now?" without defining the term "dating," Marty could say "yes" or "no" and still be honest depending on how he defines dating. If I said, "When I talk about dating, I mean regular romantic or sexual contact with the same person. Okay? Are you dating anybody right now?" If Marty says "no" to this question without mentioning Chris, he is lying.

Over Thanksgiving, I was around some younger people still out on the dating scene. They introduced me to a new question they ask potential partners: "Is there anybody that would be upset about you being with me right now?" This is a brilliantly phrased question as it gets around the regular (and therefore easy to anticipate) redefinition of dating (it also addresses the fact they might be married). This is the dating equivalent of "have you ever caused the death of another person?" The person may still lie, but they can't do so by hiding behind definitional ignorance.

Why does all of this matter? It matters because we ask pointed questions in the interview room to either get the truth, induce verbal deceptions, or provoke some sort of behavioral response that might alert us to a problem. If we ask questions with undefined or ill-defined terms that can be reinterpreted, then we are potentially missing out on all of these desired outcomes by allowing the interviewee to plead definitional ignorance. If the answer matters to you, define your terms! With well-defined terms, they have to either tell the truth or lie. They won't get to hide behind confusion.

## A List of Questions and Prompts

This isn't an exhaustive list, but perhaps you'll see some to add to your repertoire.

Why? – Perhaps the supreme question. A one-syllable prompt demanding an explanation.

In as much detail as possible, without leaving anything out…

What do you mean?
Go on.
What else?
And then?
I don't understand.
Help me understand.
Really?
Give me an example.
Such as?
Is it possible?
Would anyone say…
How did that make you feel?
Who else knew?
Tell me more about that.
What changed?
When did you first observe the change?
What happened right before that?
What happened right after that?
Who did you tell about what you did?
Did you do it?
What actions did you take to fix the situation?
How can I verify that?
Can you prove your innocence?
Who can vouch for you?
What other options did you consider?
What's the biggest lie you ever told?
What's the biggest lie the victim ever told?
You said this, but you also said this, help me understand.

## Notes

1 Turner. 2024. "Turner Forensic Psychology and Consultation." Turner Forensic Psychology and Consultation. 2024. https://www.turnerforensicpsychology.com/
2 McClish, Mark, *Don't Be Deceived* (The Marpa Group, Inc., 2012), 11.
3 McClish, *Don't Be Deceived*, 92.
4 Some of this information may be particular to Texas, where I work. Check your local laws and policy.
5 I refer to them as "Miranda rights" at times because of common usage of the phrase. I understand that they are not "rights" per se and more so a warning.
6 Again, not a lawyer. Consult with your legal team on policies and procedures.
7 Washington Post. n.d. "A Teen Wrongly Charged in a Shooting Says Police Offered Him Fast Food to Get a Confession." https://www.washingtonpost.com/nation/2022/02/23/martell-williams-waukegan/
8 Spierer, Ariel. 2017. "THE RIGHT to REMAIN a CHILD: THE IMPERMISSIBILITY of the REID TECHNIQUE in JUVENILE INTERROGATIONS." https://www.nyulawreview.org/wp-content/uploads/2018/08/NYULawReview-92-5-Spierer.pdf
9 Ferkenhoff, Eric. n.d. "Should Police Be Allowed to Lie to Minors to Get Confessions? Some States Are Banning the Practice." Des Moines Register. https://www.desmoinesregister.com/story/

news/crime-and-courts/2021/08/24/illinois-becomes-first-state-ban-police-lying-minors-confession-more-join/5506379001/

10 According to Richard A. Leo's survey of false confessions, "More than 80% of the false confessors were interrogated for more than six hours, and 50% of the false confessors were interrogated for more than twelve hours." Drizin, Steven, and Richard Leo. 2004. "The Problem of False Confessions in the Post-DNA World, 82 N.C." *L. Rev* 82 (3): 3–4. https://scholarship.law.unc.edu/cgi/viewcontent.cgi?article=4085&context=nclr

11 Not his real name.

12 I'm not a lawyer, and I probably don't work where you do. Consult lawyers and policy where you work.

13 "Frazier v. Cupp, 394 U.S. 731 (1969)." n.d. Justia Law. https://supreme.justia.com/cases/federal/us/394/731/

14 Kassin, *Duped*, 353.

15 Or anybody else, really. Imagine making lying illegal!

16 "PENAL CODE CHAPTER 37. PERJURY and OTHER FALSIFICATION." n.d. Statutes.capitol.texas.gov. https://statutes.capitol.texas.gov/Docs/PE/htm/PE.37.htm. As to fabricating evidence being criminal, let's look to our friend the Texas Penal Code:

Sec. 37.09. TAMPERING WITH OR FABRICATING PHYSICAL EVIDENCE. (a) A person commits an offense if, knowing that an investigation or official proceeding is pending or in progress, he:

(1) alters, destroys, or conceals any record, document, or thing with intent to impair its verity, legibility, or availability as evidence in the investigation or official proceeding; or
(2) makes, presents, or uses any record, document, or thing with knowledge of its falsity and with intent to affect the course or outcome of the investigation or official proceeding.
(b) This section shall not apply if the record, document, or thing concealed is privileged or is the work product of the parties to the investigation or official proceeding.
(c) An offense under Subsection (a) or Subsection (d)(1) is a felony of the third degree, unless the thing altered, destroyed, or concealed is a human corpse, in which case the offense is a felony of the second degree. An offense under Subsection (d)(2) is a Class A misdemeanor.

17 The Behavior Panel. 2021. "GUILTY? Michael Peterson Body Language Reveals ALL on the Staircase." *YouTube*. https://www.youtube.com/watch?v=rNH7GvKSnno

## References


Drizin, Steven, and Richard Leo. 2004. "The Problem of False Confessions in the Post-DNA World." *82 N.C. L. Rev* 82(3): 3–4. https://scholarship.law.unc.edu/cgi/viewcontent.cgi?article=4085&context=nclr

Ferkenhoff, Eric. n.d. "Should Police Be Allowed to Lie to Minors to Get Confessions? Some States Are Banning the Practice." Des Moines Register. https://www.desmoinesregister.com/story/news/crime-and-courts/2021/08/24/illinois-becomes-first-state-ban-police-lying-minors-confession-more-join/5506379001/

"Frazier v. Cupp, 394 U.S. 731 (1969)." n.d. Justia Law. https://supreme.justia.com/cases/federal/us/394/731/

Kassin, Saul. 2022. *Duped: Why Innocent People Confess – and Why We Believe Their Confessions*. Blue Ridge Summit: Prometheus.

McClish, Mark, *Don't Be Deceived* (The Marpa Group, Inc., 2012)

"Penal Code Chapter 37. Perjury and Other Falsification." n.d. Statutes.capitol.texas.gov. https://statutes.capitol.texas.gov/Docs/PE/htm/PE.37.htm

Spierer, Ariel. 2017. "The Right to Remain a Child: The Impermissibility of the Reid Technique in Juvenile Interrogations." https://www.nyulawreview.org/wp-content/uploads/2018/08/NYULaw-Review-92-5-Spierer.pdf

The Behavior Panel. 2021. "GUILTY? Michael Peterson Body Language Reveals ALL on the Staircase." *YouTube*. https://www.youtube.com/watch?v=rNH7GvKSnno

Turner. 2024. "Turner Forensic Psychology and Consultation." Turner Forensic Psychology and Consultation. 2024. https://www.turnerforensicpsychology.com/

*Washington Post*. n.d. "A Teen Wrongly Charged in a Shooting Says Police Offered Him Fast Food to Get a Confession." https://www.washingtonpost.com/nation/2022/02/23/martell-williams-waukegan/

Chapter 13

# Conclusion

*You* can be successful in the interview room. Learn the fundamentals. Then develop your own style. At first, lean on your strengths. If you're the friendliest person in the office, building rapport might be your strength. Be great at that. If you're a highly organized person, building timelines might be your strength. Be great at that. Once you are more comfortable in the interview room, address your weaknesses.

One example of a weakness that might be addressed: highly rational interviewers often neglect to ask questions about the suspect's feelings. For emotional offenders, questioning them about their feelings may be the key that unlocks everything else. As I write this, it was just last week I saw a detective interviewing a murder suspect. They had been at loggerheads for hours when the detective walked out. I pointed out that he hadn't asked the suspect about his feelings. I recommended he acknowledge that the suspect was probably scared and ask him about it. The detective went back in and asked those questions. The suspect immediately started crying and adding more information.

If you find yourself stalled in the interview, ask yourself if there is something you could change to get the interview moving again. In all communication, the key is to get through to the person in a way they will best receive the information. We all have our preferred way of talking to people. When our preferred style meshes with the interviewee's preferred style, the outcome is effective communication. When there is a mismatch, great interviewers adjust to meet the needs of the interviewee.

Interviewing and interrogating criminal suspects will test you in many ways. You will learn as much about yourself as you do about the various suspects. Are you willing to do what it takes to get justice for the victims? Are you willing to have an open mind to the possibility that the suspect is innocent? Are you willing to do the work when you're tired, hungry, or held over late? Nobody else is coming to do your interview for you. It's up to you.

## First the Fundamentals

Wherever your interviewing journey takes you, I hope you will remember: First the Fundamentals. If you find yourself focusing on body language or personality types or anything to the exclusion of what the person says, you've gone off course. Those things are the extras that will take your interviewing to ever higher levels of proficiency … later.

For now, study your case and prepare your questions. Ask questions one at a time. Be patient. Be pleasant. Build rapport. Always interview before interrogating. Only interrogate when their guilt is reasonably certain. An interview built on the fundamentals discussed in this book will be successful more often than not.

DOI: 10.4324/9781003663904-14

### Questioning

The concepts in effective questioning techniques are not difficult to learn, but they do require discipline to use consistently. Some of the concepts discussed in this book:

- Questions are most effective when they start as open as possible and work down to specifics.
- Don't interrupt the person as they speak.
- Ask one question at a time.
- Use an encourager instead of asking a new question. "Go on." "What else?"
- Use note-taking as speed control

Along with preparation, these questioning techniques share the most foundational block of the fundamentals of interviewing and interrogation: Knowing what you are going to say (and how you are going to say it). As such, you should prioritize making these techniques automatic. The more automatic a technique is, the more brain space you have to focus on other things. Consider practicing them in everyday life. Next time you ask your spouse how their day was, use an encourager instead of asking another question. Next time your friend tells a story, don't interrupt them.

### The Strategic Use of Evidence

One of the most powerful tools at your disposal is the Strategic Use of Evidence (SUE) technique. This method allows you to methodically present evidence at the most opportune moments during an interrogation. By delaying the disclosure of key evidence, you can gather additional information and test the consistency of a suspect's statements. This technique is particularly powerful because it gives innocent suspects a chance to explain themselves while putting a great deal of pressure on deceptive suspects to disclose information they wanted to keep secret.

With a little bit of practice, you'll be able to use SUE on the fly, in the field, and with little forethought in cases like an urgent patrol call. Of course, the more time you have to think and plan, the better your results will be.

### The Pre-Miranda Monologue

The pre-Miranda monologue is one of the most effective tools you can use to get suspects to talk to you. It plays on powerful human motivators like curiosity and hope. When the suspect hears that you'll discuss the evidence with them that has pointed to them, guilty and innocent suspects alike will find it difficult to resist the urge to find out. When you let the suspect know they'll be treated fairly, you'll reduce the fear they may be experiencing. All of this increases the likelihood that they will agree to speak with you.

The monologue only takes a few minutes, and it has an outsized impact. It might be as simple as this:

> I want to talk with you today because there is evidence indicating you were involved in this crime. I want to show you that evidence. We'll look at it together. If I'm looking at it

wrong, just tell me. If you have other evidence that shows you weren't involved, we need to talk about that because I might not find it without your help. I only want the truth. If the truth is that you didn't do it, I need your help to show that. While we talk today, you will be treated with respect. If you need water, coffee, or the bathroom, just tell me, and I'll provide those for you.

## Interrogation Techniques: Frameworks and Storytelling

When it comes to interrogation, winning or losing will often come down to your ability to talk and to talk a lot. Techniques like frameworks and storytelling are invaluable. Frameworks provide structure to the interrogation, helping you to guide the conversation towards the truth. Storytelling, on the other hand, allows you to present the suspect with a narrative that aligns with their likely justifications for the crime, making it easier for them to admit their involvement.

These techniques are about creating a psychological environment where the truth can emerge. By controlling the pace and direction of the interrogation, you can keep the suspect focused more on the benefits of telling the truth than the negative consequences of lying. The key is to remain flexible, keep talking, and adapt your approach based on the suspect's responses and the evolving dynamics of the interrogation.

## A Final Word

The lessons in this book are not the kind of thing you can read once and know forever. Check back in as you gain experience. You're sure to pick up on new things as your vision expands during suspect interviews. Maybe what you need right now is the pre-Miranda monologue and theme development. Later, you may need to refine your questioning techniques. I recommend that you choose one thing at a time to focus on. If you try to do it all "right" the first time, it will be overwhelming.

Share your knowledge with your partners. Get your partners excited about interviewing and interrogation. It only takes one trained interviewer to bring up the skill level of all those around him or her.

Approach each interview with a sense of purpose, each interrogation with a sense of responsibility, and each suspect with a sense of humanity. Remember that the work you do matters. Go out there and do great work. The truth is waiting to be found, and you are the ones who will find it.

If you'd like to learn more about training opportunities, reach out at moderninterviewingsolutions.com.

You can also contact me directly at darrel.interviewing@gmail.com.

Feel free to follow my blog at lewispurdy.substack.com.

Thank you!

## Interview and Interrogation, a Roadmap

### Prepare for the interview

Look over criminal history and previous involvements
Think of questions, write them down, organize them
Assess your evidence, think of alternate explanations (see Chapter 9)

### Prepare your interview room

Do the cameras work?
Is the room set up how you want? (see Chapter 5)

### Secondary investigator greets and settles the interviewee

Check for weapons
Ask to mute phones

### Primary interviewer enters

Greet the suspect with handshake and eye contact (see Chapter 6)
Hand the suspect a bottle of water

### **Custodial issues** (see Chapter 7)

*Non-custodial*: You are not under arrest. You are free to go at any time. If you choose to leave, the door is open. You don't need my permission to leave. If you want water or coffee, I'll bring it to you. If you need a bathroom break, I'll show you where it is.

*Custodial*

*Pre-Miranda monologue*: [goal is to increase *curiosity* and *hope* and decrease fear] (See page:) I have some evidence I'd like to look over with you. We'll look at it together. If I'm looking at that evidence wrong, just tell me. (Curiosity) If you have any evidence that can clear you of involvement, point me to where it is, and I'll go find it. (Hope) While we are together, you'll be treated with respect. I'll listen to you, because I want to understand. (Reduce Fear).

*Miranda warnings*: [vary by jurisdiction]

### **Rapport** (see Chapter 8)

One goal is to establish a baseline for how the suspect acts and talks
Another goal is to come across as trustworthy and likable

### Transition

"We do need to talk about the issue at hand. Sometimes I ask questions I already know the answer to. I do that to make sure you are telling me the truth. Do you promise to tell me the truth today? What's your understanding of why we are here?"

**Questioning** (see Chapter 2)

Open questions as much as possible
Ask one question at a time
Take notes
Ask them if they did it

**Evidence presentation (SUE)** (see Chapter 9)

Analyze and rate evidence / think of alternate explanations / prepare questions
Contact the suspect
Give suspect the chance to volunteer the information
Present the evidence from vague to specific

> I have some evidence that…
> In fact, it's really strong evidence that…
> I have [present the evidence] linking you to what happened…

**Interrogation** (see Chapter 10)

Accuse them
Present a theory or theme as to why they did it
Ignore denials
Storytelling
Accuse
Frameworks
Accuse
Alternative question

# References


A Coach's Diary. (2023, September 26). *Kobe Bryant | Confidence Comes from Preparation.* YouTube. https://www.youtube.com/watch?v=YkPODCYd100

Alison, Emily et al., "Observing Rapport-Based Interpersonal Techniques (ORBIT)," *Investigative Interviewing: Research and Practice* 12, no. 1 (2021)

*BBC News.* 2019. "Transcript in Full: Prince Andrew's Interview," November 17, 2019, sec. UK. https://www.bbc.com/news/uk-50449339

Brandon, Susan E., and Simon Wells. 2019. *Science Based Interviewing*, 1st ed. BookBaby.

"California v. Beheler, 463 U.S. 1121 (1983)." n.d. Justia Law. https://supreme.justia.com/cases/federal/us/463/1121/

Cialdini, Robert B. 2021. *Influence: Science and Practice.* 5th ed. Harlow: Pearson Education.

"CODE of CRIMINAL PROCEDURE CHAPTER 38. EVIDENCE in CRIMINAL ACTIONS." n.d. Statutes.capitol.texas.gov. https://statutes.capitol.texas.gov/Docs/CR/htm/CR.38.htm

"Confession Transcript." n.d. Riverfront Times. https://web.archive.org/web/20240804170123/https://www.riverfronttimes.com/news/confession-transcript-2465504

"Davis v. United States, 512 U.S. 452 (1994)." n.d. Justia Law. https://supreme.justia.com/cases/federal/us/512/452/

"Detecting Lies and Deception Using Statement Analysis®." 2024. Statementanalysis.com. 2024. https://www.statementanalysis.com/

Drizin, Steven, and Richard Leo. 2004. "The Problem of False Confessions in the Post-DNA World." *82 N.C. L. Rev* 82(3): 3–4. https://scholarship.law.unc.edu/cgi/viewcontent.cgi?article=4085&context=nclr

Ferkenhoff, Eric. n.d. "Should Police Be Allowed to Lie to Minors to Get Confessions? Some States Are Banning the Practice." Des Moines Register. https://www.desmoinesregister.com/story/news/crime-and-courts/2021/08/24/illinois-becomes-first-state-ban-police-lying-minors-confession-more-join/5506379001/

Finkle, Jim, and Anna Mehler Paperny. 2018. "Shoes, Bodies Strewn on Toronto Street after van Attack." *Reuters*, April 24, 2018. https://www.reuters.com/article/world/shoes-bodies-strewn-on-toronto-street-after-van-attack-idUSKBN1HV065/

Fisher, Ronald P., and Edward R. Geiselman. 1992. *Memory-Enhancing Techniques for Investigative Interviewing: The Cognitive Interview.* Springfield, IL: Charles C. Thomas.

"Frazier v. Cupp, 394 U.S. 731 (1969)." n.d. Justia Law. https://supreme.justia.com/cases/federal/us/394/731/

"Fueled by Jealousy, Kaitlin Armstrong Fatally Shot an Elite Cyclist and Then Led Officials on an International Manhunt." 2024. NBC News. April 5, 2024. https://www.nbcnews.com/news/us-news/kaitlin-armstrong-killed-cyclist-mo-wilson-fit-jealousy-led-officials-rcna146267

"Guilty until Proven Innocent." n.d. www.youtube.com. https://www.youtube.com/watch?v=BemHqUqcpI8

"I Know It When I See It." Wikipedia. Wikimedia Foundation. November 14, 2019. https://en.wikipedia.org/wiki/I_know_it_when_I_see_it

Inbau, Fred Edward. 2015. *Essentials of the Reid Technique: Criminal Interrogation and Confessions.* Burlington, MA: Jones & Bartlett Learning.

Interrogations. 2022. "Michael Bailey - Exposed in Walmart Full Interrogation." *YouTube.* January 24, 2022. https://www.youtube.com/watch?v=-xjWVahqihk

James, A, Taylor Girtman, Jala Washington, and Mercedez Hernandez. 2023. "2 Arrested after Gun Goes off inside Man's Pocket in 6th Street Bar, Affidavit Says." KXAN Austin. July 24, 2023. https://www.kxan.com/news/local/austin/2-arrested-after-gun-goes-off-inside-austin-6th-street-bar/

JCS - Criminal Psychology. 2020. "The Bizarre Case of Stephen McDaniel." *YouTube*. https://www.youtube.com/watch?v=HkRjIq8Cp2A

"Jussie Smollett FULL Interview on Alleged Attack | ABC News Exclusive." 2019. YouTube Video. *YouTube*. https://www.youtube.com/watch?v=pXLx5OY21Bk

"Jussie Smollett Hate Crime Hoax." 2023. Wikipedia. March 28, 2023. https://en.wikipedia.org/wiki/Jussie_Smollett_hate_crime_hoax

Kassin, Saul. 2022. *Duped: Why Innocent People Confess – and Why We Believe Their Confessions*. Blue Ridge Summit: Prometheus.

Law&Crime Network. 2023. "Florida Deputies Interrogate Circle K Gas Station Killer - the Case Uncovered." *YouTube*. February 4, 2023. https://www.youtube.com/watch?v=bxkOBBTET6U

Lembke, Anna. 2021. *Dopamine Nation: Finding Balance in the Age of Indulgence*. New York: Dutton.

McClish, Mark. 2012. *Don't Be Deceived*. The Marpa Group, Inc.

"Miranda: Post-Invocation Questioning." n.d. https://le.alcoda.org/publications/files/MIRANDA-POSTINVOCATION.pdf

Navarro, Joe, and Marvin Karlins. 2008. *What Every BODY Is Saying: An Ex-FBI Agent's Guide to Speed-Reading People*. New York, Ny: Harper Collins.

News, KOCO 5. 2018. "Watch: Moore Police Interrogate Former State Sen. Ralph Shortey after Being Found in Motel with Teen." YouTube Video. *YouTube*. https://www.youtube.com/watch?v=WJQ6_khlxnc

Nichols, Ralph G., and Leonard A. Stevens. 1957. "Listening to People." Harvard Business Review. September 1957. https://hbr.org/1957/09/listening-to-people

O'Connor, John, and Sophia Tareen. 2024. "Jussie Smollett's Conviction Overturned in 2019 Attack on Himself." AP News. November 21, 2024. https://apnews.com/article/jussie-smollett-conviction-overturned-chicago-91178cf27f6ef0aec8a5eef67a3a6125

Partida, Maria Guadalupe. 2022. "1966: Miranda v. Arizona." Library of Congress. 2022. https://guides.loc.gov/latinx-civil-rights/miranda-v-arizona

"Penal Code Chapter 37. Perjury and Other Falsification." n.d. Statutes.capitol.texas.gov. https://statutes.capitol.texas.gov/Docs/PE/htm/PE.37.htm

"Police Interrogation of Toronto van Attack Suspect 'Textbook,' Experts Say | Globalnews.ca." n.d. Global News. https://globalnews.ca/news/5961942/alek-minassian-interrogation-reaction/

Purdy, Lewis. 2022. "New Video, Stephanie Lazarus." Substack.com. Interview and Interrogation For Police Detectives. March 29, 2022. https://lewispurdy.substack.com/p/new-video-stephanie-lazarus.

Purdy, Lewis. 2025 "Two Investigator Suspect Interviews," Substack.com, https://lewispurdy.substack.com/p/two-investigator-suspect-interviews

Rabon, Don, and Tanya Chapman. 2019. *Interviewing and Interrogation: Questioning, Detecting Deception and Gaining Compliance*. Durham, NC: Carolina Academic Press.

Red Circle Interrogations and Confessions. 2020. "Michael Rafferty - Police Interrogation - Part 4 - the Murder of Tori Stafford." *YouTube*. June 25, 2020. https://www.youtube.com/watch?v=NA6VIrdKMNI

Red Circle Interrogations and Confessions. 2020. "Robert Mondrian Powell - Full Murder Confession - Police Interrogation." *YouTube*. September 24, 2020. https://www.youtube.com/watch?v=vE5hSlXEFOc

Reddington, Michael. 2022. *The Disciplined Listening Method: How a Certified Forensic Interviewer Unlocks Hidden Value in Every Conversation*. Charlotte, NC: Per Capita.

Roeloffs, Mary Whitfill. 2024. "Amanda Knox Convicted of Slander in Italy—Here's What We Know." Forbes. June 5, 2024. https://www.forbes.com/sites/maryroeloffs/2024/06/05/amanda-knox-convicted-of-slander-in-italy-what-we-know-about-the-man-she-wrongly-accused-of-murder/?sh=71c6103265db

Spierer, Ariel. 2017. "The Right to Remain a Child: The Impermissibility of the Reid Technique in Juvenile Interrogations." https://www.nyulawreview.org/wp-content/uploads/2018/08/NYULaw-Review-92-5-Spierer.pdf

"The Aftermath Part 1: Kids, Schools, and the Crime Surge." 2022. Apple Podcasts. January 19, 2022. https://podcasts.apple.com/us/podcast/the-aftermath-part-1-kids-schools-and-the-crime-surge/id1570872415?i=1000548337785

The Behavior Panel. 2021. "GUILTY? Michael Peterson Body Language Reveals ALL on the Staircase." *YouTube*. https://www.youtube.com/watch?v=rNH7GvKSnno

The Cappening Channel. 2016. "Music Professor Caught on to Catch a Predator James Rauch (Audio Boost!)." *YouTube*. August 14, 2016. https://www.youtube.com/watch?v=nuX6kgww1Is

The Innocence Project. 2024. "False Confessions." Innocence Project. 2024. https://innocenceproject.org/false-confessions/

Turner. 2024. "Turner Forensic Psychology and Consultation." Turner Forensic Psychology and Consultation. 2024. https://www.turnerforensicpsychology.com/

U.S. Supreme Court. 1966. "Miranda v. Arizona." Justia. June 13, 1966. https://supreme.justia.com/cases/federal/us/384/436/.

U.S. Supreme Court. 2010. "Maryland v. Shatzer." Justia. February 24, 2010. https://supreme.justia.com/cases/federal/us/559/98/.supreme.justia.com.

Various Contributors. 2019. "Jim Rauch." To Catch a Predator Wiki. Fandom, Inc. 2019. https://to-catch-a-predator.fandom.com/wiki/Jim_Rauch

Vrij, Aldert. 2008. *Detecting Lies and Deceit: Pitfalls and Opportunities*. Chichester: Wiley.

Walsh, Dave, and Ray Bull, "Examining Rapport in Investigative Interviews With Suspects: Does Its Building and Maintenance Work?," *Journal of Police and Criminal Psychology* 27 (2012), https://doi.org/10.1007/s11896-011-9087-x

*Washington Post*. n.d. "A Teen Wrongly Charged in a Shooting Says Police Offered Him Fast Food to Get a Confession." https://www.washingtonpost.com/nation/2022/02/23/martell-williams-waukegan/

"What a 15 Year Old Mass Killer Looks Like." n.d. www.youtube.com. https://www.youtube.com/watch?v=MtNASztI83c

"WNBA Star Brittney Griner on Legislation Targeting Transgender Athletes #Shorts." n.d. www.youtube.com. Accessed May 14, 2025. https://www.youtube.com/shorts/CPHc5yJMa9Q

Youtube. 2025. https://youtu.be/Cwtk97dWSJQ?si=Ms3JDhoUIVgMXvmS

YouTube. 2025. https://youtu.be/QybphTUd-o0?si=IH8D9JXCM4KczJST

# Index

Note: *Italics* indicates figures and tables in the text and page numbers followed by "n" refer to end notes.